A Manual for
BIRD WATCHING
IN THE AMERICAS

A Manual for
BIRD WATCHING
IN THE
AMERICAS

Donald S. Heintzelman

UNIVERSE BOOKS
New York

For Theodore R. Hake,
with whom I shared
many fascinating birding adventures

Published in the United States of America in 1979
by Universe Books
381 Park Avenue South, New York, N.Y. 10016

Printed in the United States of America

79 80 81 82 83/10 9 8 7 6 5 4 3 2 1

Library of Congress Cataloging in Publication Data

Heintzelman, Donald S.
  A manual for bird watching in the Americas.

  Bibliograpy: p.
  Includes index.
  1. Bird watching. 2. Bird watching—America.
I. Title.
QL677.5.H45   598.2'073'0973   78-66169
ISBN 0-87663-336-X
ISBN 0-87663-967-8 pbk.

CONTENTS

ILLUSTRATIONS

Except as otherwise indicated, all photographs were taken by Donald S. Heintzelman.

PREFACE

The Age of Bird Watching began in this century with the publication of the first of the many fine field guides to bird identification which bird watchers now use regularly as part of their standard equipment. The extent to which the hobby has grown in recent years was demonstrated when *American Birds* reported not long ago that about half a million people now actively participate in bird watching in the United States. Actually that figure may be conservative because several million copies of the more popular field guides have been sold and sales continue to soar.

This book, however, is not intended to be a field guide. Instead, it explores in considerable detail many other aspects of bird watching ranging from the selection of equipment and books, to special types of bird watching, to participation in the hobby in areas as remote as Antarctica. Hence the book is designed to supplement information contained in standard field guides and deal with many topics not included in those guides. Probably experienced bird watchers will know much of the information presented, but less experienced birders and beginners will find the material very helpful. Even experienced bird watchers can benefit from some of the information presented.

While writing this book, I drew heavily on my extensive field experience in various parts of the Americas over a period of more than twenty years. In addition, I also made extensive use of portions of the bird watching and ornithological literature when such information was needed to augment my own experience. In a few instances, various persons supplied additional information.

James A. Tucker granted me permission to use material from his notes pertaining to the record 1973 Texas Big Day Count, and Ted Chandik sent me information on pelagic bird watching in California waters. Finally, Theodore R. Hake provided details about swan migrations in eastern Pennsylvania. I am grateful to these three.

Appreciation also is extended to the editors of the following periodicals for granting permission to quote from material originally appearing in their publications:

American Birds for the use of sample Christmas Bird Counts and Breeding Bird Censuses.

Birding for the use of portions of "An Antarctic Christmas Bird Count" by Donald S. Heintzelman (1976), and various other materials.

Explorer's Journal for the use of excerpts from "Autumn Hawk Migrations" by Donald S. Heintzelman (1975) and "Bird Survey on Aves Island" by Donald S. Heintzelman (1976).

Portions of chapter 11 were loosely adapted from my *North American Ducks, Geese & Swans* with the permission of Winchester Press. Parts of chapter 12 also were loosely adapted from my *Autumn Hawk Flights: The Migrations in Eastern North America* with the permission of Rutgers University Press, and my *Guide to Eastern Hawk Watching* with the permission of the Pennsylvania State University Press.

In addition to these sources, a number of other books also were consulted, including Allen's *Stalking Birds with Color Camera*, Bond's *Birds of the West Indies*, Broun's *Hawks Aloft*, Brudenell-Bruce's *The Birds of the Bahamas*, Edwards' *Finding Birds in Mexico*, Edwards and Loftin's *Finding Birds in Panama*, ffrench's *A Guide to the Birds of Trinidad and Tobago*, Fisher and Peterson's *The World of Birds*, Hall's *A Gathering of Shore Birds*, Harris' *A Field Guide to the Birds of Galapagos*, Haverschmidt's *Birds of Surinam*, Heintzelman's *Finding Birds in Trinidad and Tobago*, Koepcke's *The Birds of the Department of Lima, Peru*, Land's *Birds of Guatemala*, Meyer de Schauensee's *The Birds of Colombia* and *A Guide to the Birds of South America*, Peterson and Chalif's *A Field Guide to Mexican Birds*, Pettingill's *A Guide to Bird Finding East of the Mississippi*, Poole's *Pennsylvania Birds*, Smithe's *The Birds of Tikal*, Watson's *Birds of the Antarctic and Sub-Antarctic*, Wauer's *Birds of Big Bend National Park and Vicinity*, Wetmore's *The Birds of the Republic of Panama*, and Woods' *The Birds of the Falkland Islands*.

Reference also was made to a number of periodicals including *American Birds, Animal Kingdom, Atlantic Naturalist, Audubon, Auk, Birding, Cassinia, Explorer's Journal, Frontiers, Kingbird, National Geographic,* and the *Wilson Bulletin.*

Photographs are an important part of this book, and whenever possible I used my own, which are uncredited. In addition, a few photographs also were supplied by the United States Fish and Wildlife Service, Bushnell Optical Company, Droll Yankees, Inc., Swift Instruments, Inc., and Carl Zeiss, Inc. Alan Brady, Allan D. Cruickshank, Jan Sosik, and Fred Tilly also supplied important photographs. The waterfowl flyway maps appearing in chapter 11 were supplied by the United States Fish and Wildlife Service.

1
WHAT IS
BIRD WATCHING?

Bird watching (or birding as it is now commonly known) is the recreational hobby of looking at wild birds in their natural habitats coupled with the desire to list as many species new to each observer as possible.

But there is much more to the subject than just listing birds. For example, take a walk in a nearby park or woodlot on a warm May morning at the height of the spring migration and there is a feeling of life everywhere. The air buzzes with the songs of woodpeckers, nuthatches, wrens, thrushes, vireos, warblers, and sparrows. Overhead, in the tops of the tallest trees, migrating vireos and wood warblers flit from branch to branch feeding on insects and insect larvae in order to replenish the large amounts of energy they will need to continue their northward migrations to ancestral nesting grounds. This is a time of great expectation for birders because they have an opportunity, during a few brief weeks, to see and list several dozen species which will not be present in many areas again until the autumn migration. In addition, these tiny northward migrants are now in full breeding plumage and a delight to see and hear. Who will forget his first view of a Wilson's or a Canada Warbler, or the simple song of an Ovenbird ringing loudly and clearly from the interior of the woodlot? Other birds also are present and in full song, waiting to be seen and listed. Perhaps it is a lone White-throated Sparrow whose movement on the ground attracts our attention and whose simple, pure voice is among the most haunting of all bird songs. Or, if it is early in the morning (the best time to enjoy spring birding), the glorious flute-like notes of a Wood Thrush ring out from some dark corner of the woodlot and announce to the world that this most charming of all woodland birds is alive and back home again. These are the sights and sounds which birders enjoy in addition to the mere listing of species seen. Indeed, by watching birds one

A Wood Thrush at its nest. The voice of this bird is among the most haunting of all bird songs.

quickly develops a firm sense of appreciation of Nature and some basic instinctive feelings for the importance of basic ecological processes which provide the foundation for the patterns of survival of all species.

Or take a crisp autumn morning on one of the hawk lookouts in the Appalachian Mountains. The sun has just risen above the horizon and fog or mist still hides the sleepy valleys while on higher ground the forest trees are beginning to turn from their summer coat of green to autumn coats of red, yellow, and purple. Then the first Broad-winged Hawk appears in the distance, slowly circling aloft, and a sense of excitement and anticipation grips the watchers as they wait for the next hawk to appear, then the next, and then hundreds or thousands more. In the nearby treetops, vireos and warblers also are migrating southward, but now they are in dull autumn plumage quite unlike their vivid spring dress. Still, they add more excitement to the birding scene.

A birder may have read about some extraordinary birding location for years before finally being able to visit the spot. Such was the case when I visited famed Bonaventure Island in Quebec for the first time. My anticipation had been building up for ten years before I finally traveled to that fabulous seabird island, and when I arrived I was breathless with excitement. As a teenager I had studied Arthur A. Allen's splendid photographs of nesting Northern

Gannets on the island and dreamed of the day when I, too, would be able to take such photographs. Now, before me were thousands of the white birds on their nests. Other birds flew by only a few feet away, and still others engaged in spectacular courtship displays. It was a scene which birders dream about.

How involved one becomes in birding varies greatly from person to person. Some people will derive great satisfaction from watching birds coming to a backyard bird feeder and may have little desire to extend their birding activities beyond such local activities. Yet such efforts can be both exciting and rewarding. Perhaps a flock of Evening Grosbeaks will add dash and color to the feeding station throughout the entire winter, or maybe a Pine Grosbeak will appear unexpectedly, or some Pine Siskins. It is always enjoyable watching these birds. But other birders, and I am one of them, will want to travel widely to remote corners of the world to see penguins on remote Antarctic beaches, or see colorful tropical tanagers deep in Amazon jungles. Birding in such places is extraordinary and more and more people are beginning to participate in such international birding activities. Regardless of what type of birding one chooses, however, there are no rules which require birders to visit foreign lands or to remain at home. Nor are there rules which dictate how relaxed or vigorous one's birding efforts must be. Each person is free to decide how involved he or she wants to be in the subject.

A kettle of migrating Broad-winged Hawks over a hawk lookout in the Appalachian Mountains.

It is not unusual, however, for birders to become deeply involved in watching birds both at home and in foreign lands. Many birders also become involved in related activities, including wildlife conservation projects, life history studies of selected species, migration and distribution studies, bird-banding, bird photography, and advanced ornithological research. All of these activities are natural outgrowths of bird watching.

Who, then, are the people who watch birds? Almost anybody may be expected to belong to the ranks of birders. Looking back into history, one finds some very extraordinary people enjoyed looking at birds. Thomas Jefferson, for example, developed a keen interest in the birdlife around Monticello and in Washington, and the Swedish botanist Peter Kalm of colonial times made many worthwhile observations of birds in and around Philadelphia. Two extraordinary Quakers from Philadelphia, John and William Bartram, were particularly noted for their interest in birds. Indeed, William Bartram was a devoted friend and patron of Alexander Wilson, the father of American ornithology. It is possible to claim that the historic Bartram mansion beside the Schuylkill River in Philadelphia is not only the birthplace of American ornithology but also the birthplace of bird watching in America. Even today Philadelphia remains one of the leading centers of bird watching in the United States, thanks in large measure to the Delaware Valley Ornithological Club founded in 1890 at the Academy of Natural Sciences. DVOC members not only engage in bird watching locally but frequently travel from the Arctic to the Antarctic, some of the most remote corners of the world, seeking new birds for their life lists. Such activities are typical of the most active birders in North America and Europe.

Among the ranks of bird watchers are some people who are well known to the general public. Rachel Carson, the noted author and biologist, was an avid birder; James Schlesinger, our first Secretary of Energy, is another keen birder; and Prince Philip, the Duke of Edinburgh, is an excellent bird photographer. Countless other people, representing virtually all occupations, also swell the ranks of bird watchers.

It is not uncommon for some birders to go further and engage in serious scientific studies of various aspects of birds as an outgrowth of their earlier bird watching days. Some of their stories are well known. For example, John James Audubon's passion for painting birds resulted in his superb bird portraits which are both art and ornithological classics. A. C. Bent, a New England textile manufacturer, wrote his many-volumed *Life Histories of North American Birds* published by the Smithsonian Institution. Indeed, S. Dillon Ripley, the Secretary of the Smithsonian Institution, has

Hawk watchers Robert and Anne MacClay looking at hawks migrating past Bake Oven Knob, Pa. Dummy owl on pole.

Nesting Northern Gannets on Bonaventure Island, Quebec. This is one of the most famous seabird colonies in North America.

written many books about birds, among them classic volumes on the birds of India and Pakistan, waterfowl, and *Rails of the World*. An Ohio housewife (and trained zoologist), Margaret Morse Nice, watched Song Sparrows so carefully that her *Studies in the Life History of the Song Sparrow* is one of the best life history studies ever published.

Charles Broley, a retired Canadian banker, took up the hobby of climbing tall trees to band nestling Bald Eagles. He banded more than a thousand eagles before he died fighting a brush fire. Data from his project resulted in the discovery of entirely new and unexpected migration patterns for these splendid birds. Harold Mayfield watched endangered Kirtland's Warblers carefully for many years and wrote a classic book about that species. Similarly Lawrence H. Walkinshaw, now a retired dentist, studied the cranes of the world most of his adult life and wrote two classic books about them.

But the most extraordinary story is that of Roger Tory Peterson, who began his distinguished career watching birds in grade school and in 1934 published the first edition of his classic *A Field Guide to the Birds*. No book or event in the history of bird watching has had such an enormous impact on this activity as has that field guide. Indeed, one can say without reservation that the Age of Bird Watching began when Peterson's field guide appeared. Today it would be hard to name another outdoor activity that is more enjoyable and can be enjoyed almost anywhere in the world as easily as can bird watching. This book will aid birders in many aspects of this exciting activity and will be particularly helpful to beginners and novices. Come and join us!

Additional Reading

Barton, R.
> 1974   Confessions of a Bird Watcher. McGraw-Hill Book Co., New York.

Broley, M. J.
> 1952   Eagle Man: Charles L. Broley's Field Adventures with American Eagles. Pellegrini & Cudahy, Publishers, New York.

Harrison, G. H.
> 1976   Roger Tory Peterson's Dozen Birding Hot Spots. Simon & Schuster, Inc., New York.

Hickey, J. J.
> 1963   A Guide to Bird Watching. National History Library, Garden City, N.Y.

Laycock, G.
> 1976   The Bird Watcher's Bible. Doubleday & Company, Inc., Garden City, N.Y.

Pasquier, R. F.
> 1977   Watching Birds: An introduction to Ornithology. Houghton Mifflin Co., Boston.

Piatt, J.
> 1973   Adventures in Birding: Confessions of a Lister. Alfred A. Knopf, New York.

2
BIRDING EQUIPMENT

Unlike many outdoor activities, bird watching is relatively inexpensive once the basic equipment is purchased. While it is true that some birders spend large sums of money for equipment, books, and travel to remote corners of the world, all of that is optional rather than necessary. Nevertheless, some basic equipment is necessary—notably binoculars and a field guide. Hints for selecting these items are contained in this chapter and the next.

Binoculars

When selecting binoculars, buy the very best that can be afforded. Such equipment will last a lifetime if used properly. Good binoculars also help in aiding bird identification by permitting subtle but important field marks to be seen more distinctly than may be possible with equipment of poorer quality. Therefore, consider very carefully different brands, styles, and prices of equipment before buying. Cheap binoculars frequently are very inferior pieces of equipment.

Since the single most important tool used in bird watching is an adequate pair of binoculars, the instrument should have the proven efficiency of central focusing, or a rapid focus lever, rather than oculars which are focused individually, as sometimes are found on older war surplus models.

The magnification of the instrument is largely a matter of each person's preference, but it should range between 6X and 10X. Most birders prefer 7x35, 7x50, or 8x40 binoculars. Those providing the lower magnification are most useful for making observations at close range whereas those which provide the higher magnifications enable one to observe birds at greater distances but still see detail adequate for proper identification. Some people engaged in special types of birding, e. g., hawk watching or studying shorebirds, prefer

Lightweight 8 × 40 prism binoculars. Photo courtesy of Swift Instruments, Inc.

Compact 8 × 30 prism binoculars. Photo courtesy of Carl Zeiss, Inc.

10X binoculars, and a few people, myself included, use 10X models routinely for all types of birding. For the most part, however, most birders select binoculars with magnifications of 7X or 8X.

In the specifications of a pair of binoculars, such as 7x50, the first number indicates the degree of magnification and the second number the relative brightness or light gathering capability of the instrument. The higher the second number, the brighter the image for a given degree of magnification. Thus a 7x50 pair of binoculars will provide considerably brighter images than a 7x35 model. While this difference may not be too obvious under normal or bright light **conditions, it becomes very obvious in woodland with dark shadows, at dawn or dusk, or whenever light is dim. However, a**

Traditional design 7 × 35 prism binoculars. Photo courtesy of Swift Instruments, Inc.

"Insta-Focus" 7 × 35 wide angle prism binoculars. Photo courtesy of Bushnell Optical Co.

disadvantage of most binoculars with great light gathering capability is their greater size and weight which can be much in excess of other binoculars.

Another factor which influences the brightness of the image seen through binoculars is the coating applied to the lenses by the manufacturer. Such coating not only provides brighter images but also reduces unwanted reflections within the instrument. All binoculars used for bird watching should have coated lenses (the bluish or metallic tint which is visible on the outside of the lenses).

The field of view provided by a pair of binoculars also is important. Generally the greater the field of view—the distance in feet (or meters) across a scene that binoculars provide at a distance of 1,000 yards (or meters)—the easier it is to locate birds perched or in flight. Most binoculars have the field of view engraved on the instrument, e.g., 375 feet at 1,000 yards. As a rule of thumb, the higher the magnification of the binoculars the narrower the field of view.

Telescopes

Many birders use telescopes in addition to binoculars, to aid in identifying waterfowl, hawks, shorebirds, and other kinds of birds. One can select from two basic types: zoom or non-zoom. Zoom telescopes allow the user to change magnification through a continuous range (generally 20X to 60X) by turning a wheel or knob on the instrument. Non-zoom telescopes, in contrast, offer a similar range of magnification but require the user to change eyepieces when a higher or lower magnification is desired. In either case, 20X or 30X is the magnification preferred by most birders.

When one uses a telescope for birding, however, some type of support is necessary because of the high magnifications involved. Most birders mount their scopes on photographic tripods such as those commonly available in camera stores. They provide adequate support, allow the instrument to be positioned and focused on a particular bird or group of birds, and also allow other birders in the group to examine a subject without having to readjust the telescope. However, this technique is useful only for birds which remain fairly stationary. For birds in flight, such as migrating ducks or hawks, many observers prefer to mount their telescopes on wood gunstocks. This permits the user maximum flexibility to locate and focus the scope on birds flying overhead or at other awkward angles. An added advantage of using a telescope mounted on a gunstock is that there is less danger that somebody will stumble over the legs of a tripod and damage the scope. This can happen easily at

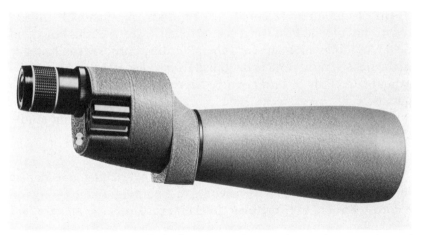

A typical zoom telescope used by bird watchers. A photographic tripod or gunstock is used to support the instrument. Photo courtesy of Bushnell Optical Co.

popular places such as hawk lookouts which sometimes become crowded with visitors.

Tape Recorders

With the ready availability of small, battery powered cassette tape recorders, bird watchers can use recordings of bird songs to aid them in their field activities. By playing the recorded songs of various species, particularly during the breeding season, birders can induce many otherwise elusive species to respond with song and to emerge into view. Tanagers, thrushes, warblers, and most other species of songbirds respond well to playbacks of their songs. Even nocturnal species show interest. Screech Owls, for example, usually respond to playbacks of their calls quickly and thus enable birders to see them (with the aid of a flashlight).

Exciting as this technique is, extreme caution is necessary in its use. Song is a fundamental part of a male bird's defense of his nest territory against other males of the same species. By repeated or prolonged playing of a recorded song during the nesting season, a bird's nesting attempts can be seriously disrupted or destroyed completely. *Never continue to play a recorded song so repeatedly or so long that a bird is driven from its territory.* Because of the danger to some birds, use of recorded bird songs in some locations is prohibited. A case in point is in Michigan where birders visiting areas used as nesting grounds by the endangered Kirtland's Warbler are prohibited from playing recorded songs of this species in an effort to locate the birds. It is possible that use of the songs of other endangered species also will be prohibited in the future if such activity might further endanger the birds in their vital nesting efforts.

21

The techniques required to produce professional quality recordings of wild bird songs are beyond the scope of this book, but field recordings adequate for general birding purposes can be made in the field by most birders or copied from some of the commercially available records of bird sounds. Some of these also are available commercially on cassettes. Thus, by a variety of methods, one can build a library of bird songs for use in the field or for home study.

Records

One of the easiest and most effective ways of learning to recognize the songs of wild birds is by listening to recordings of their songs on records. Birders are fortunate in this regard because an excellent selection of such records now is available. The titles of records listed here are available at various prices directly from the Cornell Laboratory of Ornithology, 159 Sapsucker Woods Road, Ithaca, N.Y. 14853. Many of these were made from original tape recordings in the Laboratory's world famous library of natural sounds. For example, the only authentic recording of an Ivory-billed Woodpecker, a species bordering on extinction, was made by Arthur A. Allen, one of the Laboratory's founders.

Record	*Producer*
AMERICAN BIRD SONGS (2 volumes)	Cornell Laboratory of Ornithology
BIRD SONGS IN LITERATURE	Cornell Laboratory of Ornithology
BIRD SONGS IN YOUR GARDEN	Cornell Laboratory of Ornithology
BIRD SONGS OF SOUTH CAROLINA	Cornell Laboratory of Ornithology
CARIBBEAN BIRD SONGS	Cornell Laboratory of Ornithology
DAWN IN A DUCKBLIND	Cornell Laboratory of Ornithology
AN EVENING IN SAPSUCKER WOODS	Cornell Laboratory of Ornithology
A FIELD GUIDE TO BIRD SONGS	Cornell Laboratory of Ornithology
A FIELD GUIDE TO WESTERN BIRD SONGS	Cornell Laboratory of Ornithology
FLORIDA BIRD SONGS	Cornell Laboratory of Ornithology
MEXICAN BIRD SONGS	Cornell Laboratory of Ornithology
MUSIC AND BIRD SONGS	Cornell Laboratory of Ornithology
SONGBIRDS OF AMERICA	Cornell Laboratory of Ornithology
ANTARCTICA	Saydisc Specialized Recordings Ltd.
BIRD SONG AND BIRD BEHAVIOR	Dover Publications, Inc.

BIRDS ON A MAY MORNING	Droll Yankees, Inc.
THE BROOK	Droll Yankees, Inc.
COMMON BIRD SONGS	Dover Publications, Inc.
A DAY AT FLORES MORADAS	Federation of Ontario Naturalists
A DAY AT ALGONQUIN PARK	Federation of Ontario Naturalists
FINCHES	Federation of Ontario Naturalists
PRAIRIE SPRING	Federation of Ontario Naturalists
SAPSUCKERS AND FLICKERS	Droll Yankees, Inc.
SONG SPARROW	Droll Yankees, Inc.
SONGS OF EASTERN BIRDS	Dover Publications, Inc.
SONGS OF SPRING	Federation of Ontario Naturalists
SONGS OF THE FOREST	Droll Yankees, Inc.
SONGS OF WESTERN BIRDS	Dover Publications, Inc.
SPRING MORNING	Droll Yankees, Inc.
THE SWAMP IN JUNE	Droll Yankees, Inc.
THRUSHES, WRENS AND MOCKINGBIRDS	Federation of Ontario Naturalists
WARBLERS	Federation of Ontario Naturalists

Other Equipment

One of the most important, yet least expensive, items which a birder uses is a field checklist. These checklists are small, pocket-size cards on which are printed the names of all of the species of birds known to occur in a particular area and their seasonal status in the area. Such cards can be purchased from various sources including bird clubs, the American Birding Association, and various local and regional Audubon Societies. In addition, most national wildlife refuges provide such checklists without cost. One merely stops at the information booth or center at the refuge and requests a checklist, usually forthcoming with other useful literature.

Many birders also carry with them into the field small notebooks and pencils and note interesting or unusual birds they observe. Such field notes are very important and sometimes contain raw information which is new to science! In addition, field notes and field checklists help in recalling enjoyable birding experiences over the years. Careful, accurate note-taking is very important. Notes should always include the date, location, species seen, and the numbers of each species seen.

Another inexpensive item very useful to birders is the bird "squeaker" sold by the National Audubon Society. It is surprisingly effective in attracting many songbirds. Use of this gadget frequently permits birders to see species whose presence may not have been suspected.

Kittatinny Ridg
Pennsylvania. I
217. Its' scatte
as hawk look
covers the rid

Bird watchir
during the ;
from Septe
Appalachiar
summit, pr
South Lool

This list
observed
since 19
1976, 5
those
Birding

Most
Knob
relati
dicat
the s
appe

AUTUMN BIRDS OF BAKE OVEN KNOB
Lehigh County, PA.

	Sept.	Oct.	Nov.
oon	r	u	c
sted Cormorant	u	r	
e Heron	r	r	r
S, DUCKS and GEESE			
g Swan			u
Goose	c	a	c
		c	c
Goose	r	u	u
d		r	u
can Black Duck	r	u	u
mon Pintail	u	u	r
-winged Teal		r	
d Duck			r
mmon Merganser		r	u
d-breasted Merganser	u	r	
ES, HAWKS, EAGLES, and FALCONS			
Turkey Vulture	u	u	r
Osprey	u	u	r
Northern Goshawk	r	u	u
Sharp-shinned Hawk	c	c	u
Cooper's Hawk	r	u	r
Red-tailed Hawk	u	c	c
Red-shouldered Hawk	r	u	u
Broad-winged Hawk	a	u	r
Rough-legged Hawk	r	r	r
Golden Eagle	r	r	r
Bald Eagle*	r	r	r
Northern Harrier	u	u	u
Peregrine Falcon*	r	r	r
Merlin	r	r	r
American Kestrel	u	u	r

A pocket-size field checklist

Sometimes decoys of a variety of types also can be helpful in certain types of bird watching. Artificial owls, for example, are used commonly at hawk migration lookouts to attract some hawks closer to the lookouts and give birders better views of the raptors. If an owl figure is placed in an upright position on top of a long pole, birds such as Sharp-shinned Hawks frequently dart within a few feet of the decoy and near to observers. Such artificial owls are sold in many sporting goods stores.

Weather maps also can be helpful to bird watchers during the spring and autumn migration seasons because many flights of migrating birds are closely associated with changes in weather conditions such as cold fronts and drops in barometric pressure. For instance, in autumn, low pressure and then a cold front advancing over northern New York State and lower New England tend to bring hawks flying over Pennsylvania and New Jersey shortly afterward. Weather maps can be consulted in newspapers or on television, to try to predict when the best birding conditions will occur. Many hawk watchers follow weather maps keenly.

Photographing wild birds is an extremely popular sideline of bird watching. Many birders are engaged in this activity. This is a subject in itself, however, and is beyond the scope of this book. Some of the best references on bird and nature photography are listed in the following selection of additional reading material.

Additional Reading

Allen, A. A.
  1951   Stalking Birds with Color Camera. National Geographic Society, Washington, D.C.

Angel, H.
  1972   Nature Photography: Its Art and Techniques. Fountain Press, London.

Cooper, J. D.
  1963   Photography Through Monoculars, Binoculars, and Telescopes. 2d edition. Universal Photo Books, New York.

Cruickshank, A. D. (ed.)
  1957   Hunting with the Camera: A Guide to Techniques and Adventure in the Field. Harper & Brothers, Publishers, New York.

Fisher, J., and R. T. Peterson
  1964   The World of Birds. Doubleday & Co., Garden City, N.Y.

Gulledge, J. L.
  1976   Recording Bird Sounds. *The Living Bird*, 15: 183-203.

Hartshorne, C.
  1973   Born to Sing: An Interpretation and World Survey of Bird Song. Indiana University Press, Bloomington, Ind.

Hickey, J. J.
  1963   A Guide to Bird Watching. Natural History Library, Garden City, N.Y.

Hosking, E.
  1970   An Eye for a Bird. Paul S. Eriksson, New York.

Kinne, R.
  1962   The Complete Book of Nature Photography. A. S. Barnes and Co., Inc., New York.

Reichert, R. J., and E. Reichert
  1961   Binoculars and Scopes and their Uses in Photography. Chilton Co., Philadelphia.

Remsen, J. V., Jr.
  1977   On Taking Field Notes. *American Birds*, 31 (5): 946-53.

Scofield, M.
  1978   The Complete Outfitting & Source Book for Birdwatching. Great Outdoors Trading Co., Marshall, Calif.

3
FIELD GUIDES, REFERENCES, CHECKLISTS, RARE BIRD ALERTS

Watching birds is first and foremost an outdoor activity. But how successful a birder is in that activity, and how much he or she enjoys birding, depends in no small measure upon the field guides and other references available to be consulted. Indeed, without such references modern birding as it is enjoyed today would not exist.

This chapter, therefore, contains a listing of field guides and other books of particular value to birders. No attempt is made, however, to include all of the information published about a particular area or a particular subject. Some important references are large and very expensive. One such is Joseph M. Forshaw's *Parrots of the World*. It would be just about impossible to carry this splendid tome into the field and still enjoy productive birding! Other references are highly technical and of interest mainly to professional scientists. An example of such a work is *The Birds of North and Middle America* published by the Smithsonian Institution. Still others, such as H. Kirke Swann's *A Monograph of the Birds of Prey*, are out-of-print and rare, but may be available in good libraries and large museums. Fortunately, some out-of-print books of importance to bird watchers have been reprinted in paperback editions by Dover Publications, New York, and are readily available and inexpensive. An important example of such Dover reprints is A. C. Bent's *Life Histories of North American Birds*, originally published by the Smithsonian Institution. Every serious birder should have at least some of the Bent volumes in his or her library.

Books designed for field use are marked in this chapter by an asterisk (*). They usually are of a size which will fit neatly into a coat pocket.

North America

Bull, J., and J. Farrand, Jr.
*1977   The Audubon Society Field Guide to North American Birds. Eastern Region. Alfred A. Knopf, New York.

Peterson, R. T.
*1947   A Field Guide to the Birds. 2d revised and enlarged edition. Houghton Mifflin Co., Boston.
*1961   A Field guide to Western Birds. 2d edition revised and enlarged. Houghton Mifflin Co., Boston.

Pough, R. H.
*1946   Audubon Bird Guides: Eastern Land Birds. Doubleday & Co., Garden City, N.Y.
*1951   Audubon Bird Guide: Water, Game, and Large Land Birds. Doubleday & Co., Garden City, N.Y.
*1957   Audubon Western Bird Guide. Doubleday & Co., Garden City, N.Y.

Robbins, C. S. et al.
*1966   Birds of North America: A Guide to Field Identification. Golden Press, New York.

Udvardy, M. D. F.
*1977   The Audubon Society Field Guide to North American Birds. Western Region. Alfred A. Knopf, New York.

United States

Alabama
Imhof, T. A.
1976   Alabama Birds. 2d edition. University of Alabama Press, University, Ala.

Alaska
Gabrielson, I. N., and F. C. Lincoln
1959   The Birds of Alaska. Stackpole Co., Harrisburg, Pa.

Morrin, H.
1978   Birding the 49th State: An Alaska Saga. Available from American Birding Association, P.O. Box 4335, Austin, Texas 78765.

Arizona
Lane, J. A.
*1977   Birder's Guide to Southeastern Arizona. American Birding Association, Austin, Texas (see *Morrin*, above).

Phillips, A., J. Marshall, and G. Monson
1964   The Birds of Arizona. University of Arizona Press, Tucson, Ariz.

Arkansas
Baerg, W. J.
1951   Birds of Arkansas. University of Arkansas Agricultural Experiment Station Bulletin No. 258 (revised): 1-188.

27

California

Brandt, J.
   1976   Birding Locations in and Around Los Angeles. Available
          from American Birding Association, Austin, Texas.

Dawson, W. L.
   1923   The Birds of California. 4 volumes. South Moulton Co.,
          San Diego, Calif.

Lane, J. A.
   *1976 Birder's Guide to Southern California. American Birding
          Association, Austin, Texas.

Small, A.
   1974   The Birds of California. Winchester Press, New York.

Colorado

Bailey, A. N., and R. J. Niedrach
   1965   Birds of Colorado. 2 volumes. Denver Museum of Natural
          History, Denver, Colo.

Davis, W. A.
   1969   Birds in Western Colorado. American Birding Association,
          Austin, Texas.

Lane, J. A., and H. R. Holt
   *1975 A Birder's Guide to Eastern Colorado. American Birding
          Association, Austin, Texas.

Connecticut

Proctor, N.
   1978   25 Birding Areas in Connecticut. American Birding Asso-
          ciation, Austin, Texas.

Sage, J. H., L. B. Bishop, and W. P. Bliss
   1913   The Birds of Connecticut. Connecticut State Geological and
          Natural History Survey Bulletin 20: 1-370.

Delaware

Brady, A. et al.
   *1972 A Field List of the Birds of the Delaware Valley Region.
          Delaware Valley Ornithological Club, Philadelphia.

Rhoads, S. N., and C. J. Pennock
   1905   Birds of Delaware: A Preliminary List. *Auk*, 22: 194-205.

District of Columbia

Stewart, R. E., and C. S. Robbins
   1958   Birds of Maryland and the District of Columbia. North
          American Fauna No. 62: 1-401.

Florida

Bailey, H. H.
   1925   The Birds of Florida. Williams & Wilkins Co., Baltimore,
          Md.

Bowman, M. C., and H. Kale
   1977   Where to Find Birds in Florida. American Birding Associ-
          ation, Austin, Texas.

Sprunt, A., Jr.
   1954   Florida Bird Life. Coward-McCann, New York.

Georgia
Burleigh, T. D.
   1958   Georgia Birds. University of Oklahoma Press, Norman, Okla.

Hans, D. W. (ed.)
   *1975   A Birder's Guide to Georgia. American Birding Association, Austin, Texas.

Hawaii
Berger, A. J.
   1972   Hawaiian Birdlife. University Press of Hawaii, Honolulu, Hawaii.

Munro, G. C.
   *1960   Birds of Hawaii. Revised edition. Charles E. Tuttle Co., Rutland, Vt.

Peterson, R. T.
   *1961   A Field Guide to Western Birds. 2d edition, revised and enlarged. Houghton Mifflin Co., Boston. (Includes a section on Hawaiian birds.)

Idaho
Burleigh, T. D.
   1971   Birds of Idaho. Caxton Printers, Ltd., Caldwell, Ida.

Illinois
Behrens, J.
   *1976   Birding Handbook to East-Central Illinois. American Birding Association, Austin, Texas.

Fawks, E.
   *1975   Bird Finding in Illinois. American Birding Association, Austin, Texas.

Sanders, J., and L. Yaskot
   *1975   Top Birding Spots near Chicago. American Birding Association, Austin, Texas.

Indiana
Butler, A. W.
   1898   The Birds of Indiana. Report of the State Geologist of Indiana for 1897: 515-1187.

Mumford, R., and C. Keller
   1975   An Annotated Checklist of Indiana Birds. American Birding Association, Austin, Texas.

Iowa
DuMont, P. A.
   1933   A Revised List of the Birds of Iowa. University of Iowa Studies in Natural History, 15: 1-171.

Kansas
Johnston, R. P.
   1964   The Breeding Birds of Kansas. University of Kansas Publications Museum of Natural History, 12: 575-655.

1965   A Directory to the Birds of Kansas. University of Kansas, Museum of Natural History Miscellaneous Publications No. 41.

Kentucky
Barbour, R. W. et al.
*1973   Kentucky Birds: A Finding Guide. University of Kentucky Press, Lexington, Ky.

Mengel, R. M.
1965   The Birds of Kentucky. American Ornithologists' Union Ornithological Monographs No. 3: 1-581.

Louisiana
Lowery, G. H., Jr.
1974   Louisiana Birds. 3d edition. Louisiana State University Press, Baton Rouge, La.

Maine
Palmer, R. S.
1949   Maine Birds. Bulletin Museum of Comparative Zoology, 102: 1-656.

Maryland
Robbins, C., and D. Bystrak
1977   Field List of the Birds of Maryland. American Birding Association, Austin, Texas.

Stewart, R. E., and C. S. Robbins
1958   Birds of Maryland and the District of Columbia. North American Fauna No. 62: 1-401.

Massachusetts
Forbush, E. H.
1925-29   Birds of Massachusetts and Other New England States. 3 vol. Massachusetts Department of Agriculture, Boston.
Griscom, L., and D. E. Snyder
1955   The Birds of Massachusetts: An Annotated and Revised Check List. Peabody Museum, Salem, Mass.

Michigan
Michigan Audubon Society
1973   Enjoying Birds in Michigan. Revised edition. American Birding Association, Austin, Texas.

Wood, N. A.
1951   The Birds of Michigan. University of Michigan Museum of Zoology Miscellaneous Publications No. 75.

Zimmerman, D. A., and J. Van Tyne
1959   A Distributional Check-list of the Birds of Michigan. University of Michigan Museum of Zoology Occasional Papers No. 608.

Minnesota
Eckert, K. R.
*1974   A Birder's Guide to Minnesota. Minnesota Ornithologists

Union, James Ford Bell Museum of Natural History, University of Minnesota, Minneapolis, Minn.

Green, J. C., and R. B. Janssen
  1975   Minnesota Birds: Where, When and How Many. University of Minnesota Press, Minneapolis, Minn.

Roberts, T. S.
  1936   The Birds of Minnesota. 2 volumes. 2d revised edition. University of Minnesota Press, Minneapolis, Minn.

Mississippi
Coffey, B. B., Jr.
  1936   A Preliminary List of the Birds of Mississippi. Mimeographed report.

Missouri
Bennitt, R.
  1932   Check-list of the Birds of Missouri. University of Missouri Studies, 7: 1-81.

Montana
Saunders, A. A.
  1921   A Distributional List of the Birds of Montana. Pacific Coast Avifauna No. 14.

Skaar, P. D.
  1975   Montana Bird Distribution: Preliminary Mapping by Latilong. Published privately, 501 S. Third, Bozeman, Mont.

Nebraska
Rapp, W. F., Jr. et al.
  1958   Revised Check-list of Nebraska Birds. Nebraska Ornithologists Union Occasional Papers No. 5.

Nevada
Linsdale, J. M.
  1936   The Birds of Nevada. Pacific Coast Avifauna No. 23. Supplement in *Condor*, 1951, 53: 228-49.

New Hampshire
Richards, T.
  1958   A List of the Birds of New Hampshire. Audubon Society of New Hampshire, Concord, N.H.

New Jersey
Brady, A. et al.
  *1972   A Field List of the Birds of the Delaware Valley Region. Delaware Valley Ornithological Club, Philadelphia.

Fables, D., Jr.
  1955   Annotated List of New Jersey Birds. Urner Ornithological Club, Newark, N.J.

Leck, C. F.
  1975   The Birds of New Jersey: Their Habits and Habitats. Rutgers University Press, New Brunswick, N.J.

Stone, W.
       1937   Bird Studies at Old Cape May. 2 volumes. Delaware Valley
               Ornithological Club, Philadelphia. (Reprinted by Dover
               Publications, New York.)

New Mexico
Ligon, J. S.
       1961   New Mexico Birds and Where to Find Them. University of
               New Mexico Press, Albuquerque, N.M.
Montgomery, V. A.
      *1969   Bird-Finding Localities in the Vicinity of Roswell, New
               Mexico. American Birding Association, Austin, Texas.

New York
Arbib, R. et al.
      *1966   Enjoying Birds Around New York City. Houghton Mifflin
               Co., Boston.

Beehler, B.
       1978   Birdlife of the Adirondack Park. American Birding Associ-
               ation, Austin, Texas.

Bull, J.
       1964   Birds of the New York Area. Harper & Row, Publishers,
               New York.
       1974   Birds of New York State. Doubleday/Natural History
               Press, Garden City, N.Y.
Comar, M., D. Kibbe, and D. McIlroy
       1974   Birding in the Cayuga Lake Basin. American Birding
               Association, Austin, Texas.
Pettingill, O. S., Jr., and S. F. Hoyt
      *1963   Enjoying Birds in Upstate New York. Laboratory of
               Ornithology, Cornell University, Ithaca, N.Y.

North Carolina
Carolina Bird Club, Inc.
       1977   Checklist of North Carolina Birds. American Birding
               Association, Austin, Texas.
Wray, D. L., and H. T. Davis
       1959   Birds of North Carolina. Revised edition. Bynum Printing
               Co., Raleigh, N.C.

North Dakota
Stewart, R. E.
       1975   Breeding Birds of North Dakota. Tri-College Center for
               Environmental Studies, Fargo, N.D.

Ohio
Trautman, M. B.
       1940   The Birds of Buckeye Lake, Ohio. University Michigan
               Museum of Zoology Miscellaneous Publications 44: 1-466.
Trautman, M. B., and M. A. Trautman
       1968   Annotated List of the Birds of Ohio. Ohio Journal of
               Science, 68 (5): 257-332.

Oklahoma

FIELD GUIDES, REFERENCES, CHECKLISTS, RARE BIRD ALERTS

Sutton, G. M.
- 1967   Oklahoma Birds: Their Ecology and Distribution, with Comments on the Avifauna of the Southern Great Plains. University of Oklahoma Press, Norman, Okla.

Tulsa Audubon Society
- 1973   Tulsa Audubon Society Bird Finding Guide. American Birding Association, Austin, Texas.

Oregon

Gabrielson, I. N., and S. G. Jewett
- 1940   Birds of Oregon. Oregon State College, Corvallis, Ore.

Ramsey, F. L.
- 1978   Birding Oregon. American Birding Association, Austin, Texas.

Pennsylvania

Brady, A. et al.
- *1972   A Field List of the Birds of the Delaware Valley Region. Delaware Valley Ornithological Club, Philadelphia.

Freeland, D. B.
- *1975   Where to Find Birds in Western Pennsylvania. Audubon Society of Western Pennsylvania, Pittsburgh, Pa.

Poole, E. L.
- 1964   Pennsylvania Birds: An Annotated List. Delaware Valley Ornithological Club, Philadelphia.

Street, P. B.
- 1956   Birds of the Pocono Mountains, Pennsylvania. Delaware Valley Ornithological Club, Philadelphia.
- 1975   Birds of the Pocono Mountains, 1955-1975. *Cassinia*, 55: 3-16.

Todd, W. E. C.
- 1940   Birds of Western Pennsylvania. University of Pittsburgh Press, Pittsburgh, Pa.

Wood, M.
- *1973   Birds of Pennsylvania. College of Agriculture, Pennsylvania State University, University Park, Pa.
- 1976   Birds of Central Pennsylvania. State College Bird Club, Inc., State College, Pa.

Rhode Island

Howe, R. H., Jr., and E. Sturtevant
- 1899   The Birds of Rhode Island. Published privately.
- 1903   A Supplement to the Birds of Rhode Island. Middletown, R.I.

South Carolina

Sprunt, A., Jr., E. B. Chamberlain, and E. M. Burton
- 1970   South Carolina Bird Life. Revised edition with a supplement. University of South Carolina Press, Columbia, S.C.

Tennessee

Gainer, A. F.
1933   A Distributional List of the Birds of Tennessee. Tennessee Ornithological Society, Nashville, Tenn.

Parmer, H. E.
1975   Birds of the Nashville Area. American Birding Association, Austin, Texas.

Wetmore, A.
1939   Notes on the Birds of Tennessee. Proceedings U.S. National Museum, 86: 175-243.

Texas

Kutac, E., and S. C. Caran
*1976   A Bird Finding and Naturalist's Guide for the Austin, Texas, Area. American Birding Association, Austin, Texas.

Lane, J. A.
*1978   Birder's Guide to Rio Grande Valley. American Birding Association, Austin, Texas.

Lane, J. A., and J. Tveten
*1974   A Birder's Guide to the Texas Coast. American Birding Association, Austin, Texas.

Oberholser, H. C. et al.
1974   The Bird Life of Texas. 2 volumes. University of Texas Press, Austin, Texas.

Peterson, R. T.
*1960   A Field Guide to the Birds of Texas. Houghton Mifflin Co., Boston.

Texas Ornithological Society
1975   Checklist of the Birds of Texas. American Birding Association, Austin, Texas.

Tucker, J. A.
1971   The Texas Birding Marathon. American Birding Association, Austin, Texas.

Wauer, R. H.
*1973   Birds of Big Bend National Park and Vicinity. University of Texas Press, Austin, Texas.

Utah

Behle, W., and M. L. Perry
1975   Utah Birds: Guide, Check-List and Occurrence Charts. Utah Museum of Natural History, University of Utah, Salt Lake City, Utah.

Vermont

Farrar, R. B., Jr.
1973   Birds of East-Central Vermont. American Birding Association, Austin, Texas.

Virginia

Murray, J. J.
1952   A Check-list of the Birds of Virginia. Virginia Society of Ornithology, Lexington, Va.

Washington

Jewett, S. G. et al.
    1953   Birds of Washington State. University of Washington Press,
            Seattle, Wash.

Wahl, T. R., and D. R. Paulson
    *1974   A Guide to Bird Finding in Washington. Whatcom Museum
            of History and Art, 121 Prospect St., Bellingham, Wash.

West Virginia

Brooks, M.
    1944   A Check-list of West Virginia Birds. West Virginia
            University Agricultural Experiment Station Bulletin 316.

Wisconsin

Gromme, O. J.
    1963   Birds of Wisconsin. University of Wisconsin Press,
            Madison, Wis.

Kumlien, L., and N. Hollister
    1951   The Birds of Wisconsin. Revisions by A. W. Schorger.
            Wisconsin Society for Ornithology, Madison, Wis.

Tessen, D.
    *1976   Wisconsin's Favorite Bird Haunts. American Birding
            Association, Austin, Texas.

Wyoming

McCreary, O.
    1939   Wyoming Bird Life. Revised edition. Burgess Publishing
            Co., Minneapolis, Minn.

Canada

Canada

Godfrey, W. E.
    1966   The Birds of Canada. National Museum of Canada Bulletin
            No. 203 (Biological Series): 1-428.

Stirling, D., and J. Woodford
    1976   Where to go Birdwatching in Canada. American Birding
            Association, Austin, Texas.

Alberta

Salt, W. R. , and A. L. Wilk
    1966   The Birds of Alberta. 2d (revised) edition. Alberta Depart-
            ment of Industry and Development, Edmonton, Alta.

British Columbia

Mark, D. M.
    1978   Where to Find Birds in British Columbia. American Birding
            Association, Austin, Texas.

Munro, J. A., and I. McT. Cowan
    1947   A Review of the Bird Fauna of British Columbia. British
            Columbia Provincial Museum Special Publication
            No. 2: 1-285.

35

Labrador

Todd, W. E. C.
>1963   Birds of the Labrador Peninsula and Adjacent Areas. University of Toronto Press, Toronto.

Manitoba

Jehl, J. R., and B. Smith
>1964   Birds of the Churchill Region, Manitoba. American Birding Association, Austin, Texas.

New Brunswick

Squires, W. A.
>1952   The Birds of New Brunswick. New Brunswick Museum Monograph Series No. 4.

Newfoundland

Peters, H. S., and T. D. Burleigh
>1951   The Birds of Newfoundland. Houghton Mifflin Co., Boston.

Nova Scotia

Nova Scotia Bird Society
>1976   Where to Find the Birds in Nova Scotia. American Birding Association, Austin, Texas.

Tufts, R. W.
>1962   The Birds of Nova Scotia. Nova Scotia Museum, Halifax, N.S.

Ontario

James, R. D., P. L. McLaren, and J. C. Barlow
>1976   Annotated Checklist of the Birds of Ontario. American Birding Association, Austin, Texas.

Stirrett, G.
>1973   The Spring Birds of Point Pelee National Park. American Birding Association, Austin, Texas.

Prince Edward Island

Godfrey, W. E.
>1954   Birds of Prince Edward Island. National Museum of Canada Bulletin No. 132: 155-213.

Quebec

Canadian Wildlife Service
>1973   Sea-birds of Bonaventure Island. American Birding Association, Austin, Texas.

Saskatchewan

Renaud, W. E., and D. H. Renaud
>1975   Birds of the Rosetown-Biggar District, Saskatchewan. Saskatchewan Natural History Society Special Publication No. 9: 1-120.

Yukon

Rand, A. L.
>1946   List of Yukon Birds and Those of the Canol Road. National Museum of Canada Bulletin No. 105: 1-76.

Greenland

Salomonsen, F.

1951 The Birds of Greenland. Ejnar Munksgaard, Copenhagen.

Central America

Central America

Blake, E. R.

1977 Manual of Neotropical Birds. Volume 1. University of Chicago Press, Chicago. (Additional volumes in preparation.)

Belize (British Honduras)

Russell, S. M.

1964 A Distributional Study of the Birds of British Honduras. American Ornithologists' Union Ornithological Monographs No. 1: 1-195.

Costa Rica

Slud, P.

1964 The Birds of Costa Rica. American Museum of Natural History Bulletin 128: 1-430.

El Salvador

Dickey, D. R., and A. J. Van Rossem

1938 The Birds of El Salvador. Field Museum Zoological Series, 23: 1-609.

Guatemala

Land, H. G.

*1970 Birds of Guatemala. Livingston Publishing Co., Wynnewood, Pa.

Smithe, F. B.

*1966 The Birds of Tikal. Natural History Press, Garden City, N.Y.

Honduras

Monroe, B. L., Jr.

1968 A Distributional Survey of the Birds of Honduras. American Ornithologists' Union Ornithological Monographs No. 7: 1-458.

Mexico

Alden, P.

*1969 Finding the Birds in Western Mexico. University of Arizona Press, Tucson, Ariz.

Blake, E. R.

*1953 Birds of Mexico: A Guide for Field Identification. University of Chicago Press, Chicago.

Davis, L. I.

*1972 A Field Guide to the Birds of Mexico and Central America. University of Texas Press, Austin, Texas.

37

Edwards, E. P.
*1968   Finding Birds in Mexico. 2d edition, revised and enlarged. Ernest P. Edwards, Sweet Briar, Va.
*1972   A Field Guide to the Birds of Mexico. Ernest P. Edwards, Sweet Briar, Va.

Peterson, R. T., and E. L. Chalif
*1973   A Field Guide to Mexican Birds and Adjacent Central America. Houghton Mifflin Co., Boston.

Panama
Edwards, E. P., and H. Loftin
*1971   Finding Birds in Panama. 2d edition, revised and enlarged. Ernest P. Edwards, Sweet Briar, Va.

Ridgely, R. S.
*1976   A Guide to the Birds of Panama. Princeton University Press, Princeton, N.J.

Wetmore, A.
1965   The Birds of the Republic of Panama. 4 volumes. Smithsonian Institution Press, Washington, D.C.

South America

There are no completely adequate field guides to identification of South American birds available. In some instances birders can use books detailing the birdlife of nearby countries, such as *Birds of Surinam* or *A Guide to the Birds of Venezuela*, for much of northeastern South America including the Amazon basin. Likewise, *The Birds of the Department of Lima, Peru* is useful for much of the western slopes of South America. Unfortunately the only book available for all of South America, *A Guide to the Birds of South America*, is helpful but difficult to use. Thus birding in South America is both a challenge and an adventure. One never knows what strange or rare bird might appear. Indeed, new species still are being discovered in Peru and elsewhere on the continent.

South America
Blake, E. R.
1977   Manual of Neotropical Birds. Volume 1. University of Chicago Press, Chicago. (Additional volumes in preparation.)

Meyer de Schauensee, R.
*1970   A Guide to the Birds of South America. Livingston Publishing Co., Wynnewood, Pa.

Antarctica
Watson, G. E.
*1975   Birds of the Antarctic and Sub-Antarctic. American Geophysical Union, Washington, D.C.

Argentina
Humphrey, P. S. et al.
  1970   Birds of Isla Grande (Tierra del Fuego). University of Kansas Museum of Natural History, Lawrence, Kan.

Brazil
Mitchell, M. H.
  1957   Observations on Birds of Southeastern Brazil. University of Toronto Press, Toronto.

Chile
Humphrey, P. S. et al.
  1970   Birds of Isla Grande (Tierra del Fuego). University of Kansas Museum of Natural History, Lawrence, Kan.

Johnson, A. W.
  1965-67   The Birds of Chile & Adjacent Regions of Argentina, Bolivia & Peru. 2 volumes. Buenos Aires.
  1972   Supplement to the Birds of Chile & Adjacent Regions. Buenos Aires.

Colombia
Meyer de Schauensee, R.
  *1964   The Birds of Colombia and Adjacent Areas of South and Central America. Livingston Publishing Co., Narberth, Pa.

Ecuador
Harris, M.
  *1975   A Field Guide to the Birds of the Galapagos. Taplinger Publishing Co., New York.

Falkland Islands
Woods, R. W.
  1975   The Birds of the Falkland Islands. Lindblad Travel, Inc., N.Y.

Guyana
Snyder, D. E.
  *1966   The Birds of Guyana. Peabody Museum, Salem, Mass.

Peru
Johnson, A. W.
  1965-67   The Birds of Chile and Adjacent Regions of Argentina, Bolivia and Peru. 2 volumes. Buenos Aires.
  1972   Supplement to the Birds of Chile and Adjacent Regions. Buenos Aires.

Koepcke, M.
  *1970   The Birds of the Department of Lima, Peru. Livingston Publishing Co., Wynnewood, Pa.

Surinam
Haverschmidt, F.
  1968   Birds of Surinam. Oliver & Boyd, Edinburgh.

Venezuela
Meyer de Schauensee, R., and W. H. Phelps, Jr.
  1978   A Guide to the Birds of Venezuela. Princeton University Press, Princeton, N.J.

West Indies and Bermuda

West Indies

Bond, J.

 *1971   Birds of the West Indies. 2d edition. Houghton Mifflin Co., Boston.

Bahamas

Brudenell-Bruce, P. G. C.

 *1975   The Birds of the Bahamas. Taplinger Publishing Co., N. Y.

Bermuda

Wingate, D.

 *1973   A Checklist and Guide to the Birds of Bermuda. Available in book shops in Bermuda.

Puerto Rico

Leopold, N. F.

 1963   Checklist of Birds of Puerto Rico and the Virgin Islands. Puerto Rico Agricultural Experiment Station Bulletin 168.

Trinidad and Tobago

Bond, J.

 *1970   Native and Winter Resident Birds of Tobago. Academy of Natural Sciences of Philadelphia, Philadelphia.

ffrench, R.

 *1973   A Guide to the Birds of Trinidad and Tobago. Livingston Publishing Co., Wynnewood, Pa.

Heintzelman, D. S.

 *1973   Finding Birds in Trinidad and Tobago. D. S. Heintzelman, 629 Green St., Allentown, Pa.

Special Guides and References

General Bird Finding

Geffen, A. M.

 1978   A Birdwatcher's Guide to the Eastern United States. Barron's, Woodbury, N.Y.

Kitching, J.

 1976   Birdwatcher's Guide to Wildlife Sanctuaries. Arco Pub. Co., New York.

Pettingill, O. S., Jr.

 *1953   A Guide to Bird Finding West of the Mississippi. Oxford University Press, New York. (New edition in preparation.)

 *1977   A Guide to Bird Finding East of the Mississippi. 2d edition. Oxford University Press, New York.

Hawk Watching

Brett, J. J., and A. C. Nagy

 *1973   Feathers in the Wind: The Mountain and the Migrations. Hawk Mountain Sanctuary Association, Kempton, P.

Heintzelman, D. S.

    *1972   A Guide to Northeastern Hawk Watching. Published privately, Lambertville, N.J. (Out of print.)

    1975   Autumn Hawk Flights: The Migrations in Eastern North America. Rutgers University Press, New Brunswick, N.J.

    *1976   A Guide to Eastern Hawk Watching. Pennsylvania State University Press, University Park, Pa.

    *1979a   A Guide to Hawk Watching in North America. Pennsylvania State University Press, University Park, Pa.

    1979b   Hawks and Owls of North America. Universe Books, N.Y.

Pelagic Birding

Alexander, W. B.

    *1954   Birds of the Ocean. New and revised edition. G. P. Putnam's Sons, New York.

Brown, R. G. B. et al.

    1975   Atlas of Eastern Canadian Seabirds. Canadian Wildlife Service, Ottawa.

King, W. B.

    *1967   Seabirds of the Tropical Pacific Ocean: Preliminary Smithsonian Identification Manual. Smithsonian Institution, Washington, D.C.

Murphy, R. C.

    1936   Oceanic Birds of South America. 2 volumes. American Museum of Natural History, New York.

Palmer, R. S. (ed.)

    1962   Handbook of North American Birds. Volume 1. Yale University Press, New Haven, Conn.

Stallcup, R.

    1976   Pelagic Birds of Monterey Bay, California. American Birding Association, Austin, Texas.

Watson, G. E.

    *1966   Seabirds of the Tropical Atlantic Ocean. Smithsonian Press, Washington, D.C.

Waterfowl Birding

Bellrose, F. C.

    1976   Ducks, Geese & Swans of North America. Stackpole Books, Harrisburg, Pa.

Heintzelman, D. S.

    1978   North American Ducks, Geese & Swans. Winchester Press, New York.

Johnsgard, P. A.

    1975   Waterfowl of North America. Indiana University Press, Bloomington, Ind.

Kortright, F. H.

    1953   The Ducks, Geese and Swans of North America. Stackpole Co., Harrisburg, Pa.

Palmer, R. S. (ed.)

>1976 Handbook of North American Birds. Volumes 2 and 3. Yale University Press, New Haven, Conn.

Scott, P.

>*1968 A Coloured Key to the Wildfowl of the World. The Wildfowl Trust, Slimbridge, England.

Bird Names

Choate, E. A.

>1973 The Dictionary of American Bird Names. Gambit, Boston.

Gruson, E. S.

>1972 Words for Birds: A Lexicon of North American Birds with Biographical Notes. Quadrangle Books, New York.

Bird Families

Austin, O. L., Jr.

>1961 Birds of the World. Golden Press, New York.

>1971 Families of Birds. Golden Science Guide, Golden Press, New York.

Gilliard, E. T.

>1958 Living Birds of the World. Doubleday & Co., Inc., New York.

Van Tyne, J., and A. J. Berger

>1959 Fundamentals of Ornithology. John Wiley & Sons, Inc., New York.

World Bird Checklists

Clements, J. F.

>1974 Birds of the World: A Check List. Two Continents Publishing Group, Ltd., New York.

Edwards, E. P.

>1974 A Coded List of Birds of the World. Ernest P. Edwards, Sweet Briar, Va.

Gruson, E. S.

>1976 Checklist of the World's Birds. Quadrangle Books, New York.

North American Bird Checklists

American Birding Association

>1975 A.B.A. Checklist. American Birding Association, Austin, Texas.

American Ornithologists' Union

>1957 Check-List of North American Birds. 5th edition. Port City Press, Inc., Baltimore, Md. (Order from American Ornithologists' Union.)

Major References to Selected Bird Families

Waterfowl

Delacour, J.
1954-64   The Waterfowl of the World. 4 volumes. Country Life Ltd., London.

Johnsgard, P. A.
1978   Ducks, Geese, and Swans of the World. University of Nebraska Press, Lincoln, Neb.

Ogilvie, M. A.
1978   Wild Geese. Buteo Books, Vermillion, S.D.

Curassows

Delacour, J., and D. Amadon
1973   Curassows and Related Birds. American Museum of Natural History, New York.

Hawks, Eagles, and Falcons

Brown, L., and D. Amadon
1968   Eagles, Hawks and Falcons of the World. 2 volumes. McGraw-Hill Book Co., New York.

Pheasants

Beebe, W.
1926   Pheasants: Their Lives and Homes. 2 volumes. Doubleday, Page & Co., Garden City, N.Y.

Cranes

Walkinshaw, L.
1973   Cranes of the World. Winchester Press, New York.

Rails

Ripley, S. D.
1977   Rails of the World. David R. Godine, Publisher, Boston.

Pigeons and Doves

Goodwin, D.
1967   Pigeons and Doves of the World. British Museum (Natural History), London.

Parrots

Forshaw, J. M.
1973   Parrots of the World. Doubleday & Company, Inc., N. Y.

Owls

Burton, J. A. (ed.)
1973   Owls of the World. E. P. Dutton & Co., Inc., New York.

Hummingbirds

Greenewalt, C. H.
1960   Hummingbirds. Doubleday & Company, Inc., Garden City, N.Y.

Crows

Goodwin, D.
1976   Crows of the World. Cornell University Press, Ithaca, N.Y.   43

Wood Warblers

Chapman, F. M.
  1907   The Warblers of North America. D. Appleton & Co., N.Y.
Griscom, L., and A. Sprunt, Jr.
  1957   The Warblers of America. Devin-Adair Co., New York.

Rare Bird Alerts

In many cities in the United States and Canada bird clubs and
Audubon Societies have established telephone numbers connected
to tape recorders which provide messages about rare birds seen
recently in the community. These messages are changed at frequent
intervals. The area codes and telephone numbers listed here were in
operation recently. Since they may change from time to time check
with your local bird club or Audubon Society to determine if an
alert is now operating in your area.

California
    Southern California   (213) 874-1318
    Northern California   (415) 843-2211
District of Columbia
    Washington, D.C.   (301) 652-1088
    Washington, D.C.   (202) 652-3295
Georgia
    Atlanta   (404) 634-5497
Massachusetts
    Eastern Massachusetts   (617) 259-8805
    Western Massachusetts   (413) 566-3590
Michigan-Ontario
    Detroit-Windsor   (313) 893-8020
    Minneapolis   (612) 933-6682
New Jersey
    Entire State   (201) 766-2661
New York
    Buffalo   (716) 896-1271
    New York City   (212) 832-6523
    Schenectady-Albany   (518) 377-9600
Ohio
    Cleveland   (216) 696-8186
    Columbus   (614) 221-9736
Pennsylvania
    Philadelphia   (215) 236-2473
    Western Pennsylvania   (412) 486-2090
Vermont
    Woodstock   (802) 457-2779
Washington
    Seattle   (206) 455-9722

4
BIRDING AND ORNITHOLOGICAL ORGANIZATIONS

Although a solitary observer can take up bird watching and enjoy it, many birders prefer to join birding and ornithological organizations where they can associate with people with similar interests. There are many advantages in doing so, and it will be worthwhile to examine some of them.

One very important advantage of joining a birding club is that association with fellow club members alerts birders to the local presence of rare birds which otherwise might not be heard of until it is too late to find and see them. The birding grapevine is vital to one's field efforts, and birders eager to add species to their life lists will find this source of information a distinct advantage of club membership. For example, at the frequent meetings of the Delaware Valley Ornithological Club in Philadelphia, some fifty to sixty members usually are present, and an extensive summary of unusual birds found in the area is presented along with full details about where the birds can be seen. Sometimes lively discussions accompany such presentations. Members of that organization soon develop a thick skin as a result of the sharp questioning which sometimes follows reports of exceptionally unusual species! The new reports of interesting birds also are added to the DVOC birding hotline (Rare Bird Alert), which allows other birders in the area who are not club members to share in the information.

Another very important privilege of membership in a bird club is the opportunity to attend lectures on a variety of topics relating to birds and ornithology. Not infrequently such programs are of a local focus and are presented by club members, but at the larger organizations such as the Delaware Valley Ornithological Club and the Linnaean Society of New York people of national and international reputation occasionally are featured. Such programs generally are outstanding and allow club members to view slides or motion pictures, or hear tape recordings, made on expeditions to distant lands and hear firsthand about some of the significant results of such field studies.

Participation in the field trips organized by most bird clubs also allows less experienced birders to learn directly from other more experienced birders. This is important because it effectively reduces the amount of time necessary to become skilled in bird watching. Indeed, beginning birders sometimes do not know that there are many subtle features of birds which are not always included in the illustrations or text of standard field guides yet which can be useful in making an identification of some birds. For example, in identifying accipiters in flight, it is a help to see flight style, size of bird, and shape of tail (notched or rounded). Such fine points of identification can be learned most easily by direct association with good birders with years of field experience. In addition, field trips not infrequently turn up new bird records for an area which often are of scientific value. To cite one instance, the forays conducted by members of the Brooks Bird Club of West Virginia commonly result in important new information about an area.

Finally, most of the larger bird clubs and ornithological organizations publish journals which contain a variety of original articles and notes detailing the birdlife of a particular area or region or some other aspect of birdlife. Such publications not only contain the basic raw materials for developing bird conservation programs but frequently also provide the basic facts needed for proper regional planning. In addition, the articles and notes published in birding and ornithological journals also provide the necessary historical foundation upon which knowledge of the birdlife of a given area is based and refined. Thus, for example, the important new information secured on the Brooks Bird Club's field forays is published in the club's journal *The Redstart*. Similar information is published in the DVOC's journal *Cassinia*. And, on a national and international level, the American Birding Association's fine magazine *Birding* contains a wealth of useful information on a great many topics in each issue. Not the least useful items are the birding inserts which detail outstanding birding locations and specific birds which one might expect to find at such spots.

Wildlife periodicals published by various state agencies sometimes contain articles dealing with bird watching, as do magazines issued by many conservation organizations.

There are hundreds of birding and ornithology organizations in the United States and Canada along with a few elsewhere in the Americas. Unfortunately, most do not have permanent addresses because of frequent changes of officers. However, the following clubs and groups do have permanent addresses and also publish noted journals. They can, therefore, be contacted without difficulty. For other birding organizations, consult Jon Rickert's *A Guide to North American Bird Clubs* (Avian Publications, 1978).

International

American Birding Association, Inc.
P.O. Box 4335
Austin, Texas 78765

Journal: *Birding*

American Ornithologists' Union
c/o National Museum of Natural
    History
Smithsonian Institution
Washington, D.C. 20560

Journal: *The Auk*

Cornell Laboratory of Ornithology
159 Sapsucker Woods Road
Ithaca, N.Y. 14850

Journal: *The Living Bird*

National Audubon Society
950 Third Avenue
New York, N.Y. 10022

Journal: *American Birds*

Wilson Ornithological Society
c/o Division of Birds
Museum of Zoology
University of Michigan
Ann Arbor, Mich. 48104

Journal: *The Wilson
    Bulletin*

California

Golden Gate Audubon Society
P.O. Box 103
Berkeley, Calif. 94701

Journal: *The Gull*

Connecticut

Audubon Society for the State of
    Connecticut
2325 Burr St.
Fairfield, Conn. 06430

Journal: *Bulletin of
    Connecticut Audubon
    Society*

District of Columbia

Audubon Naturalist Society of
    the Central Atlantic States
8940 Jones Mill Road
Washington, D.C. 20015

Journal: *Atlantic
    Naturalist*

Florida

Florida Audubon Society
P.O. Drawer 7,
Maitland, Florida 32751

Journal: *Florida Field
Naturalist*

Maine

Maine Audubon Society
118 Old Route One
Falmouth, Maine 04105

Journal: *Maine Field
Naturalist*

Maryland

Maryland Ornithological Society
Cylburn Mansion
4915 Greenspring Ave.
Baltimore, Md. 21209

Journal: *Maryland
Birdlife*

Massachusetts

Massachusetts Audubon Society
South Great Road
Lincoln, Mass. 01773

Journal: *Massachusetts
Audubon*

Michigan

Michigan Audubon Society
7000 North Westnedge
Kalamazoo, Mich. 49001

Journal: *Jack-Pine
Warbler*

Minnesota

Minnesota Ornithologists' Union
c/o James Ford Bell Museum of
    Natural History
University of Minnesota
Minneapolis, Minn. 55455

Journal: *The Loon*

Nebraska

Nebraska Ornithologists' Union
University of Nebraska State Museum
Lincoln, Neb. 68508

Journal: *The Nebraska
Bird Review*

New Hampshire

Audubon Society of New Hampshire
3 Silk Farm Road
Concord, N.H. 03301

Journal: *The New
Hampshire Audubon
Quarterly*

New Jersey

New Jersey Audubon Society
790 Ewing Avenue
Franklin Lakes, N.J. 07417

Journal: *New Jersey Audubon*

New York

Federation of N. Y. State Bird Clubs
c/o Cornell Laboratory of Ornithology
159 Sapsucker Woods Road
Ithaca, N.Y. 14853

Journal: *The Kingbird*

North Carolina

Carolina Bird Club
Shuford Memorial Sanctuary
P.O. Box 1220
Tryon, N.C. 28782

Journal: *The Chat*

Oregon

Oregon Audubon Society
Pittock Bird Sanctuary
5151 Northwest Cornell Road
Portland, Ore. 97210

Journal: *Audubon Warbler*

Pennsylvania

Delaware Valley Ornithological Club
c/o Academy of Natural Sciences
19th and The Parkway
Philadelphia, Pa. 19103

Journal: *Cassinia*

Rhode Island

Audubon Society of Rhode Island
40 Bowen St.
Providence, R.I. 02903

Journal: *The Narragansett Naturalist*

West Virginia

Brooks Bird Club
707 Warwood Avenue
Wheeling, W.Va. 26003

Journal: *The Redstart*

Wisconsin

Wisconsin Society for Ornithology
821 Williamson St.
Madison, Wis. 53703

Journal: *The Passenger Pigeon*

5
LIFE LISTS

During the last century and early in this one, collecting the eggs of wild birds, as well as the preserved skins of the birds themselves, was an extremely popular hobby among amateur naturalists. Thousands of eggs were taken from nests, and some avid collectors even took great pride in accumulating shockingly large numbers of eggs of prized species such as Ospreys and Peregrine Falcons. Indeed, the competition among certain egg collectors to secure Peregrine Falcon eggs was so keen that some Peregrine eyries failed to produce nestlings year after year. Even birds such as the California Condor, which is now a critically endangered species, were vulnerable to the activities of egg collectors. As one might imagine, the destruction to birdlife was enormous.

Today modern wildlife conservation laws prohibit such activities except under authority of rigidly regulated federal and state permits to scientists engaged in valid research programs and to certain other persons. Instead of egg collecting, a number of wildlife-related activities, including bird watching and bird photography, now are in vogue. But in a curious sort of way the collector's urge still survives among birders today. What are now collected, however, are the names of birds observed by a person for the first time rather than the dead birds themselves. The result is each bird watcher's life list. It is merely a list on which is recorded the name of every species of bird observed by that person. Related information, such as the location and date seen, usually is also included on the list. Thus, each bird watcher's life list is unique. The objective, of course, is to see as many different species of birds as possible in order to develop as large a life list as one can.

As one might imagine, there are many kinds of life lists of birds which a person can develop. Among the most popular among American birders are: (1) world life lists, (2) North American life lists, (3) state life lists, (4) local life lists, and (5) yearly lists. Some other bird lists might include species seen only in one's backyard, on a particular tree in one's backyard, or seen or heard on television programs. Still other life lists include those for specific parks or refuges, vacation areas, hawk watching lookouts, or other locations. A life list might even be developed from pictures of birds printed on postcards from various parts of the world.

Although bird watchers have heatedly discussed adopting specific standards for life lists, no such standards exist at this time. Nevertheless, it is more or less common knowledge among birders that birds will only be added to a life list if they are wild individuals which have not (to the best knowledge of the birder) been captured and released immediately prior to being observed. Most birders, however, accept as new for their life lists species which are noted by sound or by sight. For my own life list, however, I accept only birds that I have seen distinctly in the wild. In a few instances where both sight and sound, or sound alone, are necessary to make an identification, both criteria are used.

World Life Lists

Ornithologists currently recognize about 8,600 species of birds living in various parts of the world. In theory, therefore, it is possible for a bird watcher to develop a life list containing about that number of species. In fact, however, the exact number of bird species in the world is unknown. New species of birds still are being discovered occasionally by scientists. Such new species include Murphy's Petrel, the Elfin Woods Warbler in Puerto Rico, and twenty-one new species from Peru, among them the Long-whiskered Owlet, Bar-winged Wood-Wren, and Pardusco.

Extinction and near extinction of species is another important factor governing how many birds one is able to add to a life list. The fabulous Ivory-billed Woodpecker probably is extinct, perhaps only one or two Eskimo Curlews still survive, and fewer than forty

American Coots are among the many North American species bird watchers can include on their North American life lists.

California Condors struggle for survival in California. On
Bermuda, only about two dozen Bermuda Petrels still survive. I
consider it one of the highlights of my birding and ornithological
career to have been shown one of these rare birds on its nest by
Bermuda's leading ornithologist, David Wingate. Elsewhere in the
tropics, massive destruction of rain forests and other habitats is
bringing many splendid species to the brink of extinction. Finally,
new ornithological knowledge sometimes makes it necessary to
reduce species of birds merely to subspecies. When that happens,
bird watchers have "lost" a potential new addition to their lists.
Thus, champion birders such as Joe Taylor have been forced several
times to regain goals already attained in their life lists.

Another important factor which influences the number of birds
available for a life list is the location in the world where they are
found. Some species occur in extremely remote corners of the
world, such as interior New Guinea or Amazonia, whereas others
occur only in countries which are not currently open to American
visitors because of world political policies. In spite of such
problems, however, bird watchers such as Roger Tory Peterson and
Stuart Keith have set for themselves goals of about 4,300 species for
their life lists. Stuart Keith already has passed the one-half mark for
world species and so has seen more than 4,300 species, but it took
him more than 26 years of vigorous and expensive effort. A few
other birders also are approaching the 4,300 mark or have passed it.

What, then, is the ultimate goal? Who knows? Changing
conditions in the environment certainly will influence the ultimate
number of species which it is possible to see. Nevertheless, if a
person has almost unlimited time and money to roam the world
doing little except birding it might be possible to see 6,000 or even
7,000 species in a lifetime. For most bird watchers, however, a life
list containing perhaps 1,000 or 1,500 species will be outstanding
and a realistic goal to work toward.

North American Life Lists

In marked contrast to the staggering number of possible bird
species which might be included in a world life list, the number
available for a North American list is much less. Indeed, any birder
listing over 700 species in North America has reached a very
impressive mark. To do so one would have to travel from the subtropical corners of southern Florida and Texas to the high Arctic
corners of Alaska and Canada.

Sometimes, however, a North American life list can be
augmented in unexpected ways. This is particularly true when
accidentals (birds seen far outside of their normal geographic

ranges) occur here perhaps only once. I was lucky enough to observe one such accidental at Hawk Mountain in eastern Pennsylvania on October 3, 1959, a few days after a hurricane spent itself south of Pennsylvania. I joined about forty other hopeful observers on the lookout that day waiting for a break in the weather and the mist which hung over the mountain and hoping for hawks to begin migrating again. The prospect of seeing much was dismal, however, and many people left during the morning. But suddenly, at about one o'clock in the afternoon, a dark seabird with a conspicuous patch of white on each wing appeared low over the area now used as Hawk Mountain's South Lookout. It soared skillfully and, moments later, circled very low over the North Lookout for the next five minutes. Maurice Broun and the other observers on the lookout were nearly dumbfounded.

The moment the bird appeared, I began filming it with my 16mm motion picture camera. Nobody knew what the bird was aside from the obvious fact that it was a seabird and didn't belong over Hawk Mountain, so a photographic record was vital. Shortly after the film was processed, I sent it to Robert Cushman Murphy, a noted seabird authority at the American Museum of Natural History, and asked for his expert opinion regarding the bird's identity. He wrote·

> The short strip of motion pictures of your seabird is far more revealing than I had anticipated. It is not a Sooty Shearwater. That species has a white wing lining as conspicuous as the Black Duck's. Furthermore, your bird is not a *Puffinus* of any sort. Its bill and its style of flight show that it is a member of the genus *Pterodroma*.
>
> On geographic grounds, the most likely petrel would be *P. arminjoniana* from the South Atlantic which has once been taken at Ithaca, New York after a hurricane. Careful examination of the film appears, however, to rule out that species. My final conclusion is that this petrel can be nothing else than *P. neglecta* in the dark plumage phase. There is no other species that shows the conspicuous white wing patch against a generally black plumage.

Thus the only North American record of the Kermadec Petrel was observed, much to the delight of the bird watchers on the lookout. An accident of weather had allowed us to add a new species to our life lists—and one which birders in North America probably never again would be able to see on this continent! Unfortunately, a great debate later developed over the identification of the bird, but recent study of the film by other noted seabird experts has confirmed Dr. Murphy's original identification.

If one adds Central America (Mexico through Panama) to North America there are about 1,652 species which could be seen. It is doubtful if any bird watcher will see all of them, but it might be possible for a few keen and vigorous birders to see a large portion of them, exclusive of accidentals.

A view of the Kermadec Petrel observed at Hawk Mountain, Pa., in 1959. Photo by Donald S. Heintzelman from a 16mm motion picture film

State Life Lists

One of the first life lists which every bird watcher begins to expand is his or her state or provincial list because it is obviously the most easily expanded. Each state or province, of course, has a different number of species to be seen, and no list of known species for a state or province remains static for long. New species are continually being added to the avifauna of every state or province. Some states such as California, with a great diversity of habitats, offer birders large numbers of possible sightings, whereas many inland states cannot be expected to have as many species on their lists. Regardless of where one lives, however, keeping a state or provincial life list can be a rewarding and worthwhile experience.

Local Life Lists

Local life lists, perhaps of a county or a specific area within a county, also are very important and worthwhile because they usually are the most easily maintained and secured of all such lists. Moreover, they are developed at the least cost per bird. Frequently such local lists contain valuable scientific information if prepared by a capable birder. One's bird watching activities may actually add to local ornithological knowledge.

A case in point is the list of birds observed over a period of twenty years at Bake Oven Knob, Lehigh County, Pennsylvania. This site is used mainly as an autumn hawk migration lookout, but the combined efforts of a number of bird watchers have resulted in no less than 158 species of birds being identified there at one time or another. Included in the list are such interesting species as Double-crested Cormorant, Brant, White-fronted Goose, Black Vulture, Bald Eagle, Golden Eagle, Gyrfalcon, Peregrine Falcon, Merlin, Ruffed Grouse, Wild Turkey, Sandhill Crane, Pileated Woodpecker, Red-headed Woodpecker, Olive-sided Flycatcher, Boreal Chickadee, Pine Grosbeak, Red Crossbill, White-winged Crossbill, Lincoln's Sparrow, and Snow Bunting.

Bird watchers in many other sections of the United States and Canada have similarly concentrated on particular locations and have not only added many new species to their life lists but also added to the ornithological knowledge of an area by making repeated visits to a site for many years.

Yearly Lists

Another variation in bird listing is a yearly list. This is a list of all of the species of birds observed by a birder within one given year regardless of where the birding was done. Thus both domestic and foreign locations are included when the list is developed. Moreover, a new list is prepared every year. Thus there can be much overlapping from one list to another in respect to world life lists, North American life lists, etc.

Additional Reading

Roberson, D.
    1977   The 700 Club. *Birding*, 9 (3): 97-101.
Small, A.
    1976   The White-headed Piping Guan or How I Found My 4,000th Life Bird in Surinam. *Birding*, 8 (3): 145-48.
Tucker, J.
    1975   500 in One State: A New Landmark. *Birding*, 7 (4): 237-38.

6
CHRISTMAS
BIRD COUNTS

One of the highlights of the birding year for thousands of bird watchers is participation in a Christmas Bird Count. These one-day field trips are restricted to a circle of fifteen miles in diameter starting from an assigned center which remains fixed each year. The objective is to count as many of the species and individuals of birds in the assigned circle as possible. This includes birds seen in a variety of habitats as well as birds visiting backyard feeders.

The counts were begun in 1900 by ornithologist Frank M. Chapman of the American Museum of Natural History to replace the then popular hobby of shooting birds and collecting their preserved skins. The new Christmas Bird Counts caught on and now are organized and coordinated by the National Audubon Society in cooperation with the United States Fish and Wildlife Service. Each count is conducted by local bird watchers, whose numbers may range from a handful of people to hundreds of participants, representing one or more of the hundreds of bird clubs and Audubon Societies in North and Central America. Occasionally, Christmas Bird Counts are also conducted in foreign lands outside of the Americas, but generally these counts are not included in the special issue of *American Birds* which once each year prints the results of the latest counts. In recent years, over one thousand such counts have been reported upon.

The seventy-fifth year of Christmas Bird Counts was celebrated in 1974. Included in the magazine were 1,102 counts, including reports from Canada, the United States, Mexico, Belize, Guatemala, Panama, the Canal Zone, Cuba, the Dominican Republic, Puerto Rico, the Bahamas, and the U.S. Virgin Islands.

In the United States, birders from San Diego, California, counted the largest number of species (202).

Over the years, Christmas Bird Counts have been made in some very exotic places, but not until December 21, 1975, was a C.B.C. held in the Antarctic. Then birding history was made. On that date, a party of nine bird watchers and ornithologists from the M. S. *Lindblad Explorer* landed on remote Deception Island, in the South Shetland group off the west coast of the Antarctic Peninsula, and spent 12 hours (four on board ship, eight on foot ashore) counting as many of the island's birds as possible.

This unique C.B.C. began when some friends of Elise Friend of Connecticut dared her to conduct an Antarctic count. When she mentioned the idea to me, we decided to conduct a full-scale count. Observers participating included Roland Clement, Elise Friend, Harvey Gilston, Francois Gohier, Louise Greene, Georgi Legoe, Richard Penney, Lester Peterson, and myself (ship's ornithologist and count compiler).

The areas covered were Deception Island (Neptunes Bellows, Whalers Bay, and the area around the old whaling station, named Hector, Fumarole Bay, and a large penguin rookery on the outer coastline) and its immediately adjacent waters. Fortunately, the weather cooperated (variable cloudiness, wind WNW at Beaufort 2, air temperature 2.2°C., water temperature 1.6°C., visibility less than ten miles, and calm seas), but icebergs didn't! Our entrance to Neptunes Bellows was blocked for several hours by a small berg which finally drifted enough to allow the ship to sail through into the island's large, flooded volcanic caldera.

We were on our way—especially when Lester Peterson discovered a lone, immature Emperor Penguin on a snow slope behind the old whaling station. Only in our wildest dreams had we hoped to see an Emperor, and it was the only one that we did see. Indeed, the bird seems to be a new station record for the species!

By noon we had ticked off most of the island's common birds and returned to the ship for lunch. But we still had not seen large numbers of penguins. That situation changed rapidly in the afternoon, however, when we again went ashore and some of the more hardy and adventure-seeking people made a rugged hike across snow fields and the island's steep volcanic walls to view a large Chinstrap Penguin rookery on the outer coast. After several futile attempts at trying to count the thousands of nesting birds, I finally devised a method of estimate based upon the approximate number of birds filling one binocular field. I then slowly moved over the entire colony, binocular field by binocular field, to arrive at the final estimated count. Result? At least 25,000 Chinstraps—not including eggs or chicks.

In all, our Deception Island C.B.C. resulted in 13 species seen:

Emperor Penguin—1
Adelie Penguin—5 plus
Chinstrap Penguin—25,000
Gentoo Penguin—5
Southern Giant Fulmar—5
Cape Pigeon—325
  (on eggs)
Wilson's Storm Petrel—5

Blue-eyed Shag—2
American Sheathbill—3
South Polar Skua—1
Brown Skua—10 (on eggs)
Southern Black-backed
  Gull—60
Antarctic Tern—100 (plus
  eggs and chicks)

By seven o'clock that evening everybody was again back on board the ship, well satisfied with the day's efforts and heading south through the ice toward the Antarctic Circle—visions of Antarctic Petrels dancing in our heads. It was a day which Edward Adrian Wilson, the brilliant ornithologist on Robert Falcon Scott's ill-fated race to the Pole, would have been proud of.

Far more typical of a Christmas Bird Count, however, is a group of bird watchers hiking through snow across open fields or along a woodlot looking for Ring-necked Pheasants, Red-tailed Hawks, or perhaps a Downy Woodpecker. A typical case in point is a Count made in Buffalo Creek Valley, Pennsylvania, by members of the Audubon Society of Western Pennsylvania who recorded the following species one December 22:

Pied-billed Grebe 6; Great Blue Heron 2; Canada Goose 12; Mallard 166; Black Duck 1; Canvasback 1; Lesser Scaup 2; Com. Goldeneye 12; Sharp-shinned Hawk 2; Cooper's Hawk 5; Red-tailed Hawk 9; Red-shouldered Hawk 3; Marsh Hawk 1; Am. Kestrel 4; Ruffed Grouse 31; Ring-necked Pheasant 6; Killdeer 1; Rock Dove 92; Mourning Dove 194; Screech Owl 5; Great Horned Owl 3; owl, sp. 1; Belted Kingfisher 10; Com. Flicker (Yel.-sh) 4; Hairy Woodpecker 14; Downy Woodpecker 81; Horned Lark 4; Blue Jay 50; Com. Crow 1,508; Black-capped Chickadee 283; Tufted Titmouse 154; White-breasted Nuthatch 78; Red-breasted Nuthatch 1; Brown Creeper 12; *House Wren* 2; Winter Wren 5; Carolina Wren 54; E. Bluebird 3; Golden-crowned Kinglet 18; Ruby-crowned Kinglet 1; Cedar Waxwing 3; Starling 386; House Sparrow 155; Rusty Blackbird 5; Brown-headed Cowbird 2; Cardinal 223; Evening Grosbeak 3; Am. Goldfinch 42; Rufous-sided Towhee 1; Dark-eyed (Slate-col.) Junco 431; Tree Sparrow 301; Field Sparrow 5; White-crowned Sparrow 1; White-throated Sparrow 62; Song Sparrow 91.

In all, a total of 4,552 individuals of 54 species were tallied on that particular Christmas Bird Count.

Although there is marked difference of opinion among ornithologists regarding the scientific importance of the information compiled as Christmas Bird Counts, various uses have been made of these data. One of the most important is the preparation of a series of Early Winter Distribution maps for selected species. Each of the maps illustrates the geographic distribution and relative abundance of a selected species in North America. The maps can be used for a variety of conservation and management purposes.

Aside from the scientific aspects of Christmas Bird Counts, they provide important recreational opportunities to a large number of bird watchers. Perhaps this is the most important gain from this activity. Participants have an opportunity to spend a day in the field watching birds, learning about them, and appreciating them as major wildlife resources. These real but intangible benefits frequently lead to other important wildlife conservation projects or, at the very least, to a better appreciation of birds and wildlife in general.

Christmas Card Bird Counts

Perhaps the newest and most unusual variation on the theme of Christmas Bird Counts is to count the number of recognizable species of birds printed on the Christmas cards one receives each year. This novel idea was suggested by Gordon M. Meade, who listed 32 species of birds on his cards one season. A friend of his listed 33 species, and between them they listed an astonishing 50 species! My own efforts have not been nearly as successful, but I once received a Christmas card featuring a very unusual bird. It was a Guianan Cock-of-the-Rock painted by the famous bird artist Louis Agassiz Fuertes.

Developing Christmas Card Bird Counts is an activity which anyone can participate in, especially on stormy winter days, and it will be interesting to see who accumulates the largest counts in years to come. Dare we expect 100 species? Or 250 species? Or even 500 species?

Additional Reading

Heintzelman, D. S.
    1976   An Antarctic Christmas Bird Count. *Birding*, 8 (5): 330-31.

Meade, G. M.
    1976   A New Kind of Christmas Count. *Birding*, 8 (5): 319-20.

7
BIG DAY COUNTS

Mention a Big Day Count to an avid bird watcher and the first thing that comes to mind is a warm spring morning, thousands of birds migrating through an area, and exceptional opportunities to observe these creatures. Few activities in a bird watcher's calendar of events are as eagerly looked forward to or enjoyed as much as each year's Big Day Count. What, then, is this event? It is simply one day spent in the field during which a birder attempts to observe and identify as many different species of birds as possible simply for the fun of doing so. Eager bird watchers always begin their Big Day Counts before dawn and continue them well into the night in order to add owls and other nocturnal species to their lists. Besides extending their hours, birders try to visit as many different types of habitats as possible in order to enhance the chances of seeing the largest possible variety of species. In addition, birders try to pick the peak day of the spring migration when the largest numbers of migrating species will be seen.

Make no mistake about it, however, participation in a Big Day Count can be exhausting. One must avoid at all costs spending too much time in an area which is not producing birds even though it may have been an excellent birding area at other times. The rule of thumb is to check an area, tick off as many species of birds as can be located rapidly, then move on to the next area even if some generally common species normally seen now fail to appear. If the species are common enough they probably will be seen elsewhere. The ardent birder doesn't waste time. He keeps moving. The key to success is to keep adding birds to the list.

Results of such Big Day Counts sometimes can be very impressive. Many bird watchers report their results in *Birding*, which annually publishes a summary of each state's highest counts. Of course, the number of species counted in each state varies greatly. Generally those states with the highest number of species reported are on coasts, where the marine environment offers a variety of birds unavailable elsewhere. For example, one of the largest Big Day Counts ever reported came from Texas. On April 28, 1973, a party of keen bird watchers including Kenn Kaufmann, Stuart Keith, Joe Taylor, and Jim Tucker spent about 18 hours racing along a 550-mile route beginning in downtown Houston, continuing through eastern woodland habitats en route to Galveston, then to Freeport and on to the King Ranch south of Corpus Christi. From there the party continued to semi-tropical forest around Santa Ana and finally ended at Bentsen-Rio Grande Valley State Park. The operation was planned like a military invasion. The area was scouted ahead of time. Nothing was overlooked. Not a moment of time was wasted. The goal was to get that bird. If an area didn't produce, the team moved on. That—plus a little luck—was the key to success. But what a result! Listed below are the 229 species which this enterprising group tallied on their famous record-breaking Texas Big Day Count.

Common Loon	Blue-winged Teal
Eared Grebe	American Wigeon
Least Grebe	Northern Shoveler
Pied-billed Grebe	Wood Duck
American White Pelican	Redhead
Double-crested Cormorant	Canvasback
Neotropic Cormorant	Lesser Scaup
Great Blue Heron	Turkey Vulture
Green Heron	Black Vulture
Little Blue Heron	Mississippi Kite
Cattle Egret	Sharp-shinned Hawk
Reddish Egret	Red-tailed Hawk
Great Egret	Red-shouldered Hawk
Snowy Egret	Broad-winged Hawk
Louisiana Heron	Swainson's Hawk
Black-crowned Night Heron	White-tailed Hawk
Yellow-crowned Night Heron	Harris' Hawk
American Bittern	Northern Harrier
White-faced Ibis	Crested Caracara
White Ibis	American Kestrel
Roseate Spoonbill	Plain Chachalaca
Black-bellied Whistling Duck	Greater Prairie Chicken
Fulvous Whistling Duck	Common Bobwhite
Mottled Duck	Wild Turkey
Gadwall	King Rail
Common Pintail	Clapper Rail

Virginia Rail
Sora
Common Gallinule
American Coot
Semipalmated Plover
Snowy Plover
Wilson's Plover
Killdeer
American Golden Plover
Black-bellied Plover
Ruddy Turnstone
Common Snipe
Whimbrel
Upland Sandpiper
Spotted Sandpiper
Solitary Sandpiper
Willet
Greater Yellowlegs
Lesser Yellowlegs
Pectoral Sandpiper
Least Sandpiper
Dunlin
Short-billed Dowitcher
Long-billed Dowitcher
Stilt Sandpiper
Semipalmated Sandpiper
Western Sandpiper
Hudsonian Godwit
Sanderling
American Avocet
Black-necked Stilt
Wilson's Phalarope
Herring Gull
Ring-billed Gull
Laughing Gull
Franklin's Gull
Gull-billed Tern
Foster's Tern
Common Tern
Least Tern
Royal Tern
Sandwich Tern
Caspian Tern
Black Tern
Black Skimmer

Red-billed Pigeon
Rock Dove
White-winged Dove
Mourning Dove
Common Ground Dove
Inca Dove
White-fronted Dove
Yellow-billed Cuckoo
Greater Roadrunner
Groove-billed Ani
Barn Owl
Screech Owl
Elf Owl
Barred Owl
Chuck-Will's-Widow
Pauraque
Common Nighthawk
Lesser Nighthawk
Chimney Swift
Ruby-throated Hummingbird
Buff-bellied Hummingbird
Belted Kingfisher
Common Flicker
Pileated Woodpecker
Red-bellied Woodpecker
Golden-fronted Woodpecker
Red-headed Woodpecker
Downy Woodpecker
Ladder-backed Woodpecker
Eastern Kingbird
Tropical Kingbird
Western Kingbird
Scissor-tailed Flycatcher
Greater Kiskadee
Great Crested Flycatcher
Wied's Crested Flycatcher
Acadian Flycatcher
Vermilion Flycatcher
Horned Lark
Tree Swallow
Bank Swallow
Rough-winged Swallow
Barn Swallow
Cliff Swallow
Purple Martin

Blue Jay
Green Jay
American Crow
Carolina Chickadee
Tufted Titmouse
Black-crested Titmouse
Verdin
House Wren
Bewick's Wren
Carolina Wren
Cactus Wren
Long-billed Marsh Wren
Short-billed Marsh Wren
Northern Mockingbird
Gray Catbird
Brown Thrasher
Long-billed Thrasher
American Robin
Wood Thrush
Swainson's Thrush
Eastern Bluebird
Blue-gray Gnatcatcher
Ruby-crowned Kinglet
Cedar Waxwing
Loggerhead Shrike
European Starling
White-eyed Vireo
Yellow-throated Vireo
Solitary Vireo
Red-eyed Vireo
Warbling Vireo
Black-and-White Warbler
Prothonotary Warbler
Swainson's Warbler
Blue-winged Warbler
Tennessee Warbler
Orange-crowned Warbler
Nashville Warbler
Northern Parula Warbler
Yellow Warbler
Magnolia Warbler
Cape May Warbler
Black-throated Green
   Warbler

Chestnut-sided Warbler
Bay-breasted Warbler
Blackpoll Warbler
Pine Warbler
Ovenbird
Northern Waterthrush
Kentucky Warbler
Common Yellowthroat
Yellow-breasted Chat
Hooded Warbler
Wilson's Warbler
American Redstart
House Sparrow
Eastern Meadowlark
Yellow-headed Blackbird
Red-winged Blackbird
Orchard Oriole
Black-headed Oriole
Northern Oriole
Brewer's Blackbird
Great-tailed Grackle
Common Grackle
Brown-headed Cowbird
Bronzed Cowbird
Scarlet Tanager
Summer Tanager
Northern Cardinal
Pyrrhuloxia
Rose-breasted Grosbeak
Blue Grosbeak
Indigo Bunting
Painted Bunting
Dickcissel
Pine Siskin
American Goldfinch
Olive Sparrow
Rufous-sided Towhee
Savannah Sparrow
Seaside Sparrow
Lark Sparrow
Cassin's Sparrow
White-crowned Sparrow
White-throated Sparrow
Lincoln's Sparrow

It is exciting to know that it is possible to see such large numbers of birds on a Big Day Count if a bird watcher visits the right locations, but most counts produce far fewer numbers of species. In Pennsylvania or New Jersey, for example, an outstanding Big Day Count might produce 125 to 150 species.

In addition to the traditional Big Day Counts, some bird watchers have invented variations on these counts. For example, the Delaware Valley Ornithological Club of Philadelphia conducts a Big Day Roundup each spring during which the counts are combined from a dozen or more Big Day Counts made in Pennsylvania, New Jersey, Maryland, and Delaware. The largest number of species resulting from such Roundups is 248 for May 10, 1970. Many members of the DVOC participated in that effort in order to achieve that outstanding record.

Not all bird watchers, of course, will want to throw as much effort into making a Big Day Count as was necessary to achieve the examples described. Some birders prefer a more relaxed pace and are quite satisfied with the largest number of species they can find easily on their Big Day Counts. That birding style, too, is perfectly acceptable if the participants enjoy their day in the field. It is up to each bird watcher to decide how much or how little effort he or she wishes to put into making a Big Day Count.

Additional Reading

Clark, T.
    1977   The Big Day. *Birding*, (1): 43-45.

Eckert, K. R.
    1977   1976 Big Day Report. *Birding*, 9 (1): 46-52.

Tucker, J.
    1976   1975 Big Day Report. *Birding*, 8 (1): 66-73.

King Penguins at a rookery on South Georgia

A King Penguin rookery on South Georgia

A Black-browed Albatross with its chick on West Point Island, Falklands

A Light-mantled Sooty Albatross on its nest on South Georgia

A Southern Giant Fulmar or Giant Petrel nesting on South Georgia

A Macaroni Penguin nesting on South Georgia

Adelie Penguins nesting at Hope Bay, Antarctica

Whistling Swans in southeastern Pennsylvania

A Chipping Sparrow perched near a small natural spring which serves as a birdbath

Male Mallard on a lake in Allentown, Pennsylvania

A male Cardinal bathing in a small spring

A Greater Flamingo feeding in a shallow lagoon in the Galapagos Islands

A male Great Frigatebird displaying its throat sac on Tower Island, Galapagos

A Red-footed Booby (brown phase) near its nest on Tower Island, Galapagos

An adult Galapagos Hawk on James Island, Galapagos

Swallow-tailed Gulls on South Plaza Island, Galapagos

8
BREEDING BIRD PROJECTS

In addition to participating in Christmas Bird Counts and Big Day Counts, bird watchers can pursue a variety of exciting field projects involving breeding birds. Often, the watcher can make valuable contributions to ornithological knowledge. Were it not for the work of many amateur bird watchers much less would be known about the nesting requirements and general life histories of many North American birds, let alone many species in Central and South America. However, relatively few bird watchers engage in these projects, perhaps because such an intensive task frequently is more demanding and time consuming and requires greater skill than merely watching birds.

While it is true that some studies of breeding birds are best left to professional ornithologists, there are at least two major *short-term* breeding bird projects in which bird watchers can play important roles: (1) the North American Nest Record Program, and (2) a breeding bird census with the results published in *American Birds*. A third activity, *long-term* life history studies, requires much more time and effort but some bird watchers are well equipped to engage in these investigations and many have done so in the past. Indeed, some of the best life history studies ever completed were done by amateur bird watchers and ornithologists. One outstanding example is Margaret Morse Nice's classic *Studies in the Life History of the Song Sparrow*. Another is her *Development of Behavior in Precocial Birds*. Both were published by the Linnaean Society of New York.

Nest Record Program

Perhaps the easiest and most enjoyable breeding bird project in which bird watchers can participate at their leisure is the North American Nest Record Program fostered by the Laboratory of

Bird watchers along coastal New Jersey have studied nesting Ospreys for decades and made important contributions to our knowledge of this species.

Ornithology at Cornell University. This program basically is centered around the collection of special cards and/or computer-stored records containing clutch and/or nestling information on thousands of North American bird nests of hundreds of species from the Arctic to the tropics. Anybody can participate in the program and new cooperators are always welcome to join in the effort, which represents a major fund of information on the breeding biology of North American birds.

How does one assist? The answer is very simple. Any bird watcher who finds an occupied bird nest, with either eggs or young birds, simply counts the number of eggs and/or young, and fills in this basic information along with date, location, and certain other necessary details, including the species involved, on a printed card provided without cost by the Laboratory of Ornithology. If a person can make only one visit to a nest, that is satisfactory. Far more valuable, however, is the information gained from making a series of visits to the nest and gathering egg and nestling data over a period of several weeks or, in the case of some species, longer. Great care and caution, of course, is taken not to damage the eggs or nestlings or to disturb the nest for long periods of time. Such prolonged activities could result in damage or destruction of the nesting effort. Very brief visits, however, rarely cause any serious damage. After the basic information is completed for a particular nest the cards containing the data are mailed to the Laboratory of Ornithology where the information is added to the files and made 66 available to scientists needing such data for research purposes.

A Horned Lark at its nest. Information on nesting birds can be sent to the North American Nest Record Program at Cornell University.

Nestling Black-crowned Night Herons in a Pennsylvania rookery. Special care must be taken, when studying night herons and other colonial nesting birds, to avoid too much disturbance to nests or birds.

Bird watchers should realize that any species of bird is of interest to the operators of the program. Thus, an American Robin nesting on one's backyard tree is of just as much interest as is the nest of a Lincoln's Sparrow or some rare species seldom found nesting.

Perhaps the only exception to the general request for data of breeding birds involves endangered species such as Bald Eagles or Peregrine Falcons where special permits are necessary to work with the birds and where damage could result to the birds, nestlings, or

Nest and eggs of a Double-crested Cormorant

Nest and eggs of a Ring-necked Pheasant

eggs if certain special precautions are not carefully followed in visiting such nests. It is best, therefore, that most bird watchers not try to gather information on the nests of any endangered species without first discussing their plans with trained professional ornithologists, and the operators of the nest record program at Cornell.

But for common songbirds, which are the most likely species bird watchers report on, routine caution is generally adequate when gathering nest information. *A Field Guide to Birds' Nests* by Hal H. Harrison will be of particular value in helping people to identify nests and eggs correctly. Of course, it is not enough merely to look at a nest; one should always make an effort to actually see the species of bird using a nest before concluding what species is nesting there.

Those wishing to participate in this program can secure full details, instructions, and a supply of cards without cost by writing to the Laboratory of Ornithology, Cornell University, Ithaca, N.Y. 14853.

Breeding Bird Census

The second major project involving breeding birds in which bird watchers can participate is a breeding bird census. While this requires somewhat more skill than some other bird watching activities such as the more popular Christmas Bird Counts, it is perhaps of more biological importance. In 1977, 181 such breeding bird censuses were completed and the results published in *American Birds*, which devotes a special issue to this activity each year.

Persons making breeding bird censuses do not just drive to the nearest woodlot or field and look at birds. Rather, special requirements and techniques are established, among them detailed description and identification of the site selected and careful identification of the birds which have established territories on the area selected for study. What one does, then, is to carefully count all of the individuals and species of birds observed and/or heard on the study plot during a series of early morning visits. Study plots usually correspond to easily recognized types of habitats or ecosystems such as old fields, virgin tallgrass prairie, hemlock-white pine-hardwood forest, upland lichen woodland, or even urban residential areas. Thus any type of habitat or ecosystem can be censused; the selection is up to each participating bird watcher. However, the more years a given study plot is studied the more valuable the overall effort is because such long-term studies help scientists to document and define the normal changes of birdlife of an area as the vegetation on a site changes toward a mature forest or other ecosystem. Complete details on participating in a breeding bird census are available from

Breeding bird data are needed for common birds such as this Great Crested Flycatcher as well as for rarer species.

the editor of *American Birds* at the National Audubon Society. Two
sample censuses, reported in *American Birds*, are reprinted here.

9. MOUNTAIN TOP. OAK-MAPLE FOREST. —Location:
Pennsylvania; Westmoreland Co., 10 miles SSW of Ligonier, 6 miles
S of Laughlintown in Forbes State Forest on the top of Laurel
Mountain; 40°07'37"N, 79°10'50"W, Ligonier Quadrangle, USGS.
Continuity: Established 1974. Size: 6.07 ha = 15 acres (rectangular,
300 x 1980 ft, measured). Description of Plot: See AB 28: 993, 1974.
A major physical change is two openings cut in the forest, each
measuring approximately 300 x 150 ft; one on either side of the study
area but not opposite each other. Weather: Windy, rain and cold for
2 days; warm and clear for 2 days. Coverage: June 7-8, 14-15. Hours:
0500 to 0930, 1200 to 1300, and 1700 to 1930. Total party-hours: 17.5.
Census: Red-eyed Vireo, 5 (82, 33); Ovenbird, 4 (66,27); Rufous-
sided Towhee, 3.5 (58, 23); Dark-eyed Junco, 3 (49, 20); Wood
Thrush, 2; Chipping Sparrow, 2; E. Wood Pewee, 1.5; Brown
Creeper, 1.5; Scarlet Tanager, 1.5; Veery, 1; Solitary Vireo, 1; Black-
throated Green Warbler, 1; Rose-breasted Grosbeak, 1; Blue Jay,
0.5; White-breasted Nuthatch, 0.5; Com. Yellowthroat, 0.5; Hairy
Woodpecker, +; Great Crested Flycatcher, +; Com. Grackle, +. Total:
19 species, 29.5 territorial males (486/km², 197/100 acres). —R.
CARRELL ABBOTT, *Audubon Society of Western Pennsylvania,
Carnegie Museum, Pittsburgh, Pa. 15213.*

108. CALIFORNIA-BAY-BUCKEYE-MIXED FOREST. —Loca-
tion: California; Marin Co., 3.5 miles NW of Bolinas, just inside the
southern boundary of Point Reyes National Seashore: 37°55'N,
122°45'W, Bolinas Quadrangle, USGS. Continuity: Established
1972; 4 consecutive years. Size: 4ha = 10 acres (irregular, measured).
Description of Plot: See AB 26: 979, 1972. Weather: See Census 117.
Coverage: May 7, 16, 20, 30; June 10. Total man-hours: 12. Trips
made between 0630 and 1030 hours. Census: Wilson's Warbler, 6
(148, 60); Com. Bushtit, 4 (99, 40); Wrentit, 4; Bewick's Wren, 4;
Western Flycatcher, 3.5 (86, 35); Chestnut-sided Chickadee, 3 (74,
30); Winter Wren, 3; Am. Robin, 3; Swainson's Thrush, 3; Warbling
Vireo, 3; Black-headed Grosbeak, 3; Olive-sided Flycatcher, 2; Am.
Goldfinch, 2; Brown Towhee, 1.5; Violet-green Swallow, 1; Steller's
Jay, 1; Hutton's Vireo, 1; Purple Finch, 1; Rufous-sided Towhee, 1;
Scrub Jay, 0.5. Total: 22 species; 60 territorial males (1483/km²,
600/100 acres). Remarks: Nest found: Chestnut-backed Chickadee,
2. One male Warbling Vireo banded as an adult in 1966 was 10 years
old. Contribution No. 113, PRBO. —ROBERT M. STEWART,
Point Reyes Bird Observatory, Bolinas, Calif. 94924.

Nest Box Projects

One of the most exciting bird conservation activities in which bird
watchers can participate very effectively during the avian nesting
season is the construction and placement of nest boxes. Some
species such as Mountain Bluebirds and Eastern Bluebirds readily
70 accept boxes for nesting and a number of bird watchers have

Eastern Bluebirds naturally nest in holes in trees and posts, but they also readily accept man-made bird boxes in which to nest.

established Bluebird Trails in various parts of the United States and Canada. Canadian bird watchers have built, placed, and patrolled over 7,000 nest boxes for Mountain Bluebirds along a 500-mile-long route extending between North Battleford, Saskatchewan, and MacGregor, Manitoba, as well as along 1,500 miles of side trails. This extraordinary effort resulted in 1976 in some 8,000 Mountain Bluebirds being reared and fledged!

One of the most devoted students of Eastern Bluebirds is Dr. Lawrence Zeleny, a retired agricultural biochemist from Maryland, who also established a nest box trail in his state and has even published a book, *The Bluebird*, on the subject. Although the 85 nest boxes on his trail are modest in number compared with some similar efforts, over 1,000 Eastern Bluebirds were raised during a five year period in these boxes. Similar results are reported from other trails, and it is clear that nest box trails are major conservation efforts for these birds.

In addition to Mountain and Eastern Bluebirds, other birds will accept boxes as nest sites. Tree Swallows, for example, frequently use the boxes built for bluebirds, thus adding to the overall productivity of such nest box projects. At one site I studied for 71

American Kestrel eggs in a man-made nest box. The debris around the eggs remained in the box from the earlier activities of other birds.

several years near Pennington, New Jersey, almost every box placed beside a pond and in nearby fields was used either by Eastern Bluebirds or by Tree Swallows.

Certain birds of prey such as American Kestrels and Screech Owls also accept boxes of the correct size if they are placed near the tops of tall trees beside open fields in agricultural areas. At one site in eastern Pennsylvania, for example, an American Kestrel nest box project is established in parts of several counties and dozens of these falcons are reared every year in these structures. Elsewhere in the United States, operators of similar projects are reporting similar results. Clearly, local populations of American Kestrels and Screech Owls can be augmented to a considerable extent when nest boxes are built for them.

Wood Ducks also are willing users of nest boxes. Major conservation programs for these strikingly beautiful birds have been established not only by the United States Fish and Wildlife Service and most state wildlife agencies, but also by many sportsmen's organizations and private citizens. The net result of this effort is that local Wood Duck populations in many areas have increased markedly in recent years.

It is clear, therefore, that bird watchers seeking some worthwhile
conservation program to augment their birding activities can do no

better than build bird boxes for various selected species and add to such nest box projects from year to year.

Life History Studies

It is not unusual that many bird watchers become interested in certain species of birds to such an extent that they begin long-term, detailed field studies of the life histories of these birds in an effort to learn as much as possible about them. Sometimes nest box projects lead to such life history studies. For example, my own investigations into the life history of the American Kestrel began while I was in college because a readily available population of these birds used nesting boxes at a site nearby. Hundreds of days over a period of several years were spent watching the birds at their nest boxes, counting and measuring eggs and nestlings, banding birds, weighing birds, and generally trying to learn as much as possible about the falcons. Particular attention was given to the food habits of the birds during several nesting seasons. The result of this activity was a series of scientific articles published in a leading ornithological journal.

Other bird watchers also have conducted life history studies of various species from time to time as an outgrowth of their birding activities. Harold Mayfield spent years making exceptionally detailed field studies of the nesting activities of Kirtland's Warblers in Michigan. Eventually he wrote and published a major book on

Amateur ornithologist Lawrence H. Walkinshaw is the world authority on the Sandhill Crane (shown here nesting). Photo by Robert C. Twist / U.S. Fish and Wildlife Service

the species. Similarly, when Lawrence H. Walkinshaw began studying the life history of Sandhill Cranes his interest widened to include all of the species of cranes of the world. He made field trips to several continents to gather necessary information, and he has published two major books on cranes.

Bird watchers should recognize, however, that it is not necessary to select some rare or endangered species to study in detail. Very worthwhile life history studies can be done on very common species such as American Robins, European Starlings, Chipping Sparrows, or even House Sparrows. Indeed, some of the least studied species are the most common species! Nevertheless, before beginning such an effort it will be worthwhile to talk to a professional ornithologist and ask for his or her opinions and recommendations as to what birds would be best to select for such investigations. Most ornithologists and wildlife biologists will be happy to help as much as possible in providing preliminary information. Such scientists can frequently be located at museums, colleges and universities, and state and federal wildlife agencies.

Additional Reading

Harrison, H. H.
    1975   A Field Guide to Birds' Nests in the United States East of the Mississippi River. Houghton Mifflin Co., Boston.

Mayfield, H.
    1960   The Kirtland's Warbler. Bulletin 40. Cranbrook Institute of Science, Bloomfield Hills, Mich.

Nice, M. M.
    1964   Studies in the Life History of the Song Sparrow. 2 volumes. Dover Publications, York.

Walkinshaw, L. H.
    1949   The Sandhill Cranes. Bulletin 29. Cranbrook Institute of Science, Bloomfield Hills, Mich.
    1973   Cranes of the World. Winchester Press, New York.

Zeleny, L.
    1976   The Bluebird. Indiana University Press, Bloomington, Ind.
    1977   Song of Hope for the Bluebird. *National Geographic*, 151 (6): 854-65.

9
BACKYARD
BIRDING

Just about every bird watcher dreams of making an exciting expedition to remote Amazon jungles, of venturing into Antarctic waters to see spectacular penguin colonies on islands such as South Georgia, or of visiting Galapagos to see the endemic Darwin's finches and other fabulous birdlife of those equatorial Pacific islands. There is no denying that visits to such places are extraordinary birding experiences. But the truth of the matter is that it is not necessary to spend thousands of dollars, and travel halfway around the world to enjoy exciting birding. In a remarkable number of instances, fine birding can be enjoyed right in one's own backyard from the window of one's home.

Indeed, rare birds frequently appear at backyard bird feeders and bird watchers often travel great distances to visit these backyard attractions! For example, one November a Rufous Hummingbird appeared unexpectedly in a backyard in Devon, Pennsylvania, thousands of miles from its normal range in the West. Once a Painted Bunting appeared at a backyard feeder near my home— again far from its normal range. And Pine Grosbeaks, Green-tailed Towhees, and Hoary Redpolls all have been seen by bird watchers at backyard feeders far from where the birds should have occurred. Most bird watchers have even added a few new life list birds to their lists at backyard bird feeders.

At other times, backyards with plenty of trees, shrubs, and other vegetation and located along important migration routes frequently provide excellent bird watching opportunities during the spring and autumn migrations. Backyards can provide important habitat for birds and other wildlife at any season of the year if they are maintained properly. To encourage people to improve wildlife habitat in urban and suburban backyards, the National Wildlife Federation operates a Backyard Wildlife Habitat Program. A variety of information is available from the Federation on how to improve one's property for the benefit of birds and other wildlife. Some of the most important suggestions can be mentioned here.

Cover

Protective cover is one of the most important components in developing good wildlife habitat in urban areas as well as elsewhere. Fortunately, backyards measuring one-quarter acre or larger can be planted with a variety of trees and shrubs which provide excellent protective cover year round as well as producing berries, fruits, and other wildlife foods eaten by many species of birds. The section of the country will, of course, determine to some extent which trees and shrubs are best suited for backyards. Some of the most important are mentioned here.

In the Northeast, for example, plants such as Sunflowers, Panicgrass, and Timothy are helpful while the list of shrubs which can be planted includes Snowberry, Blueberry, Blackberry, and Huckleberry. Taller shrubs might include species such as Sumac, Elderberry, Dogwood, Autumn Olive, Wisteria, and Winterberry. Small trees also are vital for good wildlife cover. Among those known for their value to birdlife are Cherry, Crabapple, Flowering Dogwood, Hawthorn, Serviceberry, and Red Cedar. If room permits, some taller trees also are desirable. These include White Pines, Hemlock, and Colorado Spruce. Among deciduous species, Beech, Birch, Red Oak, White Oak, and Sugar Maple are excellent choices.

In the Southeast, somewhat different species of shrubs and trees can be selected to improve a backyard for the benefit of birds. Shrubs such as Spicebush, Bayberry, Blueberry, Blackberry, and Huckleberry all are good selections as are Dogwoods, Elderberry, and Sumac. Helpful also are small trees such as Crabapple, Red Cedar, Holly, Dogwood, Cherry, Hawthorn, Serviceberry, Persimmon, and Palmetto. Taller coniferous trees such as Longleaf, Shortleaf, and Loblolly Pine are desirable and one might select from such deciduous types as Pecan, Black Gum, Hackberry, Ash, Beech, Walnut, and Southern Red Oak.

Bird watchers living in the Northwest will find herbaceous growth such as Fiddlenecks, Sunflowers, Lupine, Turkey-mullein, and Filaree valuable. Small shrubs such as Oregon Grape, Snowberry, Blueberry, and Blackberry are useful, as are taller shrubs such as Madrone, Elderberry, Buckthorn, Bitterbush, Russian Olive, and Sumac. Hawthorn, Dogwood, and Serviceberry trees can be planted, as can Lodgepole Pine, Colorado Spruce, Douglas Fir, Western White Pine, and Ponderosa Pine. California Black Oak, Oregon White Oak, and Bigleaf Maple also are recommended.

In the Southwest shrubs including Prickly Pear, Spice-bush, Algerita, Utah Juniper, and Blackberry can be used
along with taller shrubs such as Lote Bush, Mulberry, Sumac,

Madrone, and Manzanita. Among trees, Crabapple, Mesquite, Dogwood, and Serviceberry frequently are recommended as are such conifers as Piñon Pine and Arizona Cypress and deciduous types such as Bitter Cherry, Pine Oak, and Live Oak.

It is important to remember, however, when planting various shrubs and trees, that it takes time to develop an area into a haven for birdlife. Do not expect instant results from efforts at improving a backyard for wildlife. Also, a given plot of land can support only limited numbers of species, especially during the nesting season, so hope must be tempered with the knowledge that natural population regulation factors will control what birds appear and how many. Still, far more types of birds can be expected to live in or visit a well-planned backyard than one with little vegetation and cover. If neighbors agree to cooperate in habitat improvement projects, the area covered will be larger and the results should be even more worthwhile.

Feeders

One of the great delights of backyard bird watching is looking at the parade of birds visiting a bird feeder every day during winter, or year round. Just what type of feeder one selects is entirely up to the individual's wishes. Some can be very simple and inexpensive homemade devices constructed from old planks, logs, or other materials. Others can be of the commercially manufactured bird

A typical backyard bird feeder. Photo courtesy of Droll Yankees, Inc.

Another variation of a backyard bird feeder. Photo courtesy of Droll Yankees, Inc.

feeders, of which a considerable variety are available. In either case, a wealth of birdlife can be expected to use feeders if they are well stocked with an assortment of sunflower seeds, cracked corn, suet, perhaps peanut butter, and even stale doughnuts obtained from local bakeries. In general, the larger the selection of food offered, the larger the variety of birds which may use a feeder.

Just which species of birds will visit a feeder depends to some extent upon where in the country it is located. But, in general, species such as woodpeckers, jays, chickadees, nuthatches, finches, and sparrows routinely visit most backyard feeding stations in winter. Some typical northeastern species, for example, include Hairy and Downy Woodpeckers, Blue Jays, Black-capped Chickadees, White-breasted Nuthatches, European Starlings, Northern Cardinals, House Finches, Evening Grosbeaks, and White-throated Sparrows.

It is extremely important, however, to keep a feeding station well stocked with food and in continous operation for the duration of the winter months in the more northern states because birds quickly become dependent upon the food provided and may perish if their food supply suddenly vanishes because a feeder is removed or neglected. The rule of thumb in backyard bird feeding is to begin in late autumn and continue until the next spring when more natural food supplies again become available. Or, if you wish, continue feeding throughout the entire year. In summer, some birds will still visit feeders despite the availability of natural foods, and in the case of hummingbirds these charming creatures can be attracted by special glass feeders filled very frequently with red sugar water. However, all hummingbird feeders *must* be kept filled constantly if they are in use because of the large amounts of food which these tiny birds need throughout each day and the frequency with which they feed at the glass feeders. Despite the work required to maintain hummingbird feeders, anybody who has watched hummingbirds at close range at sugar water feeders will quickly agree that the effort is well worthwhile. These birds are truly extraordinary creatures!

Water

An adequate supply of water is another requirement in any backyard habitat improvement program. Birds need water for drinking and bathing, so be certain to build a birdbath, or a little pool, close to some protective vegetation or to a brushpile and supply it with a continuous supply of fresh water. Many birds find such small pools into which water is dripping slowly extremely attractive and visit such spots regularly. An ordinary garden hose can sometimes be used to supply water to such pools or birdbaths,

A male Ruby-throated Hummingbird at a sugar water feeder

or more expensive and elaborate pipe arrangements can be installed. At one natural pool I visited some years ago, a small spring provided a steady supply of pure water to the shallow pool and all summer long a steady stream of Chipping Sparrows, American Robins, Brown Thrashers, Northern Cardinals, and other species used the pool to bathe. A small photographic blind was built near the pool and it was possible to take delightful photographs of the birds almost at arm's length.

A female Ruby-throated Hummingbird at a sugar water feeder

A Brown Thrasher bathing in a small spring

Nest Sites

In addition to other habitat requirements, it also is necessary to include nest sites in a well planned backyard habitat improvement project. The importance and value of nest boxes was discussed in the last chapter, but their value should be repeated here. Bird watchers also can provide nest materials in places where birds can obtain them and carry them to their nests. Orioles, for example, frequently carry bits of heavy string and weave it into the construction of their nests. Sometimes other species also will accept string, paper, or strips of cloth and use them among the natural construction materials of their nests.

If a bird box is used by a pair of birds, it is important that they not be disturbed frequently. Some species such as House Wrens will tolerate a reasonable amount of disturbance near their nests, but in

Gray Catbirds sometimes nest in gardens close to buildings.

Mourning Doves frequently nest in spruce and pine trees in gardens and parks.

general the birds will enjoy a better chance of successfully rearing their young if they are disturbed as little as possible. This may mean some slight inconvenience for a while, particularly if a nest is occupied near the door to a house, but it is a small price to pay for having these wild creatures share their lives with us. Beware of the family cat, however, which may have other ideas about the value of birds!

Additional Reading

Arbib, R., and T. Soper
    1970   The Hungry Bird Book. Taplinger Publishing Co., New York.

Davison, V. E.
    1967   Attracting Birds from the Prairies to the Atlantic. Thomas Y. Crowell Co., New York.

Dennis, J. V.
    1976   A Complete Guide to Bird Feeding. Alfred A. Knopf, Inc., New York.

Lapin, B.
    1975   A Squirrel-Baffling Bird Feeder. *Birding*, 7 (4): 196-200.

Martin, A. C. et al.
    1961   American Wildlife and Plants: A Guide to Wildlife Food Habits. Dover Publications, Inc., New York.

Schultz, W. E.
    1970   How to Attract, House and Feed Birds. Bruce Publishing Co., Milwaukee, Wis.

Terres, J. K.
    1968   Songbirds in Your Garden. Thomas Y. Crowell Co., New York.

10
WATCHING
SEABIRDS ON LAND
AND AT SEA

Watching seabirds on their breeding grounds is one of the most exciting and memorable types of bird watching, as anyone who has ever visited a large seabird colony will quickly confirm. Fortunately, there are many outstanding opportunities to visit such places along both the Atlantic and Pacific coasts of the Americas. In addition, within recent years increasing numbers of bird watchers on both our Atlantic and Pacific coasts have ventured onto the high seas in small fishing boats to watch spring and autumn migrations of seabirds. Pelagic bird watching is so relatively new, however, that only limited information is available on the best places to visit although some excellent areas now are known and are worthwhile visiting.

Unfortunately good, comprehensive field guides to northern hemisphere seabird identification still are unavailable. However, the standard guides to identification of North American birds illustrate the common seabirds which appear regularly off our coasts and are adequate for solving most seabird identification problems. W. B. Alexander's *Birds of the Ocean* also is useful although it includes all of the world's seabirds which makes it necessary to sort out many species which do not occur in North American waters.

Pelagic bird watchers face other problems also. Seasickness, for example, is a frequent and often serious problem. Motion sickness pills therefore should always be available and used prior to departure by most people. Nothing can ruin a pelagic bird watching trip more effectively than becoming seasick! In addition, warm waterproof clothing always should be taken on such trips. Indeed, warm jackets or even parkas sometimes are necessary even in spring and autumn. Weather conditions frequently are much different at sea from weather on shore and, once underway, captains of most boats will not turn back until a day's trip is completed. Adequate preparation before boarding a boat is therefore necessary in order to completely enjoy a pelagic bird watching trip.

North America: Atlantic Ocean

Canadian Maritime Area

A wide range of pelagic bird watching opportunities is available in the Canadian Maritime area if one is willing to explore and to plan far in advance of a trip. Particular attention should be given to the need for warm clothing in these relatively high latitudes.

Strait of Belle Isle, Newfoundland

Good pelagic bird watching has been reported in the Strait of Belle Isle in July. Among the species reported by birders crossing the strait are: Northern Fulmar, Greater Shearwater, Sooty Shearwater, Manx Shearwater, petrels, Northern Gannet, Red Phalarope, Pomarine Jaeger, Parasitic Jaeger, Razor-billed Auk, Common Murre, Black Guillemot, Common Puffin, Glaucous Gull, Iceland Gull, Black-legged Kittiwake, and Arctic Tern.

To reach the strait, drive to Sept Iles, Quebec, and fly from there to Blanc Sablon, Quebec. Then board the ferry which makes two round trips daily between Blanc Sablon and St. Barbe, Newfoundland. The ferry takes a route across the Strait of Belle Isle. Bird watchers wishing to stay for several days at St. Barbe can arrange lodging at the Doyles Hotel, about a five-minute walk from the wharf where the ferry docks. Because the strait sometimes is extremely rough, some crossings are cancelled or delayed for six hours or more. Motion sickness medication is recommended for anyone birding these waters.

North Sydney, Nova Scotia to Argentia, Newfoundland Ferry

Three days each week (Monday, Wednesday, and Friday) the Canadian National ferry *Ambrose Shea* sails across the 265 miles of Atlantic Ocean between North Sydney, Nova Scotia, and Argentia, Newfoundland. Dense fog sometimes seriously limits pelagic bird watching but Northern Fulmars, Pomarine Jaegers, Common Murres, and Common Puffins have been seen in July crossings. Reservations for the ferry should be made well in advance of a crossing.

Cape St. Mary's Seabird Sanctuary

This important Newfoundland bird sanctuary supports a large nesting colony of Northern Gannets along with Black-legged Kittiwakes, Common Murres, and Razor-billed Auks. Bird watchers do not actually visit Bird Island, which is the main part of the sanctuary, but rather stand on nearby cliffs about 200 feet away and look over at the nesting birds without disturbing them.

To reach this sanctuary from Placentia, Newfoundland, follow Route 8 south through St. Bride's, then east for 2.3 miles. Here turn right onto another road and follow it for 8.4 miles to the St. Mary's Light. The cliff adjacent to the sanctuary is located about half a mile away.

Bonaventure Island

Bonaventure Island, located in the Gulf of St. Lawrence a few miles off the town of Percé, near the tip of Quebec's Gaspé Peninsula, is one of North America's most spectacular and famous seabird sanctuaries. In summer, tens of thousands of Northern Gannets nest on ocean-facing cliffs along with small numbers of Common Puffins, Razor-billed Auks, Common Murres, Black-legged Kittiwakes, and other birds. Anyone interested in seabirds should make at least one visit to this important and exciting sanctuary.

Nesting Northern Gannets on Bonaventure Island, Quebec

A Northern Gannet on its nest on Bonaventure Island, Quebec

The departure point is in the town of Percé, which is easily reached by automobile. From the town one takes a tourist boat to the island nearby. The boats visit the island several times each day in summer and pass close to the ocean-facing cliffs on which the Northern Gannets nest row upon row, ledge upon ledge. It is also possible to land on the island at a public dock and to walk across the top of the island to the cliffs upon which the Northern Gannets are nesting. Large numbers of the large, white birds also nest on meadows behind the edge of the cliffs and one can approach within twenty to fifty feet behind a fence. The whole scene offers superb bird watching and photographic opportunities. A July or August visit to Bonaventure Island is an unforgettable experience!

Maine

Maine's coastal and offshore waters offer pelagic bird watching areas excellent both for migrating birds and for islands upon which seabirds nest. Of the latter, only a few can be mentioned here but bird watchers may profitably refer to Helen Cruickshank's delightful *Bird Islands Down East* for a full and captivating description of Maine's seabird islands.

Bluenose Ferry

One of the famous pelagic birding experiences in Maine's offshore waters is a trip on the M.V. *Bluenose* which runs between the ferry terminal in **Bar Harbor, Maine**, and **Yarmouth, Nova Scotia**—a distance of about 95 miles. During mid- to late summer a variety of seabirds can be seen from the decks of the *Bluenose*. Species seen frequently include Greater and Sooty Shearwaters, Leach's and Wilson's Storm Petrels, Northern and Red Phalaropes, Parasitic Jaegers, Arctic Terns, and Common Puffins. Some crossings also produce Manx Shearwaters, Northern Gannets, Razor-billed Auks, and Great Skuas. Bird watchers planning a trip on the *Bluenose* should make advance reservations well ahead of their intended trip because this ferry is used very heavily during summer.

In addition to the *Bluenose*, other ferries also run daily between Portland, Maine, and Yarmouth, a distance of 187 miles, and are suitable for pelagic bird watching. A distinct advantage of riding these ferries is that about twice as much ocean is crossed in comparison with the route followed by the *Bluenose*. Therefore, bird watchers have more opportunity to look for seabirds.

Machias Seal Island

This fascinating island, located about nine miles south of Cutler, Maine, is an important nest site for Common Puffins, Razor-billed

The lighthouse and other buildings on Machias Seal Island off the Maine coast. This is an important island for nesting seabirds.

Common Puffins on Machias Seal Island

Auks, Arctic Terns, and Leach's Storm Petrels. Bird watchers should plan visits to Machias Seal Island from June to early August if they wish to observe the largest variety of birds. Food and beverages are not available on the island. Boat transportation to the island has become somewhat of a problem in recent years, but it may be possible to make arrangements with fishermen in Cutler or other nearby Maine fishing villages or towns to take you there. In the past, a boat was available in Cutler.

Old Man Island

Not far from Machias Seal Island is small and ornithologically interesting Old Man Island. Landing there is extremely difficult except when seas are nearly calm. Once on the island, however, bird watchers will find large numbers of nesting Double-crested Cormorants along with Leach's Storm Petrels, Common Eiders, Black Guillemots, Great Black-backed Gulls, and Herring Gulls. Visits to the island in summer sometimes can be arranged on boats en route to, or from, Machias Seal Island.

87

A section of Old Man Island, Maine

Nesting Double-crested Cormorants, Old Man Island, Maine

A Double-crested Cormorant on Old Man Island, Maine

Rhode Island

Cox's Ledge

Cox's Ledge, a shoal about 30 miles southeast of Point Judith, Rhode Island, is another of New England's productive spots for watching seabirds from May through October. Among the species seen regularly are Cory's, Greater, and Sooty Shearwaters,

Black Guillemots swimming offshore from Old Man Island, Maine

Northern Fulmars, Pomarine, Parasitic, and Long-tailed Jaegers, Black-legged Kittiwakes, and Great Skuas. Visits to Cox's Ledge usually are made on board fishing boats departing from Galilee, Rhode Island.

New Jersey

Hudson Canyon

The recent discovery of substantial numbers of seabirds over the deep waters of the Hudson Canyon, about 90 miles east of Brigantine, New Jersey, provides excellent pelagic bird watching opportunities from late April to October. Among the species seen are Northern Fulmars, shearwaters of five species (Cory's, Greater, Sooty, Manx, and Audubon's), Leach's and Wilson's Storm Petrels, Northern Gannets, Red and Northern Phalaropes, Great Skuas, and Parasitic and Pomarine Jaegers.

Most visits to the Hudson Canyon are made on board fishing boats departing from Atlantic Highlands and Brielle, New Jersey. To be productive, all pelagic bird watching should be done at least 75 miles offshore, and birders should ask the captains of fishing boats how far they expect to go offshore before embarking on a particular boat.

A Greater Shearwater at sea over the Hudson Canyon off coastal New Jersey. Photo by Alan Brady

A Wilson's Storm Petrel at sea over the Hudson Canyon. Photo by Alan Brady

A Pomarine Jaeger at sea over the Hudson Canyon. Photo by Alan Brady

Maryland

Baltimore Canyon

Recent pelagic bird (and mammal) watching trips from Ocean City, Maryland, to the edge of the Baltimore Canyon, about 56 miles offshore, have produced unexpected numbers of seabirds in spring and autumn. Among the species which have been seen are Northern Gannets, Red and Northern Phalaropes, Pomarine and Parasitic Jaegers, Great Skuas, Glaucous, Iceland, and Herring Gulls, Black-legged Kittiwakes, and various unidentified terns. A Yellow-nosed Albatross also was reported from this spot. An added bonus can be splendid views of Finback Whales and Atlantic (Common) Dolphins.

North Carolina

Outer Banks Gulf Stream

About 25 miles southeast of Hatteras Inlet, the Gulf Stream approaches the Carolina coastline and provides good pelagic bird watching opportunities. In July, for example, Audubon's and Greater Shearwaters, Wilson's Storm Petrels, and Bridled Terns are seen. Fishing boats going to the Gulf Stream are available from Morehead City, North Carolina.

North America: Pacific Ocean

Pelagic bird watching opportunities also are excellent off the Pacific coastline of the United States and Canada and many bird watchers have explored these waters in recent years. The most productive spots are described here.

Washington

Ocean Off Westport

From late April through early October, pelagic bird watching trips can be taken to the open ocean off Westport, where fishing boats are boarded. For the best birding, the boat should go from 40 to 60 miles offshore to the edge of the continental shelf. Among the species observed in season are Black-footed Albatrosses, Northern Fulmars, Pink-footed and Sooty Shearwaters, Leach's and Fork-tailed Storm Petrels, Red and Northern Phalaropes, Pomarine and Parasitic Jaegers, Sabine's Gulls, Arctic Terns, as well as Cassin's Auklets and Tufted Puffins. Other rarer species also seen in autumn include Flesh-footed and Buller's Shearwaters.

California

Channel Islands

In southern California, pelagic bird watching is done in spring and autumn around the Channel Islands. Such trips sometimes are scheduled by the Los Angeles Audubon Society. More details can be secured from the Society.

Farallon Islands

The Farallon Islands are a group of small, isolated islands in the Pacific Ocean about 30 miles west of San Francisco. They form the Farallon National Wildlife Refuge and are protected and administered by the United States Fish and Wildlife Service. The islands are particularly important to nesting seabirds and support the largest North American seabird colony south of Alaska. More than 250,000 birds of 12 species breed on the islands each year: Leach's Storm Petrel, Ashy Storm Petrel, Black Oystercatcher, Double-crested Cormorant, Brandt's Cormorant, Pelagic Cormorant, Western Gull, Common Murre, Pigeon Guillemot, Cassin's Auklet, Rhinoceros Auklet, and Tufted Puffin.

Landing on the islands is prohibited because visitors can cause serious damage to the nesting seabirds. However, boat trips around the islands are worthwhile in April and May and many bird watchers join in such trips. Bay Area chapters of the National Audubon Society frequently sponsor trips around the Farallons. Other boat transportation usually can be arranged on fishing boats departing from Waldo Point, Sausalito, California.

Monterey Bay

In northern California, pelagic bird watching trips to Monterey Bay frequently are made in September and October. The Golden Gate Audubon Society organizes some of these trips.

Bermuda

The birdlife of Bermuda is essentially the same as that of eastern North America, thus allowing bird watchers visiting the island the opportunity to use any of the standard North American field guides to bird identification. In addition, David B. Wingate's *A Checklist and Guide to the Birds of Bermuda* provides a very good summary of the status of the island's birdlife along with suggestions of where to go bird watching.

Among the seabirds that breed on Bermuda, or visit the waters surrounding it, are Audubon's Shearwaters, the endangered Bermuda Petrel (or Cahow), White-tailed Tropicbirds, and Common Terns. Of these species, the tropicbird (known locally as "Longtails") is the only common seabird on the island. It breeds from March to October on various cliffs around the island, including the South Shore of Southampton, St. David's Head, the North Shore of St. George's, and the Castle Harbor Islands.

Unfortunately, opportunities to observe the endangered Bermuda Petrel are normally unavailable because the entire population numbers only a few dozen birds and they breed on certain islets in a harbor at one section of the island. These breeding islets are *strictly off-limits*! The rock forming the tiny islets is extremely rotten and serious damage can be quickly inflicted upon the bird's nest burrows and tunnels by persons unfamiliar with their locations and special requirements. Do not attempt to visit these islands.

Audubon's Shearwaters and Common Terns also are rather rare birds on Bermuda or in the offshore waters. Therefore, birders should not necessarily expect to see either species.

West Indies

Seabirds in great variety fly over the waters of the West Indies. Bird watchers traveling through this area by ship can expect to see a large assortment of species. Among those which occur regularly in the waters around the Antilles are Audubon's Shearwater, Black-capped Petrel, Leach's Storm Petrel, Wilson's Storm Petrel, the Red-billed and the White-tailed Tropicbird, the Masked (Blue-faced), Brown, and Red-footed Booby, Magnificent Frigatebird, Parasitic Jaeger, the Bridled and the Sooty Tern, and the Brown Noddy. From time to time, very many other species of seabirds also have been noted in the West Indies. Many were carried there in the eyes of hurricanes.

The best references for details about pelagic bird distribution and identification in the West Indies are James Bond's *Birds of the West*

Indies and George E. Watson's *Seabirds of the Tropical Atlantic Ocean.*

South America: Atlantic Ocean

So rarely do birders watch seabirds in the Atlantic Ocean off the coast of South America that relatively little information is available on the occurrence and distribution of seabirds in this area. The best field book for voyagers sailing through tropical Atlantic waters is George E. Watson's *Seabirds of the Tropical Atlantic Ocean*; his *Birds of the Antarctic and Sub-Antarctic* provides excellent coverage for all of the species found in the colder waters off the southern coast of the continent.

Although not designed for use in the field, Robert Cushman Murphy's classic two-volume work *Oceanic Birds of South America* provides extremely detailed information on all of South America's seabirds and the islands they nest on. Many of the islands included in this great work are visited so rarely that the information provided by Dr. Murphy in 1936 still represents much of what is known about them. *Logbook for Grace*, also by Murphy, is a fascinating and historically interesting account of his year at sea on board a whaling brig studying seabirds and other marine life in South Atlantic and Antarctic waters.

My own experiences watching seabirds in the South Atlantic show that it can be rewarding to look for these birds if one has the opportunity. During the latter part of 1975, while I served as ornithologist on board the M.S. *Lindblad Explorer*, I had abundant opportunity to observe seabirds in the western South Atlantic. The ship sailed from the Amazon River to the Falkland Islands and Antarctica.

Fernando Noronha

Fernando Noronha island is located about 356 kilometers from the coast of Brazil. It is a relatively small island, some three by seven kilometers, but it contains one of the most striking geologic formations in the entire South Atlantic—a high volcanic plug known as the Pyramid. Several small islets and rocks off the north coast provide some bird watching opportunities because a variety of species of seabirds nest there. The birds can be seen at their nests, resting on rocks, and flying overhead. Among the species I have seen there are White-tailed Tropicbirds, Brown Boobies, Masked Boobies, Red-footed Boobies, Sooty Terns, and Brown and Black Noddies. The Red-footed Boobies are mostly in the spectacular white plumage phase.

On Fernando Noronha itself, bird watching is limited to a few land birds and whatever else one can see from the island. Of more

A view of The Pyramid on Fernando Noronha Island, Brazil. Fairy Terns sometimes are seen flying near the top of the volcanic plug.

than minor interest, however, is the possibility of seeing a few Fairy Terns near the top of the Pyramid where they apparently nest. If one stands near the base and stares up toward the top of the volcanic plug, a few birds may be seen from time to time. They are beautiful white terns, well worth looking for.

Ocean South of Fernando Noronha

Bird watching south of Fernando Noronha is dull in the tropical latitudes. Only a few species are likely to be seen, among them, Cory's Shearwaters and Red-billed Tropicbirds. South of Rio de Janeiro, however, more seabirds begin to appear. For example, on November 28 at 31°33′S, 49°17′W, I observed a fine display of passing seabirds from the bridge of the M.S. *Lindblad Explorer*.

Boobies flying around an islet off Fernando Noronha Island, Brazil

Included were Cory's Shearwaters, Greater Shearwaters, Atlantic Petrels, and an unidentified storm petrel. The Atlantic Petrel was a particularly attractive species in addition to being a new life list bird for me.

Bird watching continued to improve farther south. On November 29, very rough seas prevailed under a grayish-leaden sky. Strong winds lashed at the sea and birds were everywhere soaring effortlessly. Black-browed Albatrosses soared past sometimes so close I could almost touch them. Conspicuous also were lesser seabirds, including White-chinned Petrels, Cape Pigeons, and Greater Shearwaters.

The next day, both wind and sea calmed considerably and the weather was clear and sunny. Seabirds were still around, however. Among these were Black-browed Albatrosses, a Greater Shearwater, and a Southern Black-backed Gull. I also saw my first Southern Giant Fulmars. In Antarctica, I would see many of these large birds, which frequently follow in the wake of a ship.

On December 2, we reached the famous "Roaring Forties" at 42°00'S, 58°22'W en route to the Falkland Islands. These latitudes are famous for seabirds and I was not disappointed. Birds were everywhere. Included among those seen were Magellanic Penguins, Wandering Albatrosses, Black-browed Albatrosses, Yellow-nosed Albatrosses, Southern Giant Fulmars, White-chinned Petrels, Greater Shearwaters, Sooty Shearwaters, Wilson's Storm Petrels, and Brown Skuas. The albatrosses were especially abundant: 400 Black-browed and about 20 Wandering. Closer to

96

the Falklands, Black-bellied Storm Petrels also appeared.
Watching seabirds in the South Atlantic was exciting!

Falkland Islands

The Falkland Islands are located in the western South Atlantic about 350 miles east of Cape San Diego, Tierra del Fuego, South America. They provide excellent opportunities for bird watchers wishing to see nesting seabirds of various species including a variety of species of penguins. Most visitors to the Falklands arrive there by ship, such as the M.S. *Lindblad Explorer*, from various ports in South America.

Bird watchers en route to the islands find such voyages excellent for seeing seabirds. For example, during one three-day voyage to the Falklands in early December 1975, I observed the following seabirds: Magellanic Penguins, Wandering Albatrosses, Black-browed Albatrosses, Southern Giant Fulmars, Cape Pigeons, Atlantic Petrels, White-chinned Petrels, Sooty Shearwaters, Greater Shearwaters, Wilson's Storm Petrels, Black-bellied Storm Petrels, Brown Skuas, and Arctic Terns. On another trip in January 1976, from Ushuaia, Argentina, through the Beagle Channel to the Falklands, most of the above species were seen as well as a Little Shearwater, Kerguelen Diving Petrels, Southern Black-backed Gulls, and South American Terns.

A visitor to the Falklands generally plans to touch at East Falkland, one of two main islands, where Stanley, the capital, is

Port Stanley, Falkland Islands

located. Although bird watching opportunities around Stanley are somewhat limited, some gulls will be seen as well as Flightless Steamer Ducks and some land birds. If, however, a visit to Volunteer Point on East Falkland can be arranged, a small nesting colony of King Penguins (which are rigidly protected) can be seen and photographed. These splendid birds now are extremely rare in the Falklands because of years of persecution, but their numbers are slowly increasing. This colony is the only one suitable for visiting north of South Georgia in the Antarctic. Surrounding the 43 King Penguins on my visit were about 1,000 nesting Gentoo and 750 Magellanic Penguins. Other species seen in the vicinity of these penguin colonies were Southern Giant Fulmars, Upland Geese, Speckled Teal, Turkey Vultures, Magellanic Oystercatchers, Brown Skuas, Dolphin Gulls, Southern Black-backed Gulls, Tussock-birds, and Dark-faced Ground-tyrants. Birds in the Falklands are fairly tame and easy to approach.

While in the Falkland Islands one should also make every effort to visit some of the other bird-rich islands such as West Point, Carcass, and New Island, all located west of West Falkland. Each is privately owned. The M.S. *Lindblad Explorer* visits each of these islands each year and other ships occasionally do, too.

On West Point Island, for example, one sees spectacular nesting colonies of Rockhopper Penguins and Black-browed Albatrosses. These birds are carefully protected by the Roddy Napier family, which lives on the island and raises sheep. On Carcass Island,

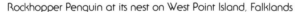

Rockhopper Penguin at its nest on West Point Island, Falklands

Black-browed Albatross in flight

Black-browed Albatross on its nest on West Point Island, Falklands

important Gentoo and Magellanic Penguin colonies are found, a few Peregrine Falcons still breed, and the rare Striated Caracara often is seen. New Island also offers exciting bird watching opportunities, especially in the vicinity of splendid headlands where there are large nesting colonies of Rockhopper Penguins, Black-browed Albatrosses, and King Shags. A very large Gentoo Penguin colony also exists behind a nearby beach not very far from the headlands. Visits to each of these privately owned islands must be arranged beforehand with the people living in the settlement on each island.

Carcass Island, Falklands

Magellanic Penguin at its nest burrow on Carcass Island, Falklands

Listed below are the species of birds I observed in the Falkland Islands on two visits.

King Penguin
Gentoo Penguin
Rockhopper Penguin
Macaroni Penguin
Magellanic Penguin
Black-browed Albatross
Southern Giant Fulmar
Slender-billed Prion
White-chinned Petrel
Sooty Shearwater
Wilson's Storm Petrel
Rock Shag
King Shag
Black-crowned Night Heron
Ruddy-headed Goose
Upland Goose
Kelp Goose
Crested Duck
Flightless Steamer Duck
Speckled Teal
Turkey Vulture

Striated Caracara
Magellanic Oystercatcher
Black Oystercatcher
Two-banded Plover
Rufous-chested Dotterel
Common Snipe
American Sheathbill
Brown Skua
Dolphin Gull
Southern Black-backed Gull
South American Tern
Blackish Cinclodes
  (Tussock-bird)
Dark-faced Ground-Tyrant
House Wren
Austral (Falkland) Thrush
Falkland (Correndera) Pipit
Long-tailed Meadowlark
Black-throated Finch
Black-chinned Siskin
House Sparrow

Persons visiting the Falkland Islands to watch birds will find that

Robin W. Woods' book *The Birds of the Falkland Islands* provides a great deal of helpful information about the islands as well as basic information, descriptions, and illustrations of the birds living there.

South America: Pacific Ocean

The Pacific Ocean off the west coast of South America contains some of the largest and most spectacular concentrations of seabirds found anywhere in the world. Here bird watchers will find ample reward for their efforts. In large measure, these spectacular seabird concentrations are due to the cold, nutrient-rich upwellings of the Humboldt and other northward-flowing currents along with the rich fish resources of the Peruvian and Chilean coasts. Robert Cushman Murphy provides excellent descriptions of the birdlife of these waters in *Bird Islands of Peru* and *Oceanic Birds of South America.* Farther north on the equator, the famous Galapagos Islands also are of extraordinary interest to bird watchers. Several endemic seabirds can be seen here, on their breeding grounds, and many other non-endemic species also occur on the islands in large numbers.

Peruvian Bird Islands

Of the many bird islands located off the coast of Peru, some of the most accessible are those a few miles off the Paracas Peninsula south of Lima. Tourist boats are available from the Hotel Paracas to take bird watchers to the islands (where landing is prohibited). Such excursions are extremely worthwhile. They can be completed in half a day and offer excellent opportunities for observation and photography. Among the species normally seen are Sooty Shearwaters, Cape Pigeons, Peruvian Diving Petrels, Wedge-rumped Storm Petrels, White-vented Storm Petrels, Wilson's Storm Petrels, Guanay Cormorants, Red-legged Cormorants, Neotropic Cormorants, Peruvian Boobies, Brown Pelicans, Peruvian Terns, Inca Terns, Gray Gulls, Southern Black-backed Gulls, Band-tailed Gulls, and Brown Skuas.

In addition to the ornithological attractions, the famous "candelabra" carved on the hillside of the Paracas Peninsula deserve a good look. Boats en route to the bird islands pass close to this carving. Field guides to the birds of this region are not equal to those for some other parts of the world, but Maria Koepcke's *The Birds of the Department of Lima, Peru* is very helpful.

Galapagos Islands

Full details about bird watching in the biologically rich Galapagos Islands are presented in chapter 20. Here, therefore, the discussion is limited to the seabirds which occur in the waters surrounding the Galapagos Islands. Those species observed most

A seabird island off Paracas, Peru. Millions of cormorants and other seabirds nest on these islands. Their guano is a major source of fertilizer for many parts of the world.

frequently include Galapagos Penguins, Waved Albatrosses, Audubon's Shearwaters, several species of storm petrels, Red-billed Tropicbirds, Brown Pelicans, Blue-footed Boobies, Masked Boobies, Red-footed Boobies, Great and Magnificent Frigatebirds, Swallow-tailed and Lava Gulls, and Brown Noddies. Most of these species nest on the islands and some are endemic to specific islands. Thus, the Waved Albatross nests only on Hood Island, and Galapagos Penguins are largely confined as breeding birds to portions of Narborough, Isabela, Santa Cruz, and a few other islands.

Since most visitors to the Galapagos Islands arrive there as part of organized tours, the operators of such tours and the national

A Magnificent Frigatebird in flight over one of the Galapagos Islands

park service guides who accompany such tours know exactly where to take visitors to see these birds without causing too much disturbance which could endanger the nesting efforts of the birds. Indeed, strict rules govern where and when visitors may visit in the islands, most of which are part of Galapagos National Park. Bird watchers visiting the Galapagos should carry with them a copy of *A Field Guide to the Birds of Galapagos* by Michael Harris.

Additional Reading

Armistead, H. T.
    1972   Pelagics: Maine, Nova Scotia, and Newfoundland. *Birding*, 4 (4): 181-82.

Brady, A.
    1977   A Summary of Recent Pelagic Trips off the New Jersey Coast. *Cassinia*, 56: 7-14.

Bushnell, B.
    1976   Pelagics: Cox's Ledge, Rhode Island. *Birding*, 8 (3): 169.

Chandik, T.
    1972   Pelagic Trips off Northern California. *Birding*, 4 (4): 175-77.

Clancy, J. J.
    1974   Common Puffin. *Birding*, 6 (3): 123.

Cruickshank, H. G.
    1941   Bird Islands Down East. Macmillan Co., New York.

DuMont, P. G.
    1973   Black-browed Albatross Sightings off the United States East Coast. *American Birds*, 27 (4): 739-40.

Harris, M.
    1974   A Field Guide to the Birds of Galapagos. Taplinger Publishing Co., Inc., New York.

Heintzelman, D. S.
    1974   The Gannets of Bonaventure Island. *Frontiers*, 38 (3): 18-21.

Koepcke, M.
    1970   The Birds of the Department of Lima, Peru. Livingston Publishing Co., Wynnewood, Pa.

Lockley, R. M.
    1974   Ocean Wanderers: The Migratory Sea Birds of the World. Stackpole Books, Harrisburg, Pa.

McDaniel, J. W.
    1973   Vagrant Albatrosses in the Western North Atlantic and Gulf of Mexico. *American Birds*, 27 (3): 563-65.

Murphy, R. C.
    1925   Bird Islands of Peru. G. P. Putnam's Sons, New York.
    1936   Oceanic Birds of South America. American Museum of Natural History, New York.

1947   Logbook for Grace. Macmillan Co., New York.

Nettleship, D. N.

1974   Seabird Colonies and Distributions Around Devon Island and Vicinity. *Arctic,* 27 (2): 95-103.

1975   A Recent Decline of Gannets, *Morus bassanus,* on Bonaventure Island, Quebec. *Canadian Field-Naturalist,* 89: 125-33.

1976   Gannets in North America: Present Numbers and Recent Population Changes. *Wilson Bulletin,* 88 (2): 300-13.

Orbison, J. L.

1976   Bonaventure Island, Quebec. *Birding,* 8 (1): 27.

Parmeter, B. D.

1974   Marbled Murrelet. *Birding,* 6 (3): 125-26.

Pettingill, E. R.

1960   Penguin Summer: An Adventure with the Birds of the Falkland Islands. Clarkson N. Potter, Inc., New York.

Pettingill, O. S., Jr.

1975   Another Penguin Summer. Charles Scribner's Sons, New York.

Rowlett, R. A.

1974   Seabirds and Marine Mammals Off Ocean City, Maryland. *Atlantic Naturalist,* 29 (4): 150-54.

1976   Clear the Decks! Pelagic Preparations and Precautions. *Birding,* 8 (2): 133-34.

Smith, P. W.

1973   Pelagics (North Carolina, Hatteras). *Birding,* 5 (4): 143.

1974   Pelagics (New Jersey, Hudson Canyon). *Birding,* 6 (3): 127-28.

1975   Hudson Canyon, N.J., Pelagics. *Birding,* 7 (3): 219-20.

Threlfall, W.

1974a   Gull Island, Newfoundland. *Birding,* 6 (1): 15-16.

1974b   Newfoundland. *Birding,* 6 (1): 29-30.

Wahl, T. R.

1976   Pelagics: Westport, Washington. *Birding,* 8 (3): 185-86.

Warham, J., and W. R. P. Bourne

1974   Additional Notes on Albatross Identification. *American Birds,* 28 (3): 598-603.

Warham, J., W. R. P. Bourne, and H. F. I. Elliott

1974   Albatross Identification in the North Atlantic. *American Birds,* 28 (3): 585-98.

Wingate, D. B.

1973   A Checklist and Guide to the Birds of Bermuda. Available in bookshops in Bermuda.

Woods, R. W.

1975   The Birds of the Falkland Islands. Anthony Nelson and Lindblad Travel, Inc., New York.

11
WATCHING WATERFOWL

Watching ducks, geese, and swans can be done at any time of the year but most people have come to recognize the thrills of watching waterfowl as signals of the beginning of spring or autumn. Who has not experienced the excitement of hearing or seeing a flock of Canada Geese migrating overhead? Or stood and watched the beauty of a flock of migrating Whistling Swans or Snow Geese against an azure sky? Waterfowl is, indeed, among the most fascinating and popular forms of wildlife to both bird watchers and hunters. Certainly every bird watcher should take advantage of the exciting opportunitites which are available in many parts of the United States and Canada for watching ducks, geese, and swans.

Migration Seasons

Waterfowl, like many other types of birds, are highly migratory over much of North America. In spring, for example, many species migrate from south to north as single individuals or in flocks. Common Goldeneyes, Redheads, and Canvasbacks all appear alone or in small numbers for brief periods of time on park and farm ponds. In other instances, large flocks of geese are conspicuous as they fly overhead. Spectacular concentrations of Whistling Swans may stop briefly to rest and feed in safe areas between their winter and summer homes. This happens in March on the lower Susquehanna River near York, Pennsylvania. Most of these birds wintered on Chesapeake Bay and gather in southeastern Pennsylvania prior to their northward migrations to the Arctic breeding grounds. Thus, for a week or two, they provide local bird watchers with an extraordinary spectacle as they fly from the river to nearby fields where they feed on corn and other grains. Some of the swans wear plastic neck collars and a few are even fitted with miniature radio transmitters placed there by Dr. William Sladen of 105

Whistling Swans in March flying from the Susquehanna River in eastern Pennsylvania to nearby fields to feed. Bird watchers from far and near visit the area every spring to enjoy the views of the birds.

Whistling Swans feeding in a field in early December near the Susquehanna River in eastern Pennsylvania.

Whistling Swans flying over the Susquehanna River in eastern Pennsylvania. Note black neck collars on several birds.

Whistling Swans standing alert

In late autumn thousands of Greater Snow Geese gather in salt meadows on Brigantine National Wildlife Refuge, New Jersey. Large numbers of birders observe and photograph the birds.

Johns Hopkins University as part of his long-term study of swan migrations. Birds from different areas of the Arctic wear collars of different colors.

White-fronted Geese are common along the Central and Pacific flyways. Photo by Jan Sosik

Similar migrations occur in autumn. Along the Atlantic coastline, bird watchers now look forward to seeing thousands of migrating Snow Geese as they stop for several months at various locations such as Brigantine National Wildlife Refuge, New Jersey, before continuing farther south to their ancestral wintering grounds. Bird watchers from many parts of the East visit the refuge when the Snow Geese are there to watch and enjoy the spectacle as clouds of the white birds take off from the salt marshes where they feed and rest.

Every year, thousands of migrating Canada Geese, along with a variety of other species, are counted in October from many of the eastern mountain lookouts used regularly by hawk watchers. The birds add great interest to the general bird watching activities at such spots and sometimes more geese than hawks are counted migrating overhead! The picture is much the same elsewhere in North America. Millions of ducks, geese, and swans migrate over the continent twice every year in extraordinary displays of animal movements. And everywhere bird watchers are quick to take advantage of the opportunities provided by these migrations.

Flyways

These millions of migrating birds do not scatter at random during their migrations. Rather, they use four great migration routes called flyways: Atlantic, Mississippi, Central, and Pacific. Not all species are equally common on each flyway. White-fronted Geese, for example, are common along the Central and Pacific flyways but uncommon along the Mississippi and rare along the Atlantic. Canada Geese are common along all four flyways, but Barnacle Geese are accidental (rarely seen) along all flyways but most likely to be seen along the Atlantic coast; they are vagrants from Europe. Canvasbacks, however, are common along the Atlantic and Pacific flyways but uncommon along the Mississippi and Central flyways. Buffleheads are common on each of the flyways except the Central where they are uncommon.

Thus each species of North American waterfowl has a unique migration pattern in its use of flyways. This fact is one of the major management tools used in setting hunting bag limits for each species each year. By careful field study of each species on its breeding ground, coupled with a knowledge of which flyways are used by birds from specific areas, bag limits and other hunting restrictions are developed for each flyway. Bird watchers can use such information effectively, too, by studying which flyway a species uses most heavily. Birding trips can then be planned to appropriate areas on such flyways to improve chances of seeing desirable species or new life list birds.

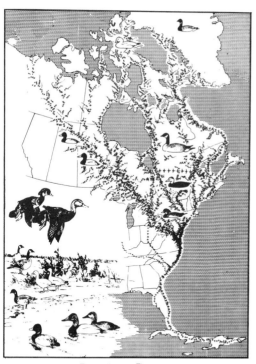

The Atlantic Flyway

The Mississippi Flyway

The Central Flyway

The Pacific Flyway

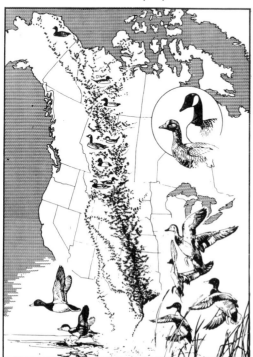

Canada Geese are common along all four North American flyways.

Concentration Areas

In addition to watching migrating waterfowl in spring and autumn, bird watchers can explore many excellent locations in the United States and Canada where impressive concentrations of ducks, geese, and sometimes swans can be seen during other seasons of the year. Among the best and most important are the many National Wildlife Refuges operated by the United States Fish and Wildlife Service. It is impossible to name them all here, but bird watchers interested in this subject will find details on all such refuges of importance to waterfowl in my *North American Ducks, Geese & Swans*; each species is illustrated with black and white or color photographs and other suggestions for enjoying waterfowl also are detailed.

Some of the most famous of our National Wildlife Refuges are worthwhile mentioning here. These would certainly include the Bear River Migratory Bird Refuge in Utah, Blackwater National Wildlife Refuge in Maryland, Bombay Hook National Wildlife Refuge in Delaware, Brigantine National Wildlife Refuge in New Jersey, Chincoteague National Wildlife Refuge in Maryland and Virginia, Lacassine and Sabine National Wildlife Refuges in Louisiana, Malheur National Wildlife Refuge in Oregon, and Mattamuskeet and Swanquarter National Wildlife Refuges in North Carolina. Still others include the famous Red Rock Lakes Migratory Waterfowl Refuge in Montana and Tule Lake, Lower Klamath, and Sacramento National Wildlife Refuges in California. Most states have at least one such federal refuge and some states have many. Bird watchers are welcome at each refuge, and many 111

Summer at Bombay Hook National Wildlife Refuge, Delaware

refuges provide free bird checklists, maps, tour route guides, and other helpful literature detailing the natural history of the site.

Some national parks also are important concentration points for waterfowl and provide excellent bird watching opportunities. In Yellowstone National Park, for example, bird watchers have opportunities to observe with relative ease small numbers of the rare Trumpeter Swan.

In addition to the various federal parks and refuges, a variety of state parks and refuges also provide excellent bird watching

Trumpeter Swans on the Malheur National Wildlife Refuge, Oregon. Photo by Ray C. Erickson / U.S. Fish and Wildlife Service

Canada Goose on Brigantine National Wildlife Refuge, New Jersey

A male Mallard on a small pond. These ducks are distributed widely in North America.

opportunities for waterfowl enthusiasts. For example, in Pennsylvania, the Pymatuning Waterfowl Area near Meadville in the western part of the state and the Middle Creek Wildlife Management Area on the Lebanon-Lancaster county border in the eastern part of the state support large concentrations of waterfowl as well as many other species of birdlife and other wildlife. Some other states have similar facilities. Details can be secured from a state's wildlife agency. Simply ask for information on waterfowl refuges or management areas. In addition, some of the regional bird finding guides mentioned in chapter 3 provide details about the best of such spots.

Various private conservation organizations own and operate wildlife sanctuaries some of which have lakes and ponds used by various species of waterfowl. In Massachusetts, for example, the Massachusetts Audubon Society's network of over two dozen sanctuaries includes some used by waterfowl. Other national or international organizations also own important waterfowl breeding areas covering millions of acres of vital wetlands. In Canada, over 1,200 such waterfowl production areas are managed by Ducks Unlimited (Canada). Most of these provide excellent bird watching opportunities.

Finally one cannot overlook the millions of small ponds and marshes on farms in the United States and Canada and their value to waterfowl either during the breeding season or during the migration season or winter. Each of these little wetlands may not be exceptionally significant by itself, but when they are considered

Mallards in flight

collectively they form a major waterfowl refuge system fully as important as our federal National Wildlife Refuge system. Refuges, also, are the local ponds and lakes in many city and town parks. At such places, ducks and geese frequently represent the most obvious and important wildlife attractions which the general public sees. Artificial lakes forming reservoirs for cities and towns also serve as important resting, feeding, and breeding areas for waterfowl while providing excellent bird watching spots for local residents.

Male Wood Ducks are vividly colored birds sometimes seen on small secluded ponds and lakes.

A male Hooded Merganser on a small pond in a city park in Allentown, Pennsylvania

It is clear, therefore, that ducks, geese, and swans not only are vital parts of our wildlife resources but also provide bird watchers with excellent opportunities to engage in their hobby. If you are a bird watcher who has not yet become a waterfowl enthusiast, why not join in the fun? You'll be in good company with countless other bird watchers!

Additional Reading

Banko, W. E.
    1960   The Trumpeter Swan. *North American Fauna* 63: 1-214.
Delacour, J.
    1954-64   The Waterfowl of the World. 4 volumes. Country Life Ltd., London.
Heintzelman, D. S.
    1978   North American Ducks, Geese & Swans. Winchester Press, New York.
Johnsgard, P. A.
    1968   Waterfowl: Their Biology and Natural History. University of Nebraska Press, Lincoln, Neb.
Scott, P.
    1972   The Swans. Houghton Mifflin Co., Boston.

12
HAWK WATCHING

One of the most exciting and enjoyable bird watching specialties, which has attracted thousands of participants in recent years, is watching migrating hawks in spring or autumn at points where natural geographic features foster concentrations. Bird watchers living in the eastern half of the continent are particularly fortunate because some of the world's finest hawk lookouts are located there. In western North America, however, ornithologists have discovered only a few outstanding hawk migration concentration points that consistently produce large numbers of migrating raptors during the appropriate season. This seeming lack of hawk lookouts in the West may not actually be the case; only limited field studies on migrating hawks have been made in that part of the continent and doubtless some new and important sites still wait to be discovered. Bird watchers can play an important role in helping to find such spots by spending some time in spring or autumn at likely locations and looking for numbers of migrating hawks.

A few hints for hawk watchers will be helpful, if such efforts are to produce the best results. For example, it is very important to scan the distant horizon at frequent intervals and attempt to detect approaching hawks before they pass a lookout. Otherwise they may be missed because they are too high overhead or too far out over valleys to be seen easily by the time they pass the observation spot. Frequent scanning is especially necessary on days with clear blue skies because migrating hawks are unusually difficult to see under those conditions when they pass overhead. It also is very helpful to have several people looking for birds. Sometimes one person will not see a bird which another person spots. In general, the more bird watchers at a lookout, the more likely it is that all of the hawks migrating past a spot will be seen and counted. There is a danger during slack periods, however, that casual conversation prevails when observers should be looking for birds, and some hawks can pass unseen. Hawk watchers should try to remain alert if they wish to see as many birds as possible passing a lookout. Finally, somebody on a lookout always should have available a field guide to general bird identification or copies of *A Guide to Eastern Hawk*

Hawk watchers on an eastern Pennsylvania hawk lookout

Watching or *A Guide to Hawk Watching in North America* to aid in identifying the birds seen. Many bird watchers are less familiar with raptor identification than with field marks of some other species of birds, and the illustrations and information contained in a hawk watching guide, or other bird guide, will prove to be very helpful even to experienced bird watchers. These hints for hawk watchers apply equally to people using both eastern and western hawk lookouts.

Migration Seasons

Spring hawk migrations in eastern North America occur from February through mid-May depending upon the location. In the Northeast and Great Lakes areas, where much of the spring hawk watching occurs, mid- to late April is particularly favorable. Large numbers of migrating hawks often are seen at the few known spring concentration points such as Derby Hill in upstate New York.

In autumn, the first of the migrating hawks begin to appear early in August. Their numbers build to peak periods of abundance from September through November with a few birds still passing some lookouts into mid-December. Within the period September through November, however, each of the species of birds of prey

A kettle of migrating Broad-winged Hawks in a thermal over an eastern Pennsylvania hawk lookout. Hawk watchers are particularly eager to see such spectacles.

that appear regularly has a fairly well defined migratory period of its own. Broad-winged Hawks, for instance, are by far the most abundant of the migrating raptors and generally occur in the largest numbers around mid-September at many northeastern lookouts. Not infrequently, September 16 or 17 produces a season's largest flight in eastern Pennsylvania. However, this can vary by a week or more earlier or later and lookouts located north or south of Pennsylvania may have somewhat different migration schedules for

A migrating eastern Red-tailed Hawk

A migrating Broad-winged Hawk

these birds. Therefore, daily watches are necessary at hawk lookouts if bird watchers wish to enjoy the spectacle of a peak flight of Broad-wings. Such flights might number from five to ten thousand birds.

Bird watchers should keep in mind, however, that lookouts which are in close proximity to each other do not always record peak hawk flights on the same days. Thus, if observers at Hawk Mountain report a peak flight of hawks on a particular day, one should not assume that another peak flight might not be seen elsewhere on a later date.

Early to mid-October produces the largest numbers of migrating Sharp-shinned Hawks. They are very exciting birds to watch as they dart past a lookout. In late October and early November, the largest flights of migrating Red-tailed Hawks occur along with Golden Eagles, Northern Goshawks, and various other species. Sometimes these days are bitterly cold and only the hardiest of hawk watchers stick to their lookouts, but the rewards are great for those who do. The great pageant of migrating Red-tails, Golden Eagles, and other species is bird watching at its very best!

Migration Routes

As there are fairly well-defined times of migration for each of the various raptors, there also are several major flyways or migration routes which these birds use in autumn but less so in spring.

Generally the northward spring migrations of hawks are widespread although some birds follow river valleys, mountains, and other prominent geographic features. An important exception to the normal widespread migration pattern is the southern shorelines of Lakes Erie and Ontario where impressive numbers of migrating hawks concentrate. One of the best locations is Derby Hill in upstate New York.

A migrating Sharp-shinned Hawk

An immature Golden Eagle

In autumn there are three very important flyways: the Atlantic coastline, the Appalachian ridges (especially those oriented in northeast to southwest directions), and the northern and western shorelines of the Great Lakes.

The bulk of the accipitrine hawks such as Sharp-shins, and falcons such as American Kestrels, follow the Atlantic coastline southward. However, buteos or soaring hawks such as Broad-wings and Red-tails, and some Sharp-shins, are more prone to follow inland mountain ridges where good updrafts provide excellent soaring conditions. Falcons, however, are relatively rare migrants along the ridges. They prefer coastal routes because of the abundant numbers of migratory songbirds which occur there and form a ready supply of food. Finally, accipitrine and soaring hawks also are abundant migrants along the northern and western shorelines of the Great Lakes.

Weather Conditions

Besides the features just discussed, weather features may correlate with large flights of migrating hawks. An understanding of weather trends is of great value to bird watchers.

In spring, for example, southerly winds along with rising air temperatures and a dropping barometer seem to correlate best with numbers of migrating hawks.

121

In autumn, general weather patterns occurring over the eastern half of the continent also play important roles in causing hawks to begin migrating southward. Generally, a low-pressure area over upstate New York and lower New England, coupled a day or two later with the passage of a cold front, produces conditions favorable for good hawk flights in Pennsylvania, New Jersey, and surrounding states. Similar combinations of conditions over the western Great Lakes also produce good hawk flights at Duluth and other hawk concentration points along the northern and western shorelines of the lakes. Moderately brisk to brisk winds are especially important. They can come from any direction but generally northwesterly winds are desirable for good flights of soaring hawks such as Red-tails. Broad-winged Hawks, on the other hand, are most dependent upon thermals (rising bubbles of warm air) and may appear in large numbers on winds with easterly or westerly components.

Hawk Flight Styles

Since most hawks are expert soaring birds, the deflective updrafts which occur along mountains such as the Kittatinny Ridge in eastern Pennsylvania and northwestern New Jersey provide excellent flyways. Surface winds strike the sides of this ridge and are deflected upward. Migrating hawks simply use these updrafts to travel without having to exert much energy for flapping flight. The hawks soar on the air currents just as sailplane pilots do. Accipiters such as Sharp-shins, however, which naturally use combinations of flapping and sailing flight, probably exert more energy than soaring hawks do.

Most of the species of migratory hawks seen in the East utilize deflective updrafts as aids to their autumnal migrations. The Broad-winged Hawk, however, is an exception and is more dependent upon thermals to carry it south around the Gulf of Mexico, through Central America, and into northern South America where it winters. Sometimes these hawks gather by the hundreds in thermals. Hawk watchers refer to these milling flocks as "kettles." They are among the most spectacular avian sights in autumn. Once inside a thermal, the entire milling kettle rides aloft in the huge air bubble. Then, as the thermal begins to cool and dissipate, the hawks glide downward in bomber-like formation until another thermal is located and the process is repeated.

Sometimes, when the birds appear in the vicinity of mountains over which good deflective updrafts occur, combinations of thermals and updrafts are used for varying distances. Such limited use of prominent geographic features is referred to as use of

An adult Turkey Vulture soaring on updrafts along an eastern Pennsylvania mountain

diversion-lines or leading-lines. In the West, Swainson's Hawks also use thermals frequently and sometimes mixed flocks of Broad-winged and Swainson's Hawks are seen in the Southwest during spring and autumn migrations.

Most soaring hawks generally are unwilling to cross large bodies of water such as the Great Lakes or the Gulf of Mexico. When such major geographic features are encountered, large numbers of hawks alter their course and follow the lake or gulf coast around the water obstacle. Ospreys and Peregrine Falcons, on the other hand, have no aversion to crossing expanses of open water and regularly migrate across the West Indies en route to South American wintering grounds or North American breeding grounds.

Hawk Lookouts

Fortunately for bird watchers, there are many excellent lookouts in the East suitable for watching migrating hawks. Anybody wishing to see a good flight of hawks should visit one or more of these places during the migration seasons. It is not at all unusual to see, also, a wide variety of other birdlife at such places so a day spent there is worthwhile from several points of view. It is not possible here to provide complete details and directions for each of the lookouts but some of the better sites are discussed briefly. Bird 123 watchers needing full details on the hawk lookouts, and on autumn hawk migration in general, will find *A Guide to Eastern Hawk Watching*, *A Guide to Hawk Watching in North America*, and *Autumn Hawk Flights* exceptionally helpful.

Perhaps the best location to enjoy hawk watching in autumn along the Great Lakes is the Hawk Ridge Nature Reserve in Duluth, Minnesota. Thousands of migrating birds of prey are counted there every year and bird watchers from far and wide make trips to the lookouts to enjoy the spectacles. Other well known and excellent autumn lookouts along the Great Lakes include Ontario's Point Pelee National Park, Holiday Beach Provincial Park, and Hawk Cliff. In spring, New York's Derby Hill on the southern shoreline of Lake Ontario is one of the best hawk lookouts.

Inland along the Appalachian mountains, Hook Mountain in New York, the Montclair Hawk Lookout Sanctuary and Raccoon Ridge in New Jersey, and Bake Oven Knob and Hawk Mountain in

Hawk watchers on the North Lookout at Hawk Mountain, Pennsylvania

eastern Pennsylvania are outstanding autumn hawk lookouts. Hawk Mountain is no doubt one of the world's best-known spots to see hawks and the story of its establishment is one of the outstanding chapters in American wildlife conservation history. Prior to the formation of the sanctuary to protect migrating hawks, thousands of the birds were shot there every autumn in the name of "sport."

Important Atlantic coastline lookouts in autumn include Brier Island in Nova Scotia, Lighthouse Point Park in Connecticut, Fire Island in New York, and Cape May Point in New Jersey. Cape May Point is one of the outstanding North American concentration areas for hawks and songbirds in autumn. A visit there in late September and early October can be unusually rewarding if northwest winds prevail. Extremely large numbers of birds are then seen, and they may include such endangered species as Peregrine Falcons.

In the western United States, two important spring hawk lookouts are located in southern Texas: Bentsen-Rio Grande Valley State Park near Mission and Santa Ana National Wildlife Refuge near McAllen. But the best autumn hawk lookout yet discovered in the West is Point Diablo near San Francisco, California.

Additional Reading

Broun, M.
   1949   Hawks Aloft: The Story of Hawk Mountain. Dodd, Mead Co., New York.

Harwood, M.
   1973   The View from Hawk Mountain. Charles Scribner's Sons, New York.

Heintzelman, D. S.
   1975   Autumn Hawk Flights: The Migrations in Eastern North America. Rutgers University Press, New Brunswick, N.J.

   1976   A Guide to Eastern Hawk Watching. Pennsylvania State University Press, University Park, Pa.

   1977   A National Inventory of Hawk Migration Lookouts. *Birding,* 9 (2): 57-58.

   1979a   Hawks and Owls of North America. Universe Books, New York.

   1979b   A Guide to Hawk Watching in North America. Pennsylvania State University Press, University Park, Pa.

Robbins, C. S.
   1956   Hawk Watch. *Atlantic Naturalist,* 11 (5): 208-17.

13
OWL WATCHING

It probably is safe to say that most bird watchers give up after dark and go home. Yet some very unusual and enjoyable bird watching is possible at night when most species of owls become active. Indeed, in recent years owl watching has become just one more of the many ways in which bird watchers can enjoy their hobby as more than one person has discovered by visiting a forest, field, or orchard after dark when most owls might be active. Once hooked on owl watching, some bird watchers even go on to make special studies of these birds including food habit investigations. These activities are both recreational and educational.

Owl Watching Techniques

Many techniques may be used to watch owls. In many instances, these techniques are somewhat different from the methods used in other types of bird watching. This is not overly surprising because owls are mostly nocturnal birds. Thus, binoculars often are exchanged for a bright flashlight and a tape recorder is used to play back recordings of the voices of the various species. It has been shown that some species of owls respond very well to recordings of their voices. This has provided bird watchers with an effective and relatively simple way to locate these birds and see them. Screech Owls, for example, readily respond to recordings of their voices. One can usually approach the birds fairly closely and shine a bright beam of light on them after they have been located by the tape recording play back method. Great Horned Owls and Saw-whet Owls also seem to respond well to recordings of their voices as do Ferruginous Pygmy-Owls in some parts of the tropics. Unfortunately full details are not yet available regarding all of the species and their willingness to react to recordings, but bird watchers easily can make copies of owl voices from records and try various sounds in the field to determine which birds react best.

As an alternative to using tape recordings of owl voices, a skillful whistler can whistle imitations of Screech Owls and other species. Many birds will respond to such whistles and approach a person nearly as closely as if recordings of their voices are used.

A red phase Screech Owl

Fortunately for people who do not wish to crash around at night looking for owls, some of these birds can be located in various ways during daylight. Long-eared Owls, for instance, sometimes can be found by walking through pine plantings and looking for whitewash (excrement) on the ground below thick branches of pines. Above such signs, owls sometimes can be seen roosting quietly in the trees. Such birds should never be disturbed. Rather, owl watchers should simply observe them quietly, then leave as quickly as possible. 127

Another technique which is used to locate owl nests is to walk through a woodlot or wooded area in spring and examine the rims of old crow nests with binoculars for tufts of fresh down clinging to the edges of the nests. When down is found on an old platform, it generally means that a hawk or owl is using the platform as a nest. Careful examination generally will reveal the identity of the bird. If it is a Great Horned Owl or Long-eared Owl the bird often can be seen incubating eggs or young. While some individuals will vigorously defend a nest by flying at an intruder and attempting to strike him, other individuals merely sit tight and watch quietly.

Saw-whet Owls respond well to tape recordings of their voices. Photo by Alan Brady

A Barn Owl at its nest in an old building. Photo by Allan D. Cruickshank

Other species of owls, notably Barn Owls, commonly nest in old buildings, quarries, or hollows of trees. In such places, Barn Owl nests can sometimes be found and studied for long periods of time. Indeed, it is not unusual for these birds to use such a site for many years. One can frequently count on seeing the birds at will if they are not disturbed too often.

In a few instances, some species of owls are more or less diurnal in their habits. Observing these birds is fairly easy if they can be located. Thus, Snowy Owls frequently are seen during daylight hours during those winters when they arrive in southward invasions from the Arctic. Many bird watchers have seen their first Snowy Owls perched on telephone poles, television antennae, or rooftops. Sometimes Short-eared Owls also are seen hunting over marshes and fields during the day. Burrowing Owls can be seen around Prairie Dog towns on the Great Plains and around some open fields at airports in some parts of the United States. The Hawk Owl of the far North also is a diurnal species but most bird watchers never have seen it because it rarely wanders south from its home in the muskegs of northern Canada and Alaska.

Listed below are the species of owls of North America and the 129

The Snowy Owl is an Arctic species. During winter it sometimes moves southward, thus giving bird watchers opportunities to see the birds in some of the lower 48 states. Photo by Allan D. Cruickshank

typical nesting habitats required by these birds. Bird watchers can use this information as an index or guide when searching for nests of owls.

Species	Typical Breeding Habitat
Barn Owl	Abandoned buildings, hollows of trees, quarries, caves, etc.
Screech Owl	Orchards, woodlots near streams, trees along roads and streets, forests, wooded canyons
Whiskered Owl	Similar to that of the Screech Owl
Flammulated Owl	Forests of fir and especially ponderosa pine
Great Horned Owl	Forests, woodlots, canyons, cliffs, river bottoms, plains, and deserts
Snowy Owl	Arctic tundra
Hawk Owl	Dense coniferous forests
Pygmy Owl	Wooded canyons, mixed wooded areas, and open coniferous woodland
Ferruginous Owl	Riverine woodland and thickets in somewhat arid areas
Elf Owl	Saguaro cactus deserts, wooded canyons, and scrub oak areas
Burrowing Owl	Fields around airports, plains, deserts, and prairies
Barred Owl	Wet woodlands and forests
Spotted Owl	Dense coniferous or mixed woodlands, forested canyons
Great Gray Owl	Dense coniferous forests, mixed woodlands adjacent to such forests
Long-eared Owl	Pine woodlands, dense forests, wooded parks, suburban areas
Short-eared Owl	Arctic tundra, marshes, wet meadows
Boreal Owl	Dense spruce forests, mixed edges of coniferous forests
Saw-whet Owl	Forests, groves, and marshes (rarely in the latter)

Owl Pellets

One of the most fascinating and educational aspects of owl watching is the study of the contents of the pellets which these birds regurgitate. Pellets are masses of fur, bones, skulls, and feathers which the birds could not digest and which are then ejected through their mouths. One can easily find pellets by searching the ground

A Long-eared Owl, shown here in a threat display, can be mistaken for the larger and more powerful Great Horned Owl.

beneath pine plantings or owl nests. Sometimes large numbers accumulate beneath trees which are used for long periods of time as roost sites. Pellets can be gathered quickly and carried home in plastic bags for later examination. In each bag, one should place a slip of paper with the location and date collected. Since most species of owls have fairly distinctive pellets, it often is possible to identify the species from which they came merely by the shape of the pellets. Large and not too compact pellets often are from Great Horned Owls, somewhat smaller pellets from Long-eared Owls, and still smaller and more compact pellets from Screech Owls. Of course, if they are gathered at an active owl nest the identity of the birds ejecting them is certain.

Studying the contents of owl pellets is fairly simple. First, they are spread out on an old newspaper and allowed to dry. Then, after they are easy to handle, they can be picked apart with forceps and the bones, skulls, and other prey remains extracted from each pellet. If they become too hard they can be soaked in a small dish of water, then the contents picked out of each pellet. Since most owls eat their food in large pieces or chunks, it is not unusual to find entire small mammal skulls intact in pellets. Such skulls can generally be identified without too much difficulty by keying them out with the aid of a good reference book on mammals. One of the best such books for the East is William H. Burt's *Mammals of the Great*

Lakes Region. It contains excellent keys to mammal skull identification. While it may take a little time to master the use of the key, particularly for non-biologists, full illustrations and instructions make it possible for anyone to learn the basic identification marks and characteristics of mammal skulls.

It is surprising how much information can be learned about the activities of owls by examining the contents of their pellets: what they feed on; the general types of habitats which the birds visited; and something about the status of prey populations in a particular area at a given season of the year. Indeed, on more than one occasion species of mammals previously unknown from a particular area were identified in owl pellets gathered below nests or roosts.

While owl pellet examination is an important tool used by research biologists, it also can be used as an excellent teaching technique when working with schoolchildren, scouts, and even groups of adults. There are few better ways of demonstrating to people the ecological importance of owls than by showing them firsthand the remains of rodent skulls and bones in the pellets of these birds. Sometimes it can be especially rewarding to examine the pellets from several different species of owls living in an area and compare their diets and general ecological impact upon other wildlife species, especially rodents, shrews, and other small mammals. Here, then, is another absorbing aspect of bird watching!

Additional Reading

Angell, T.
   1974   Owls. University of Washington Press, Seattle, Wash.

Burt, W. H.
   1957   Mammals of the Great Lakes Region. University of Michigan Press, Ann Arbor, Mich.

Burton, J. A. (ed.)
   1973   Owls of the World. E. P. Dutton & Co., Inc., New York.

Heintzelman, D. S.
   1979   Hawks and Owls of North America. Universe Books, New York.

Karalus, K. E., and A. W. Eckert
   1973   The Owls of North America. Doubleday & Co., Inc., Garden City, N.Y.

Sparks, J., and T. Soper
   1970   Owls: Their Natural and Unnatural History. Taplinger Publishing Co., New York.

Walker, L. W.
   1974   The Book of Owls. Alfred A. Knopf, Inc., New York.

14
WATCHING SHOREBIRDS

Just as there are seabird enthusiasts, waterfowl enthusiasts, hawk watching enthusiasts, and owl enthusiasts, so too are there bird watchers with keen interests in looking at shorebirds. And little wonder! Oystercatchers, avocets, stilts, plovers, godwits, curlews, sandpipers, knots, dowitchers, and snipe are just some of the many shorebirds which compete for one's attention. Indeed, watching shorebirds is one of the great challenges of bird watching and sooner or later most bird watchers turn their attention, at least in part, to these fine birds. It is useful, therefore, to consider some of the methods of watching shorebirds along with aspects of their nesting activities and migrations.

Methods of Watching Shorebirds

The methods used to study shorebirds have evolved over a period of many years from an age of great destruction to an age of great protection and appreciation. Late in the last century and early into this one, shooting shorebirds was an extremely popular activity, both for commercial and for recreational purposes. The number of birds slaughtered was staggering. Indeed, the Eskimo Curlew never recovered from the slaughter waged against it. In those days, most shorebird identifications were based upon the dead birds in the hand.

Today, modern conservation laws prevent the slaughter of these birds by shooting (water pollution and oil spills may be another matter) and we are now in the age of binoculars, telescopes, and well-illustrated field guides which make it possible for most bird watchers to identify shorebirds without too much difficulty. Telescopes are especially helpful because they allow bird watchers to examine shorebirds in detail and to carefully compare the birds they have under observation with the illustrations and text in a field guide.

Despite these aids, however, it is not always possible to identify

Watching shorebirds is one of the great adventures in bird watching. This Dowitcher sp. was seen in Alaska. Photo by Fred Tilly

all shorebirds or to identify them correctly. Mud or other stain from water might alter the legs of a bird to an unnatural color and thus mislead observers into thinking the bird is a species other than its true identity. There have been several such instances of that happening in recent years, much to the dismay of some bird watchers! That is where experience is important. To some extent, the amount of experience looking at these birds influences a bird watcher's ability to identify them correctly. A person with years of experience often is able to identify shorebirds which a beginner or a less experienced bird watcher can't. Skills at identification can be cultivated by studying shorebirds on their nesting grounds, during migration, and occasionally even in museums where preserved specimens can be handled.

When looking at shorebirds and trying to identify them, there are important points to keep in mind. For instance, the overall shape and proportions of a bird and its patterns of plumage and coloration are vital clues to the bird's identity. A curlew looks very different from a plover or sandpiper. Other clues to identification also should not be ignored. Sometimes the voice of a bird helps one to identify it. This can be especially helpful when working with yellowlegs and dowitchers.

The habitat in which a shorebird is seen is a helpful clue to species identification in some instances. A Purple Sandpiper, for example, generally would be seen near the waterline along a rocky coastline, whereas Sanderlings commonly are observed on sandy beaches 135 where they run back and forth just out of reach of the ocean waves washing ashore. On the other hand, a Spotted Sandpiper is likely to be seen along the banks of small streams, on river mudflats, or along the shorelines of farm ponds and other bodies of fresh water.

Finally, shorebird behavior also can be helpful to bird watchers. The Upland Sandpiper, for example, typically perches on fence-posts and poles in or along large fields and meadows in which it nests. Upon landing, it tends to hold its wings in an elevated position for a few moments. This is a very useful clue to identification. Unlike many shorebirds, Spotted Sandpipers teeter up and down between steps. The teetering has given away the identity of this species to many bird watchers. And Least Sandpipers often gather on mud flats away from the sand flats more preferred by Semipalmated Sandpipers, although the two species sometimes mix together in flocks. Subtle behavior patterns of other shorebirds also can help bird watchers identify these birds correctly, making it desirable to watch these birds carefully under a variety of circumstances, to achieve real skill at shorebird identification. Beginning bird watchers should not give up just because they may not be able to identify some of the birds they see. Field skills will improve with experience!

Nesting Shorebirds

To avid shorebird watchers there are few experiences more enjoyable than the opportunity to observe these birds nesting. But bird watchers must be prepared to travel long distances if they wish to see as many species as possible on breeding grounds. In general, the nesting areas used by shorebirds can be separated into five categories: Arctic and alpine, coniferous forests, prairies, seashores, and other areas.

Arctic and Alpine Areas

In North America the Alaskan and Canadian Arctic and alpine area is, by far, the most widely used breeding ground for the majority of our shorebirds. Among the species nesting on the tundra are Ringed Plovers, Semipalmated Plovers, American Golden Plovers, Black-bellied Plovers, Ruddy Turnstones, Black Turnstones, Whimbrels, Red Knots, Purple Sandpipers, Rock Sandpipers, Pectoral Sandpipers, White-rumped Sandpipers, Dunlin, Long-billed Dowitchers, Stilt Sandpipers, Semipalmated Sandpipers, Western Sandpipers, Buff-breasted Sandpipers, Bar-tailed Godwits, Hudsonian Godwits, Sanderlings, Red Phalaropes, and Northern Phalaropes.

In addition, shorebirds that might be referred to as alpine are such delightful birds as Dotterels, Mongolian Plovers, Surfbirds,

An immature Semipalmated Plover in southwestern Alaska. Photo by Fred Tilly

Wandering Tattlers, and Bristle-thighed Curlews. These are some of the species most wanted on the life lists of many bird watchers.

Not all of these shorebirds nest everywhere in the Arctic and alpine areas. Some are high Arctic birds, others low Arctic species, and still others are distributed around the globe in Arctic areas. To see a representative variety of species, a bird watcher must pick a spot with as large a selection of species as possible. Of all the best spots, none is more famous for its nesting shorebirds than the area around Churchill, Manitoba, on the shore of Hudson Bay. Here is

An adult Western Sandpiper on its breeding grounds in southwestern Alaska.
Photo by Fred Tilly

tundra and not far away timberline as well. Each summer, splendid numbers of shorebirds rush to this area to nest before the snows and ice of winter again arrive. It is an all-too-brief summer when American Golden Plovers rear their young not far from town, and when one can see without too much difficulty other species including Semipalmated Sandpipers, Semipalmated Plovers, Black-bellied Plovers, Dunlin, Stilt Sandpipers, Lesser Yellow-legs, and Whimbrels.

In this northern summer, bird watchers fight off hordes of troublesome insects in July and August, but glorious horizons of wildflowers demand attention. Sometimes, as far as one can see, carpets of orange, yellow, red, and grayish-green lichens are visible; purple, yellow, and white poppies are in bloom; green moss is thick; and dwarf willows and other trees are abundant. It is a landscape still largely untouched by man, an area rich in wildlife and plant life which has adapted itself to an environment seemingly harsh yet perfectly suited for their needs.

Elsewhere in the Arctic, other fascinating shorebirds nest every summer. One of the most interesting is the Bristle-thighed Curlew which nests on the tundra in the vicinity of Mountain Village, Alaska, yet winters in Tahiti and other beautiful South Pacific islands! What an extraordinary avian traveler it is! Few bird watchers have been lucky enough to see this bird on its nesting grounds, discovered in 1948. Exciting bird watching opportunities like this wait to be exploited in the Arctic and alpine areas of North America.

Coniferous Forest Areas

South of the extensive Arctic and alpine areas of North America are the vast tracts of coniferous forests, or boreal forests, which also serve as breeding grounds for some species of shorebirds and thus are worthy of exploring by bird watchers. Here such species as Common Snipes, Solitary Sandpipers, Greater and Lesser Yellow-legs, Least Sandpipers, and Short-billed Dowitchers nest. Some, such as the Common Snipe and Short-billed Dowitcher, prefer to live in sedge bogs, whereas others live around ponds tucked among the great forests. These are the places which eager shorebird watchers must visit if they wish to see these birds nesting.

Prairies

Farther south still, on the great prairies of North America, are found a few other species of shorebirds nesting, among them Long-billed Curlews, Upland Sandpipers, and Marbled Godwits. Bird watchers in search of nests of these birds will find the task much less difficult than is Arctic bird watching because the areas are much closer to home for most people. Indeed, in some cases such as the

Upland Sandpiper, the birds can be found nesting in meadows in states far south of Canada. Unfortunately, in many areas Upland Sandpipers are rapidly disappearing from the lists of breeding birds kept by ornithologists and bird watchers. In Pennsylvania, for example, many areas formerly used as breeding sites by these birds no longer are suitable due to development or other environmental changes. Perhaps the last and best hope for suitable nesting sites in such regions are the grassy fields around airports where the birds still occur in small numbers at times. Bird watchers should be certain to check such locations.

Seashores

Bird watchers living in states with seashores are in luck, if they wish to add some species of nesting shorebirds to their life lists. In particular, birds such as American and Black Oystercatchers, Piping Plovers, and Wilson's Plovers use such sites. Thus a shorebird watcher visiting the New Jersey coast in June will find American Oystercatchers nesting on isolated islands and shorelines here and there and may be lucky enough to find a few Piping Plovers still nesting on sand and shell bars in areas where they are not disturbed by human activities. Such sites are unfortunately becoming increasingly rare, and both the plovers and oystercatchers are not very abundant. In some cases, efforts are being made to protect the remaining habitat and to try to establish artificial nest sites for the birds. Bird watchers can help in such efforts by helping

A Killdeer on its breeding grounds in Utah. Photo by Fred Tilly

to pay for non-game and endangered species programs operated by certain states. One such state is New Jersey.

Other Areas

A variety of other areas also are used as breeding grounds by some species of shorebirds such as Jacanas, Killdeer, Snowy Plovers, Mountain Plovers, Woodcocks, Spotted Sandpipers, Avocets, Black-necked Stilts, Willets, and Wilson's Phalaropes. A bird watcher wishing to observe a Jacana nesting will have to visit tropical or sub-tropical areas in the Americas where such birds are common around wetlands. The birds are common, for example, on many islands in the West Indies, throughout Central America, and in the tropical portions of South America.

In contrast, as pointed out earlier in this chapter, Spotted Sandpipers are widespread as nesting birds in the United States along small streams, ponds, and rivers. Woodcocks prefer bogs and other wet, wooded areas. Willets commonly occur as nesting birds along seashores in the East, but inland in the West. Some of the other species prefer still other breeding habitats in the United States or Canada. Any bird watcher, therefore, can expect to see at least some nesting shorebirds without undertaking a major trip to a remote corner of our continent.

Shorebird Migrations

In addition to watching shorebirds on their breeding grounds, bird watchers have superb opportunities to see great varieties of shorebirds during their spring and autumn migrations. That is when most people look at these birds. Thousands of shorebirds then gather to feed and rest on mud flats, silt bars, and even sod farms along both our coastlines as well as along inland areas en route to or from their breeding or wintering grounds. At such places as Rockport, Texas, for example, it is not unusual to see hundreds or more of shorebirds in a single day. Brigantine National Wildlife Refuge, New Jersey, is equally famous for the enormous numbers of shorebirds which stop there during migration, thus providing shorebird watchers with splendid opportunities to see rare or unusual species. These sites and many others are famous as shorebird magnets.

But not all of the outstanding shorebird areas are along our Atlantic and Pacific coasts. Impressive numbers of these birds also migrate along some large rivers such as the Susquehanna River in eastern Pennsylvania. Curiously, many bird watchers have not become aware of this although as early as the 1950's two avid and excellent bird watchers, Theodore R. Hake and Samuel H. Dyke, made hundreds of boat trips to silt and mud flats in the river near

An American Avocet in a shallow pool. Photo by David McLauchlin / U.S. Fish and Wildlife Service

Washington Boro, Pennsylvania, and discovered large and previously unsuspected numbers of these birds during both the spring and autumn migrations. Indeed, the following 29 species were identified over the years by these two bird watchers as they made careful shorebird surveys.

Killdeer
Semipalmated Sandpiper
Pectoral Sandpiper
Least Sandpiper
Semipalmated Plover
Spotted Sandpiper
Lesser Yellow-legs
Greater Yellow-legs
American Golden Plover
Black-bellied Plover
Dunlin
Sanderling
Stilt Sandpiper
Dowitcher sp.
White-rumped Sandpiper

Western Sandpiper
Baird's Sandpiper
Solitary Sandpiper
Common Snipe
Ruddy Turnstone
Willet
Northern Phalarope
Buff-breasted Sandpiper
Whimbrel
Red Knot
Wilson's Phalarope
Hudsonian Godwit
Red Phalarope
Ruff

Every bird watcher hopes some day to discover very rare species. Sometimes such discoveries do occur. During one year, for example, all four of the world's species of godwits appeared at Brigantine National Wildlife Refuge in New Jersey and a few lucky bird watchers were able to see all four in a single day! But the most sought-after shorebird species is the presumed-extinct Eskimo Curlew. In recent years one or two individuals—probably the last of

Shorebird enthusiast Theodore R. Hake (at right) aiding bird watchers in their identification of shorebirds on a Susquehanna River mud flat

their kind—have been seen and photographed along the Texas coast and reported elsewhere. Does the species still survive? We can only hope that it does and that some unsuspecting and lucky bird watcher will scan a flock of shorebirds with a telescope and suddenly see the bird of birds. What a bird that would make for his or her life list! If such a sighting is made, however, it is likely to be made within the next few years or not at all. It is, alas, only a matter of time before the last individuals of their kind disappear from the earth forever.

A Spotted Sandpiper on its nest near a farm pond

Additional Reading

Banks, R. D.
    1977   The Decline and Fall of the Eskimo Curlew, or Why Did the
            Curlew Go Extaille? *American Birds,* 31 (2): 127-34.

Dyke, S. H.
    1955   Shorebirds on the Conejohela Flats: A Five-Year Summary.
            Atlantic Naturalist, 10 (5): 260-68.

Farrand, J., Jr.
    1977   What to Look For: Eskimo and Little Curlews Compared.
            American Birds, 31 (2): 137-38.

Hagar, J. A., and K. S. Anderson
    1977   Sight Record of Eskimo Curlew (*Numenius borealis*) on
            West Coast of James Bay, Canada. *American Birds*, 31 (2):
            135-36.

Hake, T. R.
    1952   Safe Harbor: A Way Station on the Susquehanna Flyway.
            Atlantic Naturalist, 7 (3): 124-32.
    1955   Hurricane Birds in Pennsylvania. *Atlantic Naturalist,* 11 (2):
            77-79.

Hall, H. M., and R. C. Clement
    1960   A Gathering of Shore Birds. Bramhall House, New York.

Matthiessen, P. et al.
    1967   The Shorebirds of North America. Viking Press, New York.

Weston, F. M., and E. A. Williams
    1965   Recent Records of the Eskimo Curlew. *Auk*, 82 (3): 493-96.

Yrizarry, J. C.
    1972   Black-tailed Godwit at Brigantine Refuge. *Cassinia*, 53:
            41-42.

15
WARBLER
WATCHING

One of the great bird watching specialties in North America is to watch wood warblers migrating in spring and autumn, as well as to look at them on their breeding grounds. These small, nervous woodland birds always are a delight to see. They form a family (Parulidae) native to the Americas. Not infrequently, however, watching wood warblers becomes the despair of bird watchers—especially during autumn when the warblers occur in drab immature or fall plumages. But in spring, when they are migrating northward and are dressed in colorful breeding plumage, wood warblers are much easier to identify. Even then, however, they often appear only near the tops of tall trees where they flit nervously from branch to branch, affording the watchers only fleeting glimpses. That is part of the sport of watching warblers, however, and nearly all keen bird watchers spend many pleasant May mornings looking at these birds.

Warbler Waves

Warbler waves, large groups of these birds migrating through parks, woodlots, or forested areas, are looked for with particular zeal. If such a wave is found, frequently twenty or more species can be seen and identified within a short period of time. Indeed, the only time that it is possible to observe some species, such as Blackpoll Warblers, is during the spring and autumn migrations when these birds are en route to or from their boreal breeding grounds. Unfortunately, widespread and careless uses of pesticides, let alone habitat destruction in North, Central, and South America, has seriously reduced wood warbler populations and these birds now are much less numerous than they were some years ago. Large warbler waves such as those mentioned in the older ornithological literature seldom are seen now. However, sometimes smaller groups of warblers are encountered.

Watching migrating wood warblers is one of the great specialties of bird watching. This is an adult male Yellow-rumped Warbler in May. Photo by Fred Tilly

Layering

Not very long after becoming reasonably familiar with the more common wood warblers, the bird watcher realizes that these birds forage for food and nest at various levels of the forest. Some species occur on the ground or in low vegetation, others occupy a foraging range of medium height, and still others almost always occur near or in the forest crown. This separation of species into various feeding and nesting strata sometimes is called layering. It is a useful phenomenon to keep in mind when studying wood warblers. Some typical low-ranging species (but certainly not all of them) are Canada, Connecticut, Kentucky, Kirtland's, Louisiana and Northern Waterthrushes, Prairie, Prothonotary, Swainson's, Worm-eating, Yellow-breasted Chat, and Yellowthroat. Medium-

Because the Blackpoll Warbler nests in the boreal forests, most bird watchers see it only during its spring and autumn migrations. Photo by Fred Tilly

145

ranging warblers include such species as American Redstart, Black-and-White, Black-throated Blue, Golden-winged, Magnolia, and Tennessee. High-ranging species include the Blackburnian and Cerulean Warblers.

Knowledge of the layering preferences of the various species leads to knowing where to look for them and also to understanding of something about wood warbler ecology and the use of different food resources within the forest. A new dimension to warbler study, and bird watching in general, is thus attained.

Song

Unlike many species of songbirds which have rich and melodious songs, most wood warblers have very high pitched and "weezy" songs some of which are as high as 14,000 cycles per second (Blackpoll Warbler). In addition, many species use several songs which sound quite different from each other. Thus, bird watchers wishing to learn wood warbler songs, which frequently provide the best and quickest way of locating and identifying these birds, are faced with a difficult task. Some species, such as Ovenbirds and Yellowthroats, have very distinctive and easily remembered songs which quickly become familiar to almost all bird watchers, but most songs are considerably more difficult and complex. Many bird watchers have difficulty remembering them.

Perhaps the best way to learn warbler songs, or to refresh one's memory of them, is to listen to records or taped cassettes such as those listed in chapter 2. Several excellent recordings are available and some, such as the Peterson records, are keyed to be used with his famous field guides to bird identification. The Federation of Ontario Naturalists' outstanding recordings of wood warbler songs also are recommended highly. Many bird watchers forget many of the songs from year to year, so such records are very helpful in resharpening field skills.

Hybrids and Endangered Species

Hybrids

Watching and studying wood warblers not only includes looking for the more common species but also for several famous hybrids and several species which are so extremely rare that they are now endangered species. Unfortunately, most bird watchers never have an opportunity to see these birds but occasionally somebody is lucky and adds a unique species or form to his or her life list.

Of the hybrids, the two most famous are the so-called Brewster's and Lawrence's Warblers. Both are fertile offspring resulting from

the interbreeding of Golden-winged Warblers and Blue-winged

A Black-throated Green Warbler (at right) feeding a nestling Brown-headed Cowbird it is rearing. Cowbirds deposit their eggs in warbler nests and allow the warblers to act as foster parents.

Warblers. Normally the two parent species are geographically, and therefore reproductively, isolated from each other on their breeding grounds. However, in a few locations the two parent species have breeding areas which overlap; it is in those places that the possibility of interbreeding exists. In the rare instances when Golden-winged and Blue-winged Warblers do interbreed, Brewster's and Lawrence's Warblers are produced. Of the two resulting hybrids the Lawrence's Warbler is the rarest by far because it is a recessive form. Relatively few of these birds have ever been seen, and one of the memorable moments in my bird watching activities was the opportunity to watch at length a nesting Lawrence's Warbler mated with a Blue-winged Warbler near my home. Bird watchers came from far and wide to see this rare and beautiful bird. Many were successful in enjoying clear views of it.

The second famous example of what appears to be a hybrid is the rarely encountered Sutton's Warbler which most scientists believe results from interbreeding of Parula and Yellow-throated Warblers. Almost all sightings of this rare bird come from the vicinity of Martinsburg, West Virginia, along the Potomac River. Sometimes decades pass before an individual is reported. Thus Sutton's Warbler is one of the most prized birds for anybody's list.

Endangered Species

In addition to rarely observed hybrid wood warblers, there are two other species which are now so rare that they are considered endangered species. The best known of these is the famous Kirtland's Warbler which winters in the Bahama Islands, where almost nothing is known about its ecology and survival needs, and nests in a few counties in the upper part of the Lower Peninsula of

Michigan in Jack Pine woodland of exactly the correct age. Indeed, this species is so dependent upon these trees that the birds sometimes are called Jack Pine Warblers. Unfortunately, the population of this endangered species has decreased alarmingly in recent years, but one of the management techniques which is being used successfully to produce the necessary woodland of the correct age is controlled use of fire. Trees which are too old are deliberately burned by foresters and wildlife biologists to make way for the growth of new Jack Pines to be used eventually by the warblers.

In order to prevent needless disturbance of nesting Kirtland's Warblers, federal and state wildlife officials have recently closed to public entry all nesting areas used by these birds. However, birders still can arrange to see the birds by joining free guided tours of carefully selected areas. Tours are conducted by federal wildlife biologists. Information can be secured by writing: U.S. Fish and Wildlife Service, c/o Michigan Department of Natural Resources, P.O. Box 507, Grayling, Mich. 49738 or U.S. Forest Service, Huron National Forest, Mio, Mich. 48647. Tours are conducted twice each day between May 15 and July 15. Photography is not permitted on these tours nor is the use of tape recorders allowed.

Far rarer than even the Kirtland's Warbler, however, is the Bachman's Warbler—a bird which very few bird watchers and ornithologists have ever seen. There is even speculation that this species may be extinct. Mystery always has surrounded this bird since its discovery in 1833 by the Rev. John Bachman near Charleston, South Carolina. Bachman was a close friend of John James Audubon, and it was Audubon who named the bird in honor of his friend. After its discovery none was seen again for nearly half a century and, even now, very few individuals have ever been observed. The bird occurs in southern swamps where heavy timber still grows. According to Irston R. Barnes, who is one of the few lucky bird watchers to have seen a Bachman's Warbler (in the swamp where it was discovered originally), it is the most difficult of all birds to observe even when encountered in full song. Of all the birds sought by bird watchers, the Bachman's Warbler is among the most prized!

Other Rare Species

In addition to rare hybrids and endangered species, there also are some other rare wood warblers which bird watchers rate high on their want lists. One of these is the Connecticut Warbler, which seems to evade many bird watchers looking for it. In northern Minnesota, however, Robert Janssen discovered that Connecticut
148 Warblers can sometimes be almost common on their breeding

grounds either in tamarack and black spruce swamps or in dry jack pine uplands. The birds are best located by their songs which can be heard and memorized from records. Apparently, the best time to try to see this species in Minnesota is during June and early July. Or, bird watchers can try to see one during migration.

Another of the wood warblers high on the want list of many bird watchers is the Colima Warbler which can be seen in the United States only in Big Bend National Park in Texas. Fortunately, this species can be found fairly easily from April through June in a number of locations in the upper canyons of the Chisos Mountains, including Boot Canyon. To find the bird, one should visit oak groves and remain in them for a while to determine if the birds are active amid the heavy foliage of oaks and broadleaf trees and shrubs. Although Colima Warblers can still be found in Boot Canyon until about mid-September, along the trail above the cabin at Boot Springs, the birds tend to become somewhat rarer after the nesting season. Additional areas within the park where this warbler sometimes is seen include upper Pine Canyon, along the trail just below Laguna Meadows, and Emory Peak.

Additional Reading

Chapman, F. M.
    1907   The Warblers of North America. D. Appleton & Co., New York.

Griscom, L., and A. Sprunt, Jr.
    1957   The Warblers of America. Devin-Adair Co., New York.

Hooper, R. G., and P. B. Hamel
    1977   Nesting Habitat of Bachman's Warbler—A Review. *Wilson Bulletin*, 89 (3): 373-79.

Janssen, R.
    1977   Finding the Connecticut Warbler in Minnesota. *Birding*, 9 (1): 1-3.

Mayfield, H.
    1960   The Kirtland's Warbler. Cranbrook Institute of Science, Bloomfield Hills, Mich.

Ryel, L. A.
    1978   How to See a Kirtland's Warbler. *Birding*, 10 (2): 53-58.

Walkinshaw, L. H.
    1978   The History of a Female Kirtland's Warbler and Her Descendants. *Birding*, 10 (2): 59-62.

Wauer, R. H.
    1973   Birds of Big Bend National Park and Vicinity. University of Texas Press, Austin, Texas.

16
ARCTIC AND
SUB-ARCTIC
BIRDING

Like Antarctic bird watching (see chapter 21), bird watching in the high latitudes of the Arctic and Sub-Arctic is a relatively new activity for most bird watchers. Getting there has long been very difficult. Until recently, most of the information on Arctic birds was gathered by professional ornithologists and explorers who ventured into the North Country on well organized and supplied expeditions. Even then, the risks sometimes were considerable. To some extent that is still true today. One should never take foolish or unnecessary risks on visits to Arctic areas. But opportunities now are becoming available, often at considerable expense, for bird watchers to visit some outstanding Arctic and Sub-Arctic locations.

Some of the most important bird watching spots in the Arctic and Sub-Arctic are coastal areas and islands which are remote and very hard to reach. However, some of these spots now are visited occasionally by the M.S. *Lindblad Explorer* and other tourist ships. Like its famous Antarctic voyages described more fully in chapter 21, the *Explorer*'s Arctic and Sub-Arctic expeditions include visits to scenic areas superb for bird watching and for viewing other wildlife. Along the Atlantic coast, for example, sections of Labrador and Greenland are included. Similarly, on the Pacific coast, the spectacular and isolated Aleutian and Pribilof Islands in Alaskan waters are among the fabulous sites visited. The vast breeding colonies of seabirds there are among the most impressive bird cities in North America. Millions of auks, puffins, and related species nest on these isolated, fog-swept islands. Listed below, for example, are the species of birds known to occur in the Aleutian

Islands exclusive of casual and accidental records.

Northern Fulmars off the Alaska coast. Photo by Fred Tilly

Common Loon
Arctic Loon
Red-throated Loon
Red-necked Grebe
Horned Grebe
Black-footed Albatross
Laysan Albatross
Northern Fulmar
Sooty Shearwater
Short-tailed Shearwater
Scaled Petrel
Fork-tailed Storm Petrel
Leach's Storm Petrel
Double-crested Cormorant
Pelagic Cormorant
Red-faced Cormorant
Whooper Swan
Whistling Swan
Canada Goose
Emperor Goose
White-fronted Goose
Mallard
Gadwall
Common Pintail
Green-winged Teal

Eurasian Wigeon
American Wigeon
Northern Shoveler
Canvasback
Greater Scaup
Tufted Duck
Common Goldeneye
Bufflehead
Oldsquaw
Harlequin Duck
Steller's Eider
Common Eider
King Eider
White-winged Scoter
Surf Scoter
Black Scoter
Smew
Common Merganser
Red-breasted Merganser
Rough-legged Hawk
Bald Eagle
Northern Harrier
Gyrfalcon
Peregrine Falcon
Merlin

Emperor Geese on Amchitka Island, Alaska
Photo by Luther C. Goldman / U.S. Fish and Wildlife Service

Willow Ptarmigan
Rock Ptarmigan
Sandhill Crane
Black Oystercatcher
Semipalmated Plover
American Golden Plover
Black-bellied Plover
Ruddy Turnstone
Common Snipe
Whimbrel
Wood Sandpiper
Wandering Tattler
Lesser Yellowlegs
Rock Sandpiper
Sharp-tailed Sandpiper
Pectoral Sandpiper
Baird's Sandpiper
Least Sandpiper
Dunlin
Western Sandpiper
Bar-tailed Godwit
Sanderling

Red Phalarope
Northern Phalarope
Pomarine Jaeger
Parasitic Jaeger
Long-tailed Jaeger
Glaucous Gull
Glaucous-winged Gull
Slaty-backed Gull
Herring Gull
Mew Gull
Black-headed Gull
Black-legged Kittiwake
Red-legged Kittiwake
Sabine's Gull
Arctic Tern
Aleutian Tern
Common Murre
Thick-billed Murre
Pigeon Guillemot
Marbled Murrelet
Kittlitz's Murrelet
Ancient Murrelet

Horned Puffins on St. Paul Island, Alaska. Photo by Karl W. Kenyon / U.S. Fish and Wildlife Service

Cassin's Auklet
Parakeet Auklet
Crested Auklet
Least Auklet
Whiskered Auklet
Horned Puffin
Tufted Puffin
Snowy Owl
Short-eared Owl
Belted Kingfisher
Bank Swallow
Black-billed Magpie
Northern Raven
Northern American Dipper
Winter Wren

Hermit Thrush
Water Pipit
Northern Shrike
Yellow Warbler
Wilson's Warbler
Gray-crowned Rosy Finch
Common Redpoll
Savannah Sparrow
Golden-crowned Sparrow
Fox Sparrow
Song Sparrow
Lapland Longspur
Snow Bunting
McKay's Bunting

For those bird watchers who prefer land travel, however, other birding opportunities also are available in the Arctic and Sub-Arctic. One such spot is the Arctic Outpost Camp in Canada's Northwest Territories on the shores of Char Lake about 225 miles north of the Arctic Circle and two miles southeast of Albert Edward Bay. It provides Arctic bird watching and photography programs 153 each year during the first two weeks of July. As one might expect, bird watching here is done on foot or by using motor boats to visit spots distant from the Camp. A variety of birds nest within a short distance of the Camp. Among them are Glaucous, Sabine's, and Thayer's Gulls, and three species of jaegers. Loons, waterfowl, shorebirds of many species, and many other birds also occur in the vicinity of the Camp.

Another facility north of the Arctic Circle of interest to bird watchers is the Naturalists' Arctic Centre which operates Bathurst Inlet Lodge in the Northwest Territories. Bird watching opportunities here are more or less similar to those at the Arctic Outpost Camp.

Perhaps the most famous Arctic bird watching spot in North America is Churchill, Manitoba, described in chapter 14 on watching shorebirds. Of course, many hunting and fishing camps in the Alaskan and Canadian Arctic certainly should also provide excellent bird watching opportunities. Part of the adventure of venturing into the Arctic, therefore, is to seek out and visit such spots. Also, one should not overlook the various national wildlife refuges in Alaska, especially the huge Arctic National Wildlife Refuge, which provides visitors with superb outdoor adventures.

Do not expect modern facilities in such places, however, or roads and other easy methods of transportation. Many such sites are reached only by airplane, then on foot or boat. Camping skills are vital, as are solid foundations in survival techniques. If you are not prepared to engage in rugged outdoor life, do not try to visit the more remote Arctic locations. Instead, join well-organized expeditions such as those on the *Lindblad Explorer* or other tourist ships visiting Alaskan waters in summer. Regardless of how you get there, however, bird watching in the Arctic is exciting and very worthwhile.

Additional Reading

Alsop, F. J. III
    1974   Birding Canada's Arctic: Arctic Outpost Camp. *Birding*, 6 (3): 119-21.
Pettingill, O. S., Jr.
    1965   The Bird Watcher's America. McGraw-Hill Book Co., New York.
White, A. W.
    1976   Finding Birds on Adak. *Birding*, 8 (5): 305-12.

17
UNITED STATES
BIRDING

Within recent years, bird watching in the United States has reached a very sophisticated level due, in large measure, to four important factors. First, the country is unusually large and varied. Thus, there are many types of bird habitats, ranging from polar to subtropical areas, forests and fields, prairies and plains, swamps and bogs, deserts and huge lakes, and mountains and seashores. Each of these many types of habitats may support specific species of birds. Therefore, there are hundreds of species which bird watchers can search for, observe, and add to their life lists.

The second important reason for the sophistication of bird watching in the United States is the splendid variety of excellent references which are now published about many aspects of birds in the United States. The fine field guides we have, for example, are invaluable aids to the identification of birds in the field. Augmenting the general bird guides are additional special guides— national and regional bird finding guides, hawk watching guides, and a host of other reference books. Many of these are listed in chapter 3.

Thirdly, the quality of binoculars and telescopes now used by bird watchers has reached an excellent level, making the sight identification of most birds relatively easy. Birds can now be seen clearly at a distance whereas earlier in this century the only sure way of identifying many birds was to shoot them, then key out the specimen with the aid of reference manuals.

Finally, one of the world's best transportation systems now runs through most parts of the country. It is possible to visit many types of habitats with a minimum of cost and effort. Therefore, most of the time spent in bird watching is devoted to seeking out and looking for birds rather than reaching a place to begin such activities. To some extent, however, there is a disadvantage to this highly mobile type of bird watching. One tends not to spend very much time in any one spot, not enough time to exhaust its full bird watching possibilities.

155

Older bird watchers know well, however, that far more birds are likely to be seen in a given spot if it is slowly explored on foot and if all places where birds are likely to lurk are carefully examined. That is what Witmer Stone did for years at Cape May Point, New Jersey, and surrounding areas, before writing his charming *Bird Studies at Old Cape May*. The result was a very thorough report on the birdlife of one of New Jersey's finest bird watching spots. Clearly, one should not overlook the fine opportunities often present locally. Nevertheless, bird watching in areas farther away can be very enjoyable and rewarding. To secure maximum results, bird watchers will want to devote time to both types of birding.

Therefore, this chapter considers some examples of productive locations in the United States where bird watchers can go to enjoy their hobby fully. More detailed information on bird finding localities will be found in those essential references, Olin Sewall Pettingill's *A Guide to Bird Finding East of the Mississippi* and his *A Guide to Bird Finding West of the Mississippi*. The many regional bird finding guides sold by the American Birding Association also are extremely helpful. These are listed in chapter 3.

Special bird finding sites can be grouped into a variety of basic types: national parks, national wildlife refuges, state parks, state wildlife areas, local parks and preserves, and private sanctuaries. Most of these places are open to the public, sometimes without cost, and many are among the finest bird watching locations in North America.

National Parks

The United States has the largest and finest system of national parks of any country in the world, and most of these offer fine bird watching opportunities. This is not unexpected because one of the main goals of establishing a national park is to preserve outstanding scenic and ecological features which are characteristic of a given section of the United States. Special effort, therefore, is made to select prime locations with as little human disturbance as possible. Some typical examples of such parks are:

Acadia National Park

Coastal New England always is a delight to visit, and bird watchers will not be disappointed when they explore the splendid rocky coastline, mountains, fields, and bogs of Acadia National Park on Mount Desert Island near Bar Harbor, Maine. Miles of roads and trails reach into various corners of the park, making bird finding in this beautiful natural area relatively easy. About 320 species of birds have been recorded for the park and adjacent areas. Because of Acadia's great diversity of habitats, both water and

The Atlantic coastline, Acadia National Park, Maine. The park is an excellent bird watching spot.

land birds are well represented. Common Eiders, for example, nest on many of the park's offshore islands. Harlequin Ducks appear annually in winter at Isle au Haut and occasionally along the Schoodic Peninsula. Great Black-backed Gulls and Herring Gulls also are common coastal species. In the spruce forests, one finds Hermit, Swainson's, and Gray-cheeked Thrushes in summer. It is delightful to listen to their sweet songs early in the morning or in the evening before dark. In addition, fifteen or more species of wood warblers nest regularly in the park. Spring, summer, and early autumn are especially rewarding times to visit Acadia National Park.

Big Bend National Park

Bird watchers living or visiting in southern Texas have many excellent spots available to them for bird watching, but Big Bend National Park between El Paso and Laredo certainly is one of the most important and productive places, as is demonstrated by the list of 385 species of birds reported for the area. Indeed, as Roland H. Wauer points out in *Birds of Big Bend National Park and Vicinity*, no other national park in the United States has produced a larger list of birds. Part of the explanation for this rich variety of birdlife is the park's geographic location, but equally important are the many types of habitats found there. These include flood plains, shrub deserts, grasslands, woodlands of various types, and a section of the Rio Grande River.

157

Among the birds frequently seen in suitable parts of Big Bend National Park are Scaled Quail, Roadrunners, Flammulated Owls, Elf Owls, Lesser Nighthawks, White-throated Swifts, Blue-throated Hummingbirds, Acorn Woodpeckers, Ladder-backed Woodpeckers, Vermilion Flycatchers, Mexican Jays, Bewick's Wrens, Bell's Vireos, Colima Warblers, Summer Tanagers, Painted Buntings, Cassin's Sparrows, Black-throated Sparrows, and Lincoln's Sparrows.

Because of the large size and fairly remote location of this park, bird watchers should be certain that they take an adequate supply of food and water with them into the park's interior when looking for birds. Plans should first be discussed with park rangers or naturalists, to get their recommendations. They may be able to provide hints on particularly good bird watching areas.

Bryce Canyon National Park

Bird watchers visiting the vicinity of Bryce Junction in southwestern Utah will find it worthwhile to explore parts of nearby Bryce Canyon National Park. Within its 50 square miles, 164 species of birds have been documented plus another seventeen species of doubtful or very rare occurrence. Among the common species of interest are Black-chinned, Broad-tailed, and Rufous Hummingbirds, Ash-throated Flycatchers, Violet-green Swallows, Gray Jays, Piñon Jays, Mountain Chickadees, Pygmy Nuthatches, Sage Thrashers, Western Bluebirds, Cassin's Finches, and Brewer's Sparrows.

Crater Lake National Park

Now a flooded volcanic caldera, Crater Lake National Park is one of the most unusual links in our national park system. It is located about forty-six miles north of Klamath Falls, Oregon. Bird watchers will not find as many species of birds in this park as in some others, but at least 191 species have been seen here. Among the permanent residents are Red-tailed Hawks, Golden Eagles, Bald Eagles, Blue Grouse, Ruffed Grouse, Pygmy Owls, Black-backed Three-toed Woodpeckers, Gray Jays, Steller's Jays, Mountain Chickadees, Chestnut-backed Chickadees, North American Dippers, Cassin's Finches, and others. A trip to this park certainly is worthwhile, both to watch birds and to enjoy a strikingly beautiful natural area.

Everglades National Park

Because of its large size and subtropical location in southern Florida, about 30 miles south of Miami, Everglades National Park is a major stronghold for birds and other wildlife. No bird watcher should pass up an opportunity to visit this splendid 2,100-square-mile natural area which is unique in the United States. Perhaps the best time to visit the Everglades is in late autumn, winter, and early spring when the park's variety of birdlife reaches its maximum abundance. Then, Red-shouldered Hawks, American Kestrels, American Crows, and Boat-tailed Grackles are observed commonly along the park's main road.

Along the Anhinga Trail, one of the park's outstanding wildlife areas, bird watchers can enjoy splendid opportunities to observe many waterbirds including Great Blue Herons, Little Blue Herons, Green Herons, Louisiana Herons, Snowy Egrets, American Bitterns, and White Ibises. American Anhingas are especially well represented and often can be seen perched on shrubs and other vegetation drying their wings in the sunlight. Common Gallinules and American Coots also are frequently seen in open water areas along the Anhinga Trail, which follows an old road beside wetlands and ends with a fine elevated boardwalk extending over part of a lake and marsh. Great numbers of other species also live in the Everglades. They include Swallow-tailed Kites, Short-tailed Hawks, Bald Eagles, Roseate Spoonbills, White-crowned Pigeons, Mangrove Cuckoos, and Black-whiskered Vireos. The park has excellent visitor information centers and other facilities where rangers and naturalists can provide additional details upon request.

National Wildlife Refuges

In addition to outstanding national parks, the United States also is blessed with an extensive network of hundreds of national wildlife refuges which extend from coast to coast (and even offshore) and from the Arctic to the subtropics. Just about every type of habitat found in North America is protected within the borders of one national wildlife refuge or another. These fine areas provide essential protection for representatives of most species of birds of regular occurrence in North America. Bird watchers have been regular visitors to many of these facilities for years because they are some of the best bird watching locations in the country. A few examples of national wildlife refuges are discussed here to illustrate the importance of these areas. However, a refuge-by-refuge summary of the many national wildlife refuges of particular importance to waterfowl is contained in my *North American Ducks, Geese & Swans.*

Aransas National Wildlife Refuge

Because almost all of the world's wild Whooping Cranes winter in Aransas National Wildlife Refuge along the Texas Gulf coast near Austwell, this 54,829-acre refuge is as famous as any in the entire

Whooping Cranes in flight. Photo by Luther C. Goldman / U.S. Fish and Wildlife Service

national system. Thousands of bird watchers visit this preserve every December through February to try to see a few of these rarest of all North American cranes. They are large, magnificent birds well worth the effort to find. And they can be found either by looking for them from the refuge's observation tower or in other areas of the refuge, or by joining guided bird watching tours on a boat departing several times each week from Copano Bay about nine miles north of Rockport. Since the boat ventures into areas not possible to reach in any other way, birders on board almost always enjoy good views of the cranes along with numerous other birds in this wildlife-rich area.

A family of Whooping Cranes on the Aransas National Wildlife Refuge, Texas. Photo by Luther C. Goldman / U.S. Fish and Wildlife Service

It is an adventure all bird watchers should try to experience at least once in a lifetime.

Arctic National Wildlife Refuge

Because of its remote location in the extreme northeastern corner of Alaska, the Arctic National Wildlife Refuge rarely is visited by bird watchers. Yet within its 8,900,000-acre area are some of the finest examples of untouched Arctic and Sub-Arctic wildlife habitats in North America. Since no roads lead into the area all visits must be made by air, then on foot. About 95 species of birds are known to occur in the refuge, including large numbers of birds of prey, countless numbers of shorebirds, and large numbers of various species of waterfowl. During the short summer in July and August, when almost complete daylight prevails, birds take advantage of every moment to complete their nesting. By September, however, ice again begins to form on the lakes, ponds, and rivers and many birds are migrating southward. Because of the difficulties and dangers involved in visiting this refuge, anyone wishing to do so should first contact the refuge manager for full information, maps, and other details at P.O. Box 280, Anchorage, Alaska 99501.

Bear River Migratory Bird Refuge

One of the finest waterfowl production areas in the United States exists on the famous Bear River Migratory Bird Refuge about 15 miles west of Brigham City, Utah. About 222 species of birds are reported from the refuge and countless bird watchers from all over North America have visited this bird paradise over the years to enjoy its wildlife attractions. Within its 64,895 acres are impoundments, marshes, open water, and mud flats. Among the species of waterfowl commonly seen during one season or another are Whistling Swans, Canada Geese, Mallards, Gadwalls, Common

The Gadwall is a common duck on the Bear River Migratory Bird Refuge, Utah. Photo by Alan Brady

A female Redhead. These diving ducks are common on the Bear River Migratory Bird Refuge, Utah. Photo by Alan Brady

Pintails, Green-winged Teal, Northern Shovelers, Redheads, Canvasbacks, and Ruddy Ducks. Great numbers of shorebirds also stop at the refuge during the migration seasons, and some species nest there in limited numbers. There always is something of interest to see, and bird watchers will not be disappointed by visiting this fine refuge.

Brigantine National Wildlife Refuge

Most bird watchers on the east coast are no strangers to Brigantine National Wildlife Refuge near Oceanville, New Jersey, because it is one of the outstanding birding areas available to them. Indeed, at least 269 species have been seen within the refuge's 20,229 acres of salt marshes, saltwater inlets and bays, freshwater ponds and pools, meadows, pastures, and wooded areas. Bird watching is generally excellent here at any season of the year, but the largest numbers of birds often are present in spring, late summer, autumn, and early winter before the water freezes on the ponds and pools. Waterfowl are one of Brigantine's most common attractions and Mute Swans, Canada Geese, Brant, American Black Ducks, Common Pintails, Gadwalls, and Northern Shovelers are observed regularly. Thousands of Snow Geese also use the refuge as a resting and feeding area in late autumn and early winter and when these birds are present bird watching at Brigantine is particularly exciting. Most of the species of herons and egrets common in the East also can be seen without difficulty—often at close range. Cattle Egrets are fairly common. Glossy Ibises have increased in numbers in recent years and are now common during the warmer months of the year. In addition, some shorebirds always are present, but large numbers can be expected in spring and again in late summer and early autumn. Gulls, terns, and various hawks and songbirds likewise populate Brigantine National Wildlife Refuge and add to the bird watcher's enjoyment of the place.

Various visitor facilities are available. An auto tour route, for

Bird watchers in winter at
Brigantine National Wildlife
Refuge, New Jersey

Visitors driving along the auto tour route in Brigantine National Wildlife Refuge, New Jersey. Snow Geese fly overhead.

example, runs for several miles along dikes separating salt marshes from freshwater pools, then through woodland back to the refuge headquarters. Most bird watchers follow this route and do most of their birding right from their cars. Several tall steel observation towers are available, however, for people who wish to stop and experience a panoramic view of the refuge. Anyone seriously interested in bird watching will find a visit to Brigantine National Wildlife Refuge worthwhile.

A Laughing Gull flying over a salt meadow on Brigantine National Wildlife Refuge, New Jersey, where Laughing Gulls are common breeding birds

A Great Egret in a freshwater pool at Brigantine National Wildlife Refuge, New Jersey

A freshwater pond and marsh in Brigantine National Wildlife Refuge, New Jersey

Merced National Wildlife Refuge

Bird watchers in California have available to them a number of excellent national wildlife refuges, but one of the most important is Merced. Its 2,561 acres of marshes, creeks, cultivated fields, and grass pastures are located about 14 miles southwest of Merced in the San Joaquin Valley. From October through January, unusually large concentrations of waterfowl populate the refuge. For example, a large portion of the world's population of the little Ross' Goose winters on this refuge after migrating from their breeding grounds in the Perry River area of Canada's Northwest Territories. Other species of waterfowl which also are common at Merced National Wildlife Refuge in spring and autumn include five subspecies of Canada Geese, White-fronted Geese, Snow Geese, Mallards, Gadwalls, Common Pintails, Green-winged Teal, Cinnamon Teal, American Wigeons, Northern Shovelers, and Ruddy Ducks. In spring a variety of shorebirds stop here, including American Avocets and Black-necked Stilts. At least 177 species of birds have been reported for the refuge since it was established in 1951.

Okefenokee National Wildlife Refuge

Just before the Florida border, a visitor to southeastern Georgia will come to the famous Okefenokee Swamp, a part of which includes the Okefenokee National Wildlife Refuge. This splendid 700-square-mile wilderness area includes cypress swamps, marshes, lakes, open waterways, and prairies, all of which are a wildlife paradise for bird watchers. Late April or early May is an excellent time to visit the refuge to see nesting birds, but winter visits also are very worthwhile. Among the birds likely to be seen while exploring the refuge with a rented boat are Great Blue Herons, Little Blue Herons, Wood Storks, White Ibises, Wood Ducks, Red-shouldered Hawks, and Barred Owls. Pileated Woodpeckers are common and various wood warblers also are present, including the beautiful Prothonotary Warbler which is very common. In winter many ducks also visit the lakes in the refuge. Entrances to Okefenokee National Wildlife Refuge are located near Waycross, near Folkston, and near Fargo.

Sand Lake National Wildlife Refuge

Sand Lake is one of the many national wildlife refuges in South Dakota which provide vital habitat for waterfowl and other wildlife and which also provide superb bird watching opportunities. Its 10,240 acres are located in northeastern South Dakota along 17 miles of the James River near Columbia. Among the refuge's habitats are marshes, open water, islands within the river, and cultivated areas. At least 226 species of birds are known to occur here plus another 15 species seen only once or twice. In spring, up to half a million geese stop on the refuge, and in autumn 100,000 geese and 200,000 ducks use the refuge for resting and feeding.

Whistling Swans, Canada Geese, White-fronted Geese, Snow Geese, Mallards, Gadwalls, Common Pintails, Blue-winged Teal, Northern Shovelers, Canvasbacks, and Ruddy Ducks are all observed commonly in spring and autumn. In addition, large numbers of shorebirds visit the refuge during migration and other kinds of waterbirds also nest on the refuge. Franklin's Gulls, for instance, are abundant breeding birds and many grebes, herons, and terns also nest at Sand Lake. Bird watching is encouraged at all seasons of the year.

Santa Ana National Wildlife Refuge

Santa Ana National Wildlife Refuge, located a few miles south of Alamo, Texas, along the Rio Grande river, is one of the most famous bird watching locations in Texas because it is one of the few areas in the United States where it is possible to visit a subtropical forest and see species characteristic of that type of habitat without visiting Central or South America. The area is extremely rich in birds. Indeed, 326 species are known from Santa Ana's 2,000 acres of jungle-like forest, fields, lakes and ponds, and a section of the Rio Grande. Among the specialties are Least Grebes, Black-bellied Whistling Ducks, Hook-billed Kites (rare), Gray Hawks, Jacanas, Plain Chachalacas, Red-billed Pigeons, White-winged Doves, Groove-billed Anis, Rose-throated Becards, Green Jays, White-collared Seedeaters, and Olive Sparrows. In late March and April, huge northward migrations of Broad-winged Hawks and Swainson's Hawks sometimes are seen from the refuge. Visitors enjoy almost seven miles of self-guiding auto routes, fourteen miles of foot trails, and a number of photographic blinds. Early morning and late afternoon are especially productive times to see the area's wildlife.

State Parks

Most states have extensive park systems and many of these areas also are excellent bird watching locations. Full details about such parks generally are available from the park departments in state capitals. Here, however, a few such parks are discussed to give readers an idea of the bird watching opportunities available in such places.

Bird watchers in Alabama will find DeSoto State Park near Fort Payne typical in that it is not only an exceptionally scenic area but also supports a rich population of birds. Here, amid woodland with 167 lush growth of rhododendron, azaleas, and mountain laurel one may expect to see such birds as Pileated Woodpeckers, Yellow-throated Vireos, Black-throated Green Warblers, Yellow-throated Warblers, Ovenbirds, Scarlet Tanagers, and many other species during spring and summer.

In Indiana, Turkey Run State Park near Rockville is another fine bird watching area. Here deep canyons and coniferous and deciduous forests provide excellent habitats for a host of birds including Acadian Flycatchers, Carolina Wrens, and many vireos, wood warblers, and tanagers. In winter, more than 100 Turkey Vultures gather every evening to roost on the canyon walls, and woodpeckers are unusually common.

New Jersey also has its share of bird-rich state parks, including High Point State Park in the northwestern corner of the state. In autumn many hawk watchers use the base of the high monument within the park as a hawk migration lookout. A good variety of species is seen, including Sharp-shinned Hawks, Broad-winged Hawks, and Red-tailed Hawks. Elsewhere, in the park's Cedar Swamp, 29 species of birds have been found nesting, including Veeries, Worm-eating Warblers, and Golden-winged Warblers.

Finally, my home state of Pennsylvania also has many excellent examples of state parks which offer fine bird watching opportunities. A case in point is Presque Isle State Park near Erie. It is used constantly by birders. In May and September, many shorebirds stop here during migration and Semipalmated Plovers, Baird's Sandpipers, Dunlin, and many other species are not at all uncommon. Within the park's interior, a great variety of species also nest, and swans, geese, and diving ducks regularly frequent adjacent Erie Bay in autumn.

State Wildlife Areas

The wildlife agencies in many states own and maintain a variety of wildlife refuges or management areas which often are excellent bird watching sites during seasons of the year when hunting is not in progress. Some details about such areas usually can be obtained from each state's wildlife agency although many states may not be able to provide full details about bird watching opportunities. Nevertheless, these state wildlife lands should be used by bird watchers far more regularly than many are being used now. To illustrate the bird watching importance of such areas, I include here some descriptions of a few such areas with which I am more or less familiar and for which some good ornithological details are available.

Bake Oven Knob, in northern Lehigh County, Pennsylvania, for

Bake Oven Knob, Lehigh County, Pennsylvania, is a state game land and an important bird watching area.

example, is a state game land owned by the Pennsylvania Game Commission. It is essentially the top of the Kittatinny Ridge along which many thousands of migrating hawks and other birds pass every autumn. A spectacular rocky lookout at the top of the Knob can be reached by walking along the Appalachian Trail for about one-third of a mile. During the twenty years that bird records have been kept for this site, 158 species of autumn migrants have been identified.

Migrating birds of prey are the big attraction and all the species one would expect in the Northeast have been seen: Turkey Vulture, Black Vulture, Northern Goshawk, Sharp-shinned Hawk, Cooper's Hawk, Red-tailed Hawk, Red-shouldered Hawk, Broad-winged Hawk, Swainson's Hawk, Rough-legged Hawk, Golden Eagle, Bald Eagle, Northern Harrier, Osprey, Gyrfalcon, Peregrine Falcon, Merlin, and American Kestrel. Common Loons also are sometimes counted in large numbers in November, and Canada Geese migrate overhead by the thousands in October.

Bird watchers who arrive at the Knob early in the morning often report seeing Ruffed Grouse in the woods or along the trail and occasionally Wild Turkeys are seen. Ruby-throated Hummingbirds zip past the lookout in late August and September, and a pair or two of Pileated Woodpeckers are residents on the forested mountain slopes below the lookout. Sometimes the birds put on superb displays and fly past the lookout at eye level, but most of the time 169 they are heard rather than seen. A few Red-headed Woodpeckers migrate past the Knob and occasionally Olive-sided Flycatchers are seen perched on the tips of old dead trees in late August and early September.

Large numbers of Blue Jays migrate past the spot in October; in November, their numbers are replaced by hundreds of migrating American Crows. Many kinds of thrushes, vireos, and wood warblers are seen in the woodland around the lookout, while in good "finch years" such species as Evening Grosbeaks, Pine Grosbeaks, Purple Finches, House Finches, Pine Siskins, Red Crossbills, and White-winged Crossbills occur in varying numbers. Bake Oven Knob is a major bird observatory, especially in autumn, and thousands of bird watchers from many states and foreign countries have visited the Knob over the years. Most have been well rewarded with good hawk flights and sights of many other species of birds.

The Pennsylvania Game Commission's Middle Creek Wildlife Management Area near Kleinfeltersville, in eastern Pennsylvania, is another example of an excellent bird watching area on public wildlife land. This 5,000-acre area was established to provide for the hunting of Canada Geese and ducks, but it has many types of habitats which serve to attract a large number of other species of birds. About 229 species have been reported from the area already and more will doubtless be discovered in the years to come. Unlike many state wildlife lands, the Middle Creek Wildlife Management Area has excellent visitor facilities, a modern building which houses a small museum with fine displays of waterfowl, birds of prey, and other birds as well as an auditorium for presenting educational programs. There is also a large room with wide windows overlooking the property. Increasing numbers of bird watchers are using this facility to good advantage and Middle Creek has become one of the bird watching hot spots in eastern Pennsylvania.

Delaware bird watchers have discovered that the Little Creek State Wildlife Area near Dover is an excellent place to find impressive numbers of waterbirds. Here, four pools have been created and the marshes and open water provide ideal habitat for diving birds, herons and egrets, geese and ducks, rails, shorebirds, and gulls and terns. Among the more interesting birds reported from Little Creek are Red-necked Grebes, Cattle Egrets, Louisiana Herons, Yellow-crowned Night Herons, Least Bitterns, American Bitterns, White Ibises, Eurasian Wigeons, Yellow Rails, Black Rails, American Golden Plovers, Red Knots, White-rumped Sandpipers, Stilt Sandpipers, Western Sandpipers, Ruffs, American Avocets, Black-necked Stilts, Iceland Gulls, Forster's Terns, Caspian Terns, Black Terns, and Black Skimmers. A great ·

The 5,000 acres of the Middle Creek Wildlife Management Area in eastern Pennsylvania are a very productive bird watching area.

many other species also are known from the area. Bird watchers in Delaware consider the Little Creek State Wildlife Area one of their best birding locations.

Local Parks and Preserves

A variety of local parks and preserves are owned and operated by many county and municipal governments. How important some of these places are for birdlife varies greatly depending on the types of habitats which are preserved or created there. Some of these spots, however, are fine bird watching locations and are used regularly by people living near them. A few examples of what to expect when bird watching in such parks or preserves are provided here.

Bird watchers living near Valley Forge, Pennsylvania, often visit Mill Grove—a 120-acre estate containing John James Audubon's first home in America, open fields and lawns, and surrounding woodland. Contained within the old stone home are original paintings by Audubon, prints from his famous books, as well as a complete first edition set of the four volumes of *The Birds of America*. No bird watcher should overlook the opportunity to examine and enjoy these major ornithological art treasures. Outside, of course, bird watching can be worthwhile, especially in 171

May, and Downy Woodpeckers, White-breasted Nuthatches, Eastern Phoebes, Barn Swallows, Wood Thrushes, and many vireos and wood warblers are likely to be seen.

Not far from my home in Allentown, Pennsylvania, there is another fine bird watching spot known as Robin Hood Woods in one of our city owned parks, called Lehigh Parkway South. Here there is opportunity to explore a small deciduous woodlot, open lawn, a tiny marsh, a stream, and some woodland edge. This spot can be productive at any time of the year, but the largest number of birds generally are seen during the May migration. Then the area sometimes is alive with birds. Some of the species I have seen in the Robin Hood Woods area over the years include Great Blue Heron, Solitary Sandpiper, Yellow-billed Cuckoo, Red-bellied Woodpecker, Hermit Thrush, Swainson's Thrush, Veery, Blue-gray Gnatcatcher, Solitary Vireo, Brewster's Warbler, Magnolia Warbler, Black-throated Green Warbler, Ovenbird, Wilson's Warbler, Canada Warbler, Scarlet Tanager, Indigo Bunting, Chipping Sparrow, Field Sparrow, White-throated Sparrow, Swamp Sparrow, and Song Sparrow. Woodland paths lead through the woodlot and adjacent areas and one can easily cover the entire area in an hour or two or spend more time there if desired.

The value of local parks and preserves for providing good bird watching opportunities is not, however, confined only to smaller towns and cities. Such parks may be of even more significance in major cities such as New York City where many parks are used continually by local bird watchers. Indeed, over the years, 410 species of birds have been seen within New York City and surrounding areas! Forest Park in Queens, for example, is one of the best birding spots in New York City because it has fine old oak forests with abundant undergrowth. Large numbers of wood warblers, vireos, flycatchers, and thrushes are often seen here in May. Similarly the well-known Jamaica Bay Wildlife Refuge (a unit of the Gateway National Recreational Area), also in Queens, offers superb opportunities to see waterbirds and shorebirds in summer and autumn. In addition many herons and egrets also nest here. At least 312 species of birds have been reported from Jamaica Bay since the early 1950s.

The many fine parks within Philadelphia, Pennsylvania, also offer splendid bird watching opportunities. Rittenhouse Square, in the heart of downtown Philadelphia, is only about one block in size but in late April and early May an extraordinary assortment of birds stops here during migration. Some wood warblers and vireos are included. Brown Thrashers, American Robins, and White-throated Sparrows are among the species seen within the park early in the morning. Far more important, however, is Philadelphia's

Robin Hood Woods, part of the Allentown, Pennsylvania park system, is used regularly by local bird watchers in spring and autumn.

Fairmount Park which extends for miles through parts of the city. Areas within the park, such as the Wissahickon Ravine, are well known to local bird watchers both for the numbers of spring and autumn migrants seen there but also for the number of birds which nest there. Among those found nesting are Ring-necked Pheasants, Mourning Doves, Red-bellied Woodpeckers, Great Crested Flycatchers, Acadian Flycatchers, House Wrens, Winter Wrens, Carolina Wrens, American Robins, Veeries, Red-eyed Vireos, Worm-eating Warblers, Blue-winged Warblers, Ovenbirds, Kentucky Warblers, Scarlet Tanagers, House Finches, and many others.

Private Sanctuaries

Scattered throughout the United States are a large number of private wildlife sanctuaries many of which are very important bird watching locations. For example, there are probably somewhere around 1,000 nature centers in the country and most of these are fine 173

Corkscrew Swamp Sanctuary, Florida, is a major wildlife sanctuary owned by the National Audubon Society.

locations for bird watching. In addition, a variety of other sanctuaries are known for their rich birdlife. It is not possible to try to list them all here, but a few representative examples are discussed briefly.

Hawk Mountain Sanctuary near Kempton, Pennsylvania, is an outstanding example of a privately owned and operated wildlife sanctuary of exceptional importance for bird watching. Foremost, of course, are the splendid hawk flights which migrate past the sanctuary in autumn and which have made the place world famous. But many other bird watching opportunities also are possible at Hawk Mountain during other seasons of the year. Indeed, about 232 species of birds have been reported within the sanctuary since its establishment in 1934. Among those which nest at Hawk Mountain are Ruffed Grouse, Great Horned Owls, Ruby-throated Hummingbirds, Pileated Woodpeckers, Least Flycatchers, Black-capped Chickadees, Wood Thrushes, Red-eyed Vireos, Worm-eating Warblers, Golden-winged Warblers, Blue-winged Warblers, Brewster's Warblers, Black-throated Green Warblers, Ovenbirds, American Redstarts, Scarlet Tanagers, Indigo Buntings, and Song Sparrows. Thus, a visit to the sanctuary in spring or summer can be just as interesting as an autumn visit. Even winter is a good time to enjoy bird watching at Hawk Mountain because a very active winter bird feeding program is carried out at the new headquarters building and one generally can see lots of Evening Grosbeaks, Pine Siskins, and other species. See also chapter 12 and its "Additional Reading."

The National Audubon Society's Corkscrew Swamp Sanctuary near Immokalee, Florida, is another outstanding example of a private wildlife sanctuary with exceptional bird watching values. Within its 10,422 acres are the last remnants of virgin bald cypress in Florida as well as pine woodlands, wet prairie, and a pond-cypress swamp. One of the exciting features of Corkscrew Swamp is a mile-long elevated boardwalk which reaches into all of the area's major habitats and allows visitors to venture into these areas easily and in comfort. At various spots along the boardwalk there are glimpses of such species as Red-cockaded Woodpeckers, Brown-headed Nuthatches, Little Blue Herons, White Ibises, American Anhingas, Limpkins, and Barred Owls. No visit to Florida should omit a visit to this fine facility. There is always something of interest to be seen here.

Additional Reading

Geffen, A. M.
> 1978   A Birdwatcher's Guide to the Eastern United States. Barron's, Woodbury, N.Y.

Harrison, G. H.
> 1976   Roger Tory Peterson's Dozen Birding Hot Spots. Simon & Schuster, Inc., New York.

Heintzelman, D. S.
> 1976   A Guide to Eastern Hawk Watching. Pennsylvania State University Press, University Park, Pa.
> 1979   A Guide to Hawk Watching in North America. Pennsylvania State University Press, University Park, Pa.

Kitching, J.
> 1976   Birdwatcher's Guide to Wildlife Sanctuaries. Arco Pub. Co., New York.

Peterson, R. T.
> 1953   The Bird Watcher's Anthology. Bonanza Books, New York.

Pettingill, O. S., Jr.
> 1953   A Guide to Bird Finding West of the Mississippi. Oxford University Press, New York. (Out of print; new edition in preparation.)
> 1965   The Bird Watcher's America. McGraw-Hill Book Co., New York.
> 1977   A Guide to Bird Finding East of the Mississippi. 2d edition. Oxford University Press, New York.

Scofield, M.
> 1978   The Complete Outfitting & Source Book for Birdwatching. Great Outdoors Trading Co., Marshall, Calif.

18
WEST INDIAN
BIRDING

As more and more bird watchers leave the United States and Canada to expand the horizons of their hobby, and to add to their life lists, they are turning with increasing frequency to the tropical (called neotropical) parts of the Americas. Among the most popular of these bird watching areas are the many beautiful islands in the West Indies. They not only can be reached by jet within a few hours from New York or Miami at relatively moderate expense, but they also contain rich avifaunas which include many endemic species. Listed below are the species of birds which are endemic to the various islands in the West Indies; those marked with (E) are endangered.

Species	*Where Found*
Cuban Kite	Eastern Cuba
Gundlach's Hawk	Cuba
Ridgway's Hawk	Hispaniola
Zapata Rail	Zapata Swamp, Cuba
Ring-tailed Pigeon	Jamaica
Grenada Dove (E)	Grenada
Crested Quail Dove	Jamaica
Gray-headed Quail Dove	Cuba and Dominican Republic
Blue-headed Quail Dove	Cuba
Imperial Parrot (E)	Dominica
St. Vincent Parrot (E)	St. Vincent
St. Lucia Parrot (E)	St. Lucia
Red-necked Parrot	Dominica
Hispaniolan Parrot	Hispaniola
Yellow-billed Parrot	Jamaica
Puerto Rican Parrot (E)	Puerto Rico
Black-billed Parrot	Jamaica
Hispaniolan Parakeet	Hispaniola and Puerto Rico
Cuban Parakeet	Cuba
Chestnut-bellied Cuckoo	Jamaica

Bay-breasted Cuckoo	Hispaniola and Gonave Island
Hispaniolan Lizard Cuckoo	Hispaniola
Jamaican Lizard Cuckoo	Jamaica
Puerto Rican Lizard Cuckoo	Puerto Rico
Bare-legged Owl	Cuba and Isle of Pines
Cuban Pygmy Owl	Cuba and Isle of Pines
Jamaican Owl	Jamaica
Least Pauraque	Hispaniola and Gonave Island
Puerto Rican Emerald	Puerto Rico
Hispaniolan Emerald	Hispaniola
Blue-headed Hummingbird	Dominica and Martinique
Jamaican Mango	Jamaica
Green Mango	Puerto Rico
Streamertail	Jamaica
Bee Hummingbird	Cuba and Isle of Pines
Vervain Hummingbird	Hispaniola and Jamaica
Hispaniolan Trogon	Hispaniola
Cuban Trogon	Cuba and Isle of Pines
Cuban Tody	Cuba and Isle of Pines
Narrow-billed Tody	Hispaniola
Puerto Rican Tody	Puerto Rico
Jamaican Tody	Jamaica
Broad-billed Tody	Hispaniola and Gonave Island
Antillean Piculet	Hispaniola and Gonave Island
Fernandina's Flicker	Cuba
Puerto Rican Woodpecker	Puerto Rico and Vieques Island
Guadeloupe Woodpecker	Guadeloupe
Jamaican Woodpecker	Jamaica
Hispaniolan Woodpecker	Hispaniola
Cuban Green Woodpecker	Cuba and Isle of Pines
Jamaican Becard	Jamaica
Rufous-tailed Flycatcher	Jamaica
Greater Antillean Elaenia	Hispaniola and Jamaica
Jamaican Yellow-crowned Elaenia	Jamaica
Golden Swallow	Hispaniola and Jamaica
Jamaican Crow	Jamaica
Palm Crow	Cuba and Hispaniola
Zapata Wren	Cuba
St. Andrew Mockingbird	St. Andrew
White-breasted Thrasher (E)	Martinique and St. Lucia
White-eyed Thrush	Jamaica
La Selle Thrush	Hispaniola (Southeast Haiti)
White-chinned Thrush	Jamaica
Grand Cayman Thrush	Grand Cayman

177

Cuban Solitaire	Cuba and Isle of Pines
Cuban Gnatcatcher	Cuba
Palm-Chat	Hispaniola and Gonave Island
Flat-billed Vireo	Hispaniola and Gonave Island
Jamaican White-eyed Vireo	Jamaica
St. Andrew Vireo	St. Andrew
Cuban Vireo	Cuba and Isle of Pines
Puerto Rican Vireo	Puerto Rico
Blue Mountain Vireo	Jamaica
Elfin Woods Warbler	Puerto Rico (Sierra de Luquillo)
Arrow-headed Warbler	Jamaica
Whistling Warbler	St. Vincent
Semper's Warbler (E)	St. Lucia
Green-tailed Ground Warbler	Hispaniola and Beata Island
White-winged Ground Warbler	Hispaniola
Yellow-headed Warbler	Western Cuba and Isle of Pines
Oriente Warbler	Eastern Cuba
Orangequit	Jamaica
Jamaican Euphonia	Jamaica
Hooded Tanager	St. Vincent and Grenada
Black-crowned Palm Tanager	Hispaniola
Puerto Rican Tanager	Puerto Rico
Chat-Tanager	Hispaniola and Gonave Island
Cuban Blackbird	Cuba
Montserrat Oriole	Montserrat
St. Lucia Oriole	St. Lucia
Martinique Oriole	Martinique
Tawny-shouldered Blackbird	Cuba and Hispaniola
Yellow-shouldered Blackbird	Puerto Rico and Mona Island
Jamaican Blackbird	Jamaica
Antillean Siskin	Hispaniola
Puerto Rican Bullfinch	Puerto Rico
St. Lucia Black Finch	St. Lucia
Cuban Grassquit	Cuba
Yellow-shouldered Grassquit	Jamaica
Zapata Sparrow	Cuba

As bird watchers who have visited some of the islands in the West Indies know well, many enjoyable days can be spent on the appropriate islands looking for some of these endemics as well as looking at the many other colorful birds one encounters. An additional advantage of bird watching in the West Indies is that the number of neotropical birds encountered on any one island is large but not overwhelmingly so to a beginning or inexperienced bird watcher. Thus, a visit to the West Indies is a fine introduction to the richness of tropical birdlife.

Among the islands most commonly visited by most bird watchers are the Bahamas, Jamaica, Puerto Rico, the Virgin Islands, Martinique, St. Lucia, Tobago, and Trinidad. Fine field guides available for the birds of these islands include James Bond's *Birds of the West Indies*, P. G. C. Brudenell-Bruce's *The Birds of the Bahamas*, and Richard ffrench's *A Guide to the Birds of Trinidad and Tobago*.

Bahamas

In addition to seventeen relatively large islands, the Bahamas also contain thousands of smaller islands, cays, and rocks. New Providence and Grand Bahama are visited quite regularly by bird watchers because of their closeness to Florida. Most of the birds seen here are North American migrants or visitors, but no fewer than 40 resident species also are known. This provides birders with opportunities to add some new birds to their life lists. Among the possibilities are Zenaida Doves, Ground Doves, White-bellied Doves, Key West Quail Doves, Mangrove Cuckoos, Great Lizard Cuckoos, Bahama Woodstars, Loggerhead Kingbirds, Stolid Flycatchers, Greater Antillean Pewees, Bahama Mockingbirds, Red-legged Thrushes, Thick-billed Vireos, Bananaquits, Bahama Yellowthroats, Stripe-headed Tanagers, Greater Antillean Bullfinches, and Black-faced Grassquits.

Cuba

This bird-rich island is the home of a variety of exotic species including many rare and endemic birds. Among them are rare hawks, parrots, the world's smallest hummingbird (the Bee Hummingbird), and many other fascinating creatures. In recent years, however, little bird watching has been done in Cuba, but as international travel restrictions are relaxed bird watchers will again want to visit the island, and the Isle of Pines, to enjoy some of Cuba's important ornithological attractions.

Grand Cayman

Grand Cayman is a small island located just northwest of Jamaica. Only 8 miles wide and 22 miles long, it nevertheless offers good introductory bird watching for people wishing to make a short two-or-three-day visit to the West Indies. Some bird watchers have reported seeing as many as 65 species here within that period of time. Ira Thompson, owner and driver of a local taxi service, knows the island's wildlife well and usually is able to locate most species of birds which occur there. Among those which can be seen are Cuban Parrots, West Indian Red-bellied Woodpeckers, Loggerhead Kingbirds, Stolid Flycatchers, Caribbean Elaenias, Gray Catbirds, several vireos, and many wood warblers in winter. Unfortunately, the endemic Grand Cayman Thrush probably is extinct; none has been seen in recent years.

Jamaica

Jamaica is one of the most popular and frequently visited islands in the West Indies. Its beautiful beaches and fine scenery are splendid attractions. Bird watchers find the island's rich birdlife equally exciting. Indeed, there are no fewer than 25 endemic bird species on the island! Here is a bird watcher's goldmine of possibilities. Among the very worthwhile bird watching locations which should not be ignored are the Hope Botanical Gardens in Kingston, the coastal lowlands, the "cockpit country," and the Blue Mountains.

Coastal Lowlands

In the coastal lowlands, as many as 60 species of birds have been seen along the north shore, west of Annotto Bay, in the vicinity of Strawberry Fields Campground. Birds to be looked for in this area include Orangequits, Streamertails, Jamaican Woodpeckers, and Jamaican Todies.

"Cockpit Country"

The "cockpit country" is a region of limestone hills located in the western interior of Jamaica. Perhaps one of the best spots in this area for bird watching is the Rocklands Feeding Station where such species as Jamaican Becards and Jamaican White-eyed Vireos occur along with many other species. In addition, the Worthy Park section of St. Catherine is another fine bird watching area. Least Grebes and Ruddy Quail Doves occur here, while parrots may be seen on Long Mountain. Arrow-headed Warblers and Jamaican Crows sometimes are also reported from upland pastures and should be searched for when visiting this area.

Blue Mountains

Bird watchers visiting Jamaica should also be certain to visit the scenic and beautiful Blue Mountains where exciting birding is to be experienced. Hollywell National Forest, for example, is in one of the higher elevations (near Hardwar Gap on road maps) and is excellent because Rufous-throated Solitaires, White-eyed Thrushes, and White-chinned Thrushes occur here. Afternoon bird watching here can be particularly productive and it is not unusual to see such species as Ring-tailed Pigeons, White-collared Swifts,

Jamaican Becards, Jamaican Yellow-crowned Elaenias, and Blue
Mountain Vireos. Jamaican Blackbirds also should be looked for
among the bromeliads growing on the trees at Hardwar Gap.

The length of time one wishes to stay on an island such as Jamaica
depends entirely upon the vigor with which one engages in bird
watching, but a week of active birding here should yield a list of
about eighty species including many new to a life list.

Puerto Rico

Many excellent bird watching opportunities can be enjoyed on
Puerto Rico. American birders in particular should not ignore this
beautiful island. Just where the best bird finding locations are may
require some exploration, but some starting points can be
mentioned here. Always keep in mind that there are 12 species of
endemic birds found on the island and as many of these as possible
should be high on a want list.

Luquillo National Forest

Bird watchers exploring Puerto Rico certainly will want to visit
Luquillo National Forest because it offers excellent bird watching
opportunities from several points of view. Not the least important is
the fact that a few endangered (and endemic) Puerto Rican Parrots
still live here and there is always the possibility that one of these
birds might be seen. The best locations one should check for these
birds are areas with long views early in the morning in the vicinity of
kilometer 13 on Route 191. A number of other species of birds also
can be seen in the forest, including Red-necked Pigeons, Puerto
Rican Tanagers, Puerto Rican Emeralds, Puerto Rican Todies,
Puerto Rican Woodpeckers, and Red-legged Thrushes. The forest
also is extremely scenic and provides splendid natural history
opportunities of all types.

Las Croabas Village

The area around Las Croabas village also is known as one of the
island's better birding areas. For example, it is likely that Antillean
Crested Hummingbirds, Green-throated Caribs, and Caribbean
Elaenias can be seen here as well as a variety of other species.

Cidra

A few Plain Pigeons still are to be found in the mountains of
middle Puerto Rico near the town of Cidra. One of the better places
to look for the birds is along a stream to be crossed just before
arriving at the Treasure Island Hotel.

Culebra Island

Culebra, one of the smaller islands near Puerto Rico, is also of
interest to bird watchers. It is located east of the main island and is

reached either by airplane from San Juan or by ferry from Fajardo. There is a small hotel in the town of Dewey. Among the rich assortment of birds found on the island are large nesting colonies of Bridled Terns, Sooty Terns, and Noddy Terns in summer. Since the island serves as a firing range for the U.S. Navy, visits cannot be made when firing is in progress. Local residents should be able to inform visitors if the island is closed for naval use.

Martinique

Visitors to French-speaking Martinique will find an interesting assortment of birds. For example, in the lush rain forests near Mt. Pelée Blue-headed Hummingbirds, Lesser Antillean Swifts, and Rufous-throated Solitaires are likely to be seen. In the dry forests, fine bird watching may be enjoyed along the road running west of the town of Diamant south of Fort-de-France. This is one of the areas where the endemic Martinique Oriole should be searched for and is seen occasionally. A variety of other species also occur in the area, including Green-throated Caribs, Crested Antillean Hummingbirds, Gray Kingbirds, and Lesser Antillean Bullfinches.

Aves Island

One of the most remote islands in the West Indies is a tiny speck of land known as Aves Island. It is located about 130 miles west of Dominica and apparently serves as a major nesting site for Sooty Terns in winter. Few people have ever set foot on this low island,

Aves Island, a tiny remote dot of land in the West Indies west of Dominica, is an important seabird nesting area, as well as a resting area for migrating birds.

which has only a slim, orange, post-like marker on it to mark its ownership by Venezuela. On October 11, 1974, from the M.S. *Lindblad Explorer*, a landing was made on Aves Island and a record of the birds seen there was made. The species seen included Brown Boobies, Magnificent Frigatebirds, Peregrine Falcons, Semipalmated Plovers, Black-bellied Plovers, Laughing Gulls, Sooty Terns, Black-billed Cuckoos, Barn Swallows, and an unidentified warbler. In the unlikely event that other bird watchers should reach this remote spot, a record of the birds seen there would be of ornithological interest.

Trinidad and Tobago

Unlike most of the other islands in the West Indies which are oceanic in origin, Trinidad and Tobago are continental islands which support avifaunas reflecting the birdlife of mainland South America. Therefore a visit to these islands, especially Trinidad, is an exceptionally rich bird watching experience. Anybody who has not previously watched birds in South America can find no better introduction to the spectacular birdlife of the continent than is enjoyed in Trinidad. The birds are abundant here, but do not occur in such large numbers of species that they will overwhelm a watcher with the task of learning new birds. Nevertheless 399 species are known from Trinidad and 172 from nearby Tobago. Serious bird watchers on these islands will find Richard ffrench's *A Guide to the Birds of Trinidad and Tobago* essential. In addition, my *Finding Birds in Trinidad and Tobago* also will be helpful—especially for people visiting the islands for the first time. Interesting bird watching can be enjoyed on Trinidad and Tobago at any time of the year, but the best period is during the long dry season which extends from January through April.

To illustrate some of the splendid birding possibilities found on the islands, some of the more important locations are discussed and typical birds seen there mentioned.

Asa Wright Nature Centre

The Asa Wright Nature Centre is world famous among bird watchers as one of the best spots in Trinidad for finding large numbers of birds. It is located above the town of Arima, off the Blanchisseuse Road at the 7½-7¾-mile marker, at an elevation of about 1,200 feet. In addition to its being a working cocoa-coffee-citrus plantation, it also protects a superb example of lower montane rain forest and a major nesting colony of Oilbirds. Full visitor facilities are available and most bird watchers spend at least a week here using the Centre as their base for day-long birding trips elsewhere on the island. Among the birds likely to be seen on the 183

The Asa Wright Nature Centre, Trinidad, West Indies—extremely popular with bird watchers

Centre's grounds are Gray-headed Kites, Common Black Hawks, Smooth-billed Anis, Oilbirds, Band-rumped Swifts, Little Hermits, White-breasted Emeralds, Common Emeralds, Channel-billed Toucans, Barred Antshrikes, Bearded Bellbirds, Golden-headed Manakins, Great Kiskadees, House Wrens, Cocoa Thrushes, Yellow-breasted Peppershrikes, Purple Honeycreepers, Bananaquits, Crested Oropendolas, Violaceous Euphonias, Blue-gray Tanagers, and Silver-beaked Tanagers. It is not unusual to see many of these birds from the Centre's gallery!

Nesting Oilbirds, a major attraction on the Asa Wright Nature Centre, Trinidad

Blanchisseuse Road

Most bird watchers who have spent much time on the Blanchisseuse Road, which extends from Arima for some 24 miles across the beautiful Northern Range mountains to the Caribbean town of Blanchisseuse, will be quick to agree that it provides some of the finest bird watching experiences in all of Trinidad. Part of the reason for its rich diversity of birds is related to the fact that it touches various types of habitats including deciduous seasonal forest, secondary forest and plantations, lower montane rain forest, and other areas. A day spent birding along this road produces impressive numbers of birds, including such species as Turkey Vultures, Black Vultures, Swallow-tailed Kites, Double-toothed Kites, Short-tailed Hawks, White Hawks, Bat Falcons, Orange-winged Parrots, Squirrel Cuckoos, Ferruginous Pygmy-Owls, Chestnut-collared Swifts, White-necked Jacobins, Ruby-topaz Hummingbirds, Tufted Coquettes, White-tailed Trogons, Collared Trogons, Violaceous Trogons, Blue-crowned Motmots, and Rufous-tailed Jacamars. Other species often seen along this road include Channel-billed Toucans, Chestnut Woodpeckers, Lineated Woodpeckers, Great Antshrikes, Barred Antshrikes, Bearded Bellbirds, Golden-headed Manakins, White-bearded Manakins, Boat-billed Flycatchers, Great Kiskadees, Euler's Flycatchers, Forest Elaenias, Rufous-breasted Wrens, Cocoa Thrushes, Crested Oropendolas, Bananaquits, Purple Honeycreepers, Red-legged Honeycreepers, Green Honeycreepers, Swallow-Tanagers, Speckled Tanagers, Bay-headed Tanagers, Blue-gray Tanagers, and many other species.

Caroni Swamp

The Caroni Swamp probably is second only to the Blanchisseuse Road in importance to bird watchers in Trinidad. This splendid mangrove swamp is located a few miles from Port of Spain. It provides birders with exceptional opportunities to see large numbers of wading and water birds, including clouds of blood-red Scarlet Ibises flying into the center of the swamp to roost each evening on several small mangrove islands. It is a sight not to be forgotten. In addition, one frequently also sees Striated Herons, Long-winged Harriers, Greater Anis, Yellow-throated Spinetails White-headed Marsh-Tyrants, and Red-breasted Blackbirds in the swamp. Boats as well as guides are available at a number of locations, thus making a trip into the Caroni Swamp easy and very enjoyable. It is a must for all bird watchers.

Tobago

Bird watching on Tobago is very worthwhile even though fewer species are found on the island than on nearby Trinidad. Tobago

Seabird cliffs, Little Tobago Island, West Indies. Red-billed Tropicbirds and other seabirds nest here.

also is a very beautiful island. Among birds commonly seen at feeders at some hotels and estates are Rufous-vented Chachalacas, Blue-crowned Motmots, Red-crowned Woodpeckers, Tropical Mockingbirds, Bare-eyed Thrushes, and Bananaquits. Sometimes Rufous-tailed Jacamars and Blue-crowned Motmots are seen along the old Castara Road near the Hillsboro Dam, and milepost five along this road is probably Tobago's best spot for seeing the island's beautiful Blue-backed Manakins. In addition, a variety of other birds also are readily seen elsewhere on the island including various gulls and terns along the shore. While on Tobago, a necessary bird watching side trip also is made to nearby Little Tobago Island across Speyside Bay at the northeastern end of Tobago.

Little Tobago Island

This fine government bird sanctuary protects a variety of species of birds including nesting Red-billed Tropicbirds and Brown Boobies. Peregrine Falcons sometimes appear along the steep cliffs and various songbirds also populate the island. However, the outstanding avian attraction on Little Tobago is the presence of several Greater Birds-of-Paradise which were introduced onto the island from the Aru Islands off New Guinea in 1909. Apparently the birds one sees today on Little Tobago are the offspring from the original stock. They are spectacular birds, especially during their courtship period from December through February, and are eagerly looked for by all visiting birders. Unfortunately, they are now very rare and seen only occasionally, but many birders report hearing the birds from the interior of dense jungle-like forest. Even if the Greater Birds-of-Paradise are not seen, there is still enough of interest on Little Tobago to justify a visit there.

Additional Reading

Abramson, I. J.
    1974   Grand Cayman Island. *Birding*, 6 (5): 224-26.

Allen, R. P.
    1961   Birds of the Caribbean. Viking Press, New York.

Barnett, J. M.
    1967   Birding in Trinidad. *Canadian Audubon*, 29 (1): 15-18.

Bond, J.
    1971   Birds of the West Indies. 2d edition. Houghton Mifflin Co.,
            Boston.

Brudenell-Bruce, P. G. C.
    1975   The Birds of the Bahamas. Taplinger Publishing Co.,
            New York.

Eckelberry, D.
    1964   Bird Painting in a Tropical Valley. *Audubon Magazine,* 66:
            284-89.
    1967   Steel Bands and Tropical Birds—My Eden. *Audubon*, 69:
            44-53.

ffrench, R.
    1973   A Guide to the Birds of Trinidad and Tobago. Livingston
            Publishing Co., Wynnewood, Pa.

Heintzelman, D. S.
    1973   Finding Birds in Trinidad and Tobago. Published privately,
            629 Green St., Allentown, Pa.
    1976   Bird Survey on Aves Island. *Explorers Journal*, 54 (2): 65.

Leck, C., and M. Kuhnen
    1975   Bird Areas of Jamaica. *Birding*, 7 (1): 4-6.

Lindblad, J.
    1969   Journey to Red Birds. Collins, London.

Ross, E. S.
    1965   Birds that "See" in the Dark with their Ears. *National
            Geographic*, 127 (2): 282-90.

Snider, D. E.
    1974   Martinique. *Birding*, 6 (2): 77.

Willman, P. A.
    1972   Lesser Antilles, Island of Martinique (Oriole, Martinique).
            Birding, 4 (4): 179.
    1974   Birding in Puerto Rico. *Birding*, 6 (1): 5-7.

Worth, C. B.
    1967   A Naturalist in Trinidad. J. B. Lippincott Co., Philadelphia.

19
CENTRAL AMERICAN BIRDING

After visiting some of the islands in the West Indies, the next step in neotropical bird watching is a trip to one of the charming countries in Central America, such as Mexico, Guatemala, Costa Rica, or Panama, where one can see a variety of birds far in excess of the numbers to be found on most West Indian islands. Fortunately, bird watching in Central America has come of age and there are a number of excellent field guides and bird finding guides available for various countries (see chapter 3). In addition, several new national parks are now established in some countries and plans for others are being prepared. In the future, these areas are likely to become major bird watching locations because they preserve vital habitats for a variety of unique birds which elsewhere are rapidly being destroyed. Therefore, bird watchers have a direct stake in seeing to it that such outstanding natural areas are preserved and protected whenever possible.

Mexico

Mexico long has been a favorite starting point for bird watchers venturing into Central America. Its close proximity to the United States, coupled with its large size, varied geography, and great variety of habitat types make it an exciting place to visit. Unfortunately, habitat destruction is continuing rapidly in many parts of Mexico, as elsewhere in Latin America, and this is having a grave impact on many birds and other forms of wildlife. Nevertheless, many excellent birding areas still remain. The best of these are described in detail in Ernest P. Edwards' *Finding Birds in Mexico* and in Peter Alden's *Finding the Birds in Western Mexico*.

For those bird watchers who may not feel capable of visiting this country alone, many excellent bird watching tours are available where capable and interested tour leaders help find and identify the best birds. Such tours are offered in the pages of many magazines, including *Audubon*, *American Birds*, and *Birding*. Once experience is gained in Mexico, one can then revisit the country alone and seek new life list birds. The four field guides now available for Mexican birds will enable any bird watcher to identify most species without too much difficulty.

There are so many excellent bird watching locations in Mexico that it is not possible to discuss all of them here. Rather, I have picked a few typical examples to illustrate only a fraction of the richness of Mexican birdlife.

Atlantic Lowlands

Mexico's important Atlantic lowlands generally include the areas east of the high central mountain ranges as well as the lower mountain slopes and the coastal plain. Within the area are many typically tropical species which make the region of particular interest to bird watchers. The largest number of such birds are found in the southern sections of the Atlantic lowlands, as one would expect.

In the vicinity of the town of Coatzacoalcos in the state of Veracruz, for example, one may expect to see Roadside Hawks, Laughing Falcons, Bat Falcons, Barred Antshrikes, Spot-breasted Wrens, Clay-colored Robins, Yellow-winged Tanagers, and Black-headed Saltators, as well as other tropical species.

Similarly, Fortin de las Flores, also in the state of Veracruz, provides excellent bird watching opportunities both within the town and in the surrounding areas. Many bird watchers use the town as a base of operations when visiting this section of the Atlantic lowlands. Among the species one might expect to see are White-collared Swifts, Boat-billed Flycatchers, Social Flycatchers, Band-backed Wrens, and Common Bush-Tanagers, along with a host of other species not strictly tropical.

Still another outstanding location for bird watching in the Atlantic lowlands is the old archaeological ruin near the town of Palenque in the state of Chiapas where such species as Little Tinamous, Ruddy Ground-Doves, Collared Trogons, Violaceous Trogons, Citreoline Trogons, and Masked Tityras have been reported. Other species also known from the area include Red-legged Honeycreepers, Red-crowned Ant-Tanagers, Red-throated Ant-Tanagers, Tody Motmots, and Dot-winged Antwrens. Many additional birds occur around the old ruins and much productive bird watching is possible here.

Yucatan Area

Visits to Yucatan are of interest not only because of fine bird watching possibilities there but also because of major archaeological sites which one can and should enjoy. At Chichén Itzá, for example, the old ruins are extraordinary, and one may be hard pressed to concentrate on birds with such ancient splendors around. Nevertheless, many birds are to be seen here including Ruddy Ground-Doves, Turquoise-browed Motmots, Yucatan Flycatchers, Yucatan Jays, and Grayish Saltators. Away from the cleared areas, still more birds are likely to be seen, such as Aztec Parakeets, Ivory-billed Woodcreepers, Masked Tityras, Blue Buntings, and Blue-black Grassquits.

Bird watching in and around the city of Merida in the Yucatan area likewise is worthwhile. In the city suburbs, for instance, an early morning or late afternoon bird walk might produce Tropical Mockingbirds, Clay-colored Robins, Hooded Orioles, and Grayish Saltators. Farther afield around old archaeological sites or wooded areas, Wedge-tailed Sabrewings, Barred Antshrikes, Yucatan Flycatchers, Cave Swallows, and Yellow-faced Grassquits are some of the birds likely to appear.

Still another excellent spot to enjoy ancient ruins as well as fine bird watching is the archaeological site at Uxmal. In the cleared areas, one might expect to see Turkey Vultures, Black Vultures, Groove-billed Anis, Tropical Kingbirds, Melodious Blackbirds, and a host of other species. Nearby in wooded areas and fields, even more birds are likely to be discovered: Fork-tailed Emeralds, Fawn-breasted Hummingbirds, Gray-breasted Martins, Yucatan Wrens, Mangrove Vireos, Gray-crowned Yellowthroats, Blue Buntings, and Olive Sparrows.

The Highlands

The great highlands of Mexico run down the length of the entire country like a giant backbone. A variety of habitats and birds may be found in the area, which is largely over 5,000 feet in elevation, and fine bird watching is possible at many locations. For example, in clearings and forested mountain slopes in and around the city of Cuernavaca, Dusky Hummingbirds, Violet-crowned Hummingbirds, Rufous-backed Robins, Banded Wrens, and Happy Wrens are seen frequently. Turkey Vultures and Black Vultures are common. White-naped Swifts and Chestnut-collared Swifts also are relatively easy to see within the city. Outside Cuernavaca in wooded areas, Squirrel Cuckoos, Russet-crowned Motmots, Nutting's Flycatchers, Golden Vireos, Rufous-capped Warblers, and Striped-headed Sparrows are likely to be observed.

North of the city along the *old road* going to Mexico City, it is possible to explore areas up to 10,000 feet in elevation where Berylline Hummingbirds, Russet Nightingale-Thrushes, Chestnut-sided Shrike-Vireos, and Green-striped Brush-Finches are reported along with many other species. Much time can be spent in the area, and it is often very productive simply to walk along roads and search out some of the more unusual and interesting birds.

Pacific Lowlands

Mexico's Pacific lowlands, exclusive of Baja California, run southward the entire length of the country but extend inland only to the foothills of the high mountains and therefore reach elevations of only about 5,000 feet. As elsewhere in Mexico, a good number of exotic birds live in the region and they offer much worthwhile bird watching. For example, in addition to the waterbirds which are very common around the city of Acapulco, many other tropical birds also are to be seen in the gardens and other open areas within the city. These include Ruddy Ground-Doves, Rufous-naped Wrens, and Streak-backed Orioles. Away from the city, where wooded hillsides still occur, Orange-fronted Parakeets, White-fronted Parrots, and Squirrel Cuckoos, Citreoline Trogons, Yellow-winged Caciques, and a host of other species are likely candidates for a bird list. Additional fine birding is also possible still farther from the city where reasonably untouched habitats can be found.

In and around Mazatlán, in the state of Sinalosa, bird watchers will find Cinnamon Hummingbirds, Golden-cheeked Woodpeckers, Happy Wrens, and Streak-backed Orioles in orchards, gardens, and similar places. North of the city, a number of roads lead into farm and orchard areas where Lilac-crowned Parrots, Citreoline Trogons, Bar-vented Wrens, and Rosy Thrush Tanagers are a few of the attractions. Many waterbirds and shorebirds also frequent the beaches around Mazatlán.

In and around the town of Tehuantepec, in the state of Oaxaca, excellent bird watching is possible especially where one finds fields, woodland, and other likely bird habitats such as those to the east of town where Roadside Hawks, Inca Doves, Orange-fronted Parakeets, Citreoline Trogons, Russet-crowned Motmots, Yellow-winged Caciques, and Cinnamon-tailed Sparrows occur.

Guatemala

Many experienced bird watchers conside Guatemala to be one of the most beautiful and productive countries in Central America. Like Mexico, it has a rich variety of habitats ranging from lowland jungles to high volcanic peaks all of which provide habitats for about 667 species of birds. No wonder bird watchers are delighted by visits to this country! Some of the more important natural regions of Guatemala are described here briefly and some typical birds of such areas mentioned. Bird watchers needing more complete details will find Hugh C. Land's *Birds of Guatemala* very helpful.

Highland Areas

Birds of the highlands are mainly lower montane and montane in character. In some areas, elevations reach to 10,000 feet, and a dozen or so volcanic peaks are even higher. Tajumulco, for instance, is 12,800 feet high. Since there are various vegetation zones within the highlands, a variety of birds occur in the different zones. Typical of the cool montane locations, for example, are Horned Guans, Rufous-browed Wrens, Pink-headed Warblers, and Black-capped Siskins.

In other zones of the highlands, a variety of endemic or nearly endemic species occur. There are Atitlán Grebes (found only on Lake Atitlán), Fulvous Owls, Garnet-throated Hummingbirds, Wine-throated Hummingbirds, Belted Flycatchers, Blue-and-white Mockingbirds, and others. Additional highland birds with wider geographic distributions include White-breasted Hawks, Green-throated Mountaingems, Resplendent Quetzals (the national bird of Guatemala), Mountain Trogons, Spot-crowned Woodpeckers, and Scaled Antpittas.

There is little doubt that some of the most interesting and exciting bird watching can be done in the various areas of the highlands. Lake Atitlán, for instance, is not only the one place in the world where the Atitlán Grebe can be seen in the wild but it also is one of the ecological treasures of Guatemala and well worth a visit.

Arid Interior Areas

Although only about 75 species of birds are found as residents in Guatemala's arid interior areas, many of these birds tend to be very common. Expect sights of Common Black Hawks, Laughing Falcons, Crested Caracaras, Green Parakeets, Elegant Trogons, Lineated Woodpeckers, Masked Tityras, Tropical Kingbirds, Blue Grosbeaks, and many others.

Subtropical Areas

The subtropical areas of Guatemala include the humid slopes of the Caribbean and Pacific sides of the country along with slopes in the interior; all are generally between 3,000 and 6,000 feet in elevation. About 270 species of birds are resident in the subtropical areas, including Black-crested Coquettes, Scaly-throated Foliagegleaners, White-throated Flycatchers, Grace's Warblers, Rufous-capped Warblers, Blue-crowned Chlorophonias. Highways lead into subtropical areas on both the Caribbean and Pacific slopes and can be used by bird watchers to reach some of these areas.

Tropical Lowland Areas

The tropical lowland areas exclusive of the arid interior can be divided into those along the Caribbean, the Petén, and the Pacific lowlands. These are the sections of Guatemala with the richest birdlife; almost 350 species are resident. The Caribbean lowlands provide the best bird watching opportunities, the Pacific lowlands somewhat less so. The Petén is the least accessible of the lowlands. However, it is of great importance because of the presence of Tikal National Park where splendid Mayan temples and other ruins are preserved and open to the public and where excellent bird watching is possible. Access is ordinarily only by air from Guatemala City. Extensive information about the birdlife found at Tikal and the Petén in general is presented by Frank B. Smithe in *The Birds of Tikal* which bird watchers will find extremely useful on visits to this site. Some typical examples of common birds seen at Tikal and vicinity are Slaty-breasted Tinamous, Little Blue Herons, Turkey Vultures, Hook-billed Kites, Roadside Hawks, Orange-breasted Falcons, Bat Falcons, Great Curassows, Brown-hooded Parrots, White-crowned Parrots, Mottled Owls, Long-tailed Hermits, White-bellied Emeralds, Slaty-tailed Trogons, Citreoline Trogons, Pygmy Kingfishers, Tody Motmots, Blue-crowned Motmots, Collared Aracaris, Smoky-brown Woodpeckers, and Ruddy Woodcreepers. Some other common species include Ivory-billed Woodcreepers, Cinnamon Becards, Red-capped Manakins, Tropical Kingbirds, White-throated Spadebills, Brown Jays, Red-legged Honeycreepers, Yellow-throated Euphonias, and White-collared Seedeaters. Approximately 280 species of birds have been reported within the area forming Tikal National Park.

Costa Rica

Bird watching in Costa Rica has become increasingly popular in recent years because of the rich assortment of birds living there. The Monteverde Cloud Forest Preserve, for example, is one of the outstanding bird watching and wilderness areas in the country. It is located on the continental divide, in west-central Costa Rica, in the Cordillera de Tilaran. Mid-March to late May is the recommended time to visit the area. The preserve's four distinctive biotic communities (Elfin Forest, Cloud Forest, Middle Zone Forest, and Tall Multilayered Forest) provide the essential habitats responsible for the area's splendid birdlife. Some examples of common birds seen in one zone or another of the preserve include Highland Tinamous, Swallow-tailed Kites, Barred Forest-Falcons, Black Guans, Brown-hooded Parrots, Squirrel Cuckoos, Blue-crowned Motmots, Long-tailed Manakins, Masked Tityras, Great Kiskadees, Brown Jays, Clay-colored Robins, Slaty-backed Nightingale-Thrushes, Golden-crowned Warblers, Spangle-cheeked Tanagers, Yellow Grosbeaks, and Rufous-collared

Sparrows. A large number of other species also occur in the preserve.

Panama

Of all the Central American countries, Panama has the richest avifauna because it is nearest to the center of the great South American neotropical avifauna. Thus bird watching in Panama can be a very rewarding experience. Increasingly large numbers of bird watchers are beginning to visit this country in their quests for new life list birds. The necessary field guides and bird finding guides are now available. Of these, Robert S. Ridgely's *A Guide to the Birds of Panama* and Ernest P. Edwards and Horace Loftin's *Finding Birds in Panama* are the most useful to bird watchers.

Panama, like most other Central American countries, has a rich variety of habitats, including lowland tropical areas, dense rain forests, open savannas, and high mountains and volcanoes. For general bird watching purposes, the country can be divided into several general regions: Atlantic slope, the Canal Zone, Pacific slope, and the Highlands.

Atlantic Slope

Although large numbers of birds occur in the Atlantic slope region, those known primarily from this area include Gray-headed Doves, Gray-rumped Swifts, Snowcaps, Lattice-tailed Trogans, Chestnut-colored Woodpeckers, Cane-brake Wrens, Olive-crowned Yellowthroats, White-vented Euphonias, Olive-backed Euphonias, and Crimson-collared Tanagers. These are some of the special birds to be looked for in this section of Panama but which may not occur elsewhere in the country.

Canal Zone

One of the really outstanding areas which all bird watchers should visit while in Panama is the Canal Zone. Along the famous Pipeline Road, for example, one can drive for some 15 miles through superb jungle-like birding territory and stop at leisure to explore favorable looking spots. Some of the more common birds likely to be seen along the road are Double-toothed Kites, White Hawks, Black Hawk-Eagles, Scaled Pigeons, Orange-chinned Parakeets, Blue-headed Parrots, Long-tailed Hermits, Slaty-tailed Trogons, Black-throated Trogons, Violaceous Trogons, Keel-billed Toucans, Black-cheeked Woodpeckers, Slaty Antshrikes, Dot-winged Antwrens, Red-capped Manakins, Golden-collared Manakins, Purple-throated Fruitcrows, Red-legged Honeycreepers, Shining Honeycreepers, Green Honeycreepers, Scarlet-rumped Caciques, Bay-headed Tanagers, and Crimson-backed Tanagers. In addition, rarer birds also reported from the

Pipeline Road include Barred Forest-Falcons, Sunbitterns, Crested Owls, Pygmy Kingfishers, and Great Jacamars.

In early to mid-October enormous migrations of hawks often pass over Ancon Hill in the Canal Zone, providing bird watchers with one of the most extraordinary raptor spectacles anywhere in the Americas. Broad-winged Hawks and Swainson's Hawks often form the bulk of the birds seen in these migrations.

Pacific Slope

The Pacific slope of Panama also provides very fine bird watching opportunities with Mangrove Cuckoos, Mottled Owls, Rufous Nightjars, Vaux's Swifts, Baird's Trogons, and Rufous-breasted Wrens being some of the species primarily restricted to this area in appropriate habitats.

Highlands

A great variety of birds also occur in Panama's highlands. Some of those which are fairly restricted to these areas are Highland Tinamous, Black Guans, Ruddy Pigeons, Banded Parakeets, Bare-shanked Screech Owls, Brown Violet-ears, Green-crowned Brilliants, Collared Trogons, Red-headed Barbets, and Black Phoebes. Of course, many of the generally distributed birds also occur in some of the lower reaches of the highlands.

Widely Distributed Species

In addition to various birds with more or less restricted geographic distributions, very many species are widely distributed throughout Panama, especially in the lowland areas, and are likely to be seen in suitable habitats. Some typical examples are Great Tinamous, Little Tinamous, Black-bellied Whistling Ducks, Turkey Vultures, Black Vultures, King Vultures, Swallow-tailed Kites, Hook-billed Kites, Double-toothed Kites, Savanna Hawks, Roadside Hawks, Laughing Falcons, Crested Caracaras, Bat Falcons, Great Curassows, Ruddy Ground-Doves, Squirrel Cuckoos, Smooth-billed Anis, Little Hermits, Violaceous Trogons, Ringed Kingfishers, Blue-crowned Motmots, Great Jacamars, Lineated Woodpeckers, Crimson-crested Woodpeckers, Barred Antshrikes, as well as a large number of other species. These birds do not all occur in the same types of habitats.

Additional Reading

Brodkin, H.
  1976   Costa Rica: ABA Pilot Expedition, 1976. *Birding*, 8 (5): 313-18.

Chapman, F. M.

    1931   My Tropical Air Castle. D. Appleton-Century Co., New York.

    1938   Life in an Air Castle. D. Appleton-Century Co., New York.

Powell, G. V. N.

    1977   Monteverde Cloud Forest Preserve, Costa Rica. *American Birds*, 31 (2): 119-26.

Ridgely, R. S.

    1974   Pipeline Road, Canal Zone. *American Birds,* 29 (5): 874-79.

Smith, N.

    1973   Spectacular Buteo Migration over Panama Canal Zone, October, 1972. *American Birds*, 27 (1): 3-5.

20
SOUTH AMERICAN BIRDING

Bird watching in South America still is so relatively new that most of that vast continent's best locations still await discovery. Nevertheless, this chapter attempts to discuss in general terms the rich and varied bird watching opportunities available in South America. However, new South American bird species still are being discovered and no completely adequate field guides are available for the continent's birdlife (see chapter 3 for those which are available). Little wonder, then, that only the more skilled and dedicated bird watchers generally attempt birding here. For those who do, the rewards can be almost overwhelming. Almost 3,000 species of birds live in South America and most of them are potential life list birds for anyone without previous experience in the neotropics and southern hemisphere. Indeed whole families are restricted to sections of the continent—rheas, screamers, hoatzins, sunbitterns, seedsnipes, and plantcutters.

In addition to having the richest and largest avifauna of any continent, South America also contains an extraordinary assortment of habitats ranging from Ice Age-like conditions to the vast and still largely unexplored Amazon rain forests. Add to them important offshore islands such as the Galapagos and Peru's famous guano islands and one quickly realizes why South America is a bird watcher's El Dorado.

Colombia

Of all the countries of South America, Colombia boasts the largest number of species of birds—about 1,567 species or about 56% of the entire South American avifauna. Part of the avian richness is explained by the fact that Colombia enjoys both Atlantic and Pacific coastlines and also includes in its territory sections of the high Andes and the vast Amazon Basin. Because of the large number of species to be found in Colombia and the difficulty of identifying some of them, some bird watchers with field experience in Colombia recommend that novices first visit places like Trinidad,

Leticia, Colombia, is a small frontier town on the Amazon. Birds are abundant in the area.

Panama, or other tropical countries containing neotropical elements less abundant than those in Colombia. In addition, a visit to a good natural history museum with collections of northern South American birds will help prepare one for a bird watching trip to Colombia because specimens of many of the species can be examined and studied carefully in the hand. That experience, and a copy of Rodolphe Meyer de Schauensee's *The Birds of Colombia*, should enable good bird watchers to handle most of the identification problems they encounter. Perhaps the more energetic individuals also will want to photograph museum specimens and mount the color photographs in a small notebook, thus making a crude do-it-yourself field guide.

From a general faunistic point of view, Colombia can be divided into seven major areas, each with more or less characteristic birdlife. Bird watchers visiting this country can use these areas as general guidelines in determining the species they most eagerly want to try to see.

Amazonian Region

This is a vast region, dominated by the Amazon River. Virgin rain forests extend unbroken to the horizon. Only along the major rivers and streams is there much human activity although in such areas the forest sometimes has been severely cut and burned. About a third of Colombia is located in the Amazonian region which extends westward and northward to the lower slopes of the Eastern Andes. It is an extraordinarily beautiful area and one very rich in birds, wildlife, and plant life.

Bird watchers visiting Colombia's portion of the Amazonian 198 region probably will arrive at the frontier town of Leticia on the

Amazon River. Here hotels, meals, and guides are available. Travel to Leticia is either by ship or boat sailing up or down the Amazon or by air from one of Colombia's larger cities. Once in the town, however, an effort should be made to go by boat upriver or downriver, then into some of the smaller river and stream channels where it is possible to travel for miles into the interior and to see many interesting and beautiful birds. Some typical examples of the birdlife in the general area include Neotropic Cormorants, Green Ibises, Black Vultures, Greater Yellow-headed Vultures, Snail Kites, Black-collared Hawks, Black Hawk-Eagles, Yellow-headed Caracaras, Black Curassows, Large-billed Terns, Black Skimmers, Red-and-Green Macaws, Chestnut-fronted Macaws, Green-rumped Parakeets, Smooth-billed Anis, Ringed Kingfishers, Green Kingfishers, Chestnut Jacamars, White-throated Toucans, Black-necked Aracaris, Yellow-throated Woodpeckers, Lineated Woodpeckers, Spangled Cotingas, Lesser Kiskadees, Brown-chested Martins, Crested Oropendolas, Yellow-rumped Caciques, Red-capped Cardinals, and Lesser Seed-Finches. Occasionally, Amazonian Umbrellabirds are seen overhead, and a great many other species also may be observed. Indeed, different species often are seen on each trip afield.

Orinoco Region

Typical habitats in this area are patches of woodland, palm groves, and llanos in the general region to the north of the Rio Guaviare and eastward to the great Orinoco. Here one finds many open country birds. The Orinoco is the best pathway into this region.

Catatumbo Region

The heavy forests of this region are located at the eastern base of the Eastern Andes and contain a great many species of birds not found elsewhere in Colombia. For example, Pygmy Swifts and Red Siskins live in the area. The city of Cututa is the jumping-off point for exploring and birding this region.

Sierra Nevada de Santa Marta

The isolated mountains of this area rise from the Caribbean Sea and reach elevations at which ice and snow cover their summits. Because the mountains are isolated from the Andes they more or less form islands which contain some birds not found in other parts of Colombia. Among the unique species of these mountains are Santa Marta Parakeets, Santa Marta Sabrewings, White-tailed Star-Frontlets, Black-backed Thorn-bills, and Santa Marta Ground-Tyrants. Each of these species would be desirable on a bird watcher's life list. No towns or cities are close to this mountain range.

Caribbean Region

Colombia's coastal Carribean areas are more or less semi-arid if not actually desert-like in some places. Among the species of birds to be found in this area are Bare-eyed Pigeons, Scaled Doves, Troupials, and Vermilion Cardinals.

Central Mountains Region

The central part of Colombia includes the area from the western slopes of the Eastern Andes westward to the western slopes of the Western Andes. In all, three major mountain chains dominate the area (the Western, Central, and Eastern Andes) along with two major central valleys. Bird watching here is both varied and very rich, although extensive destruction of original forests has ruined many formerly important areas and probably exterminated some endemic species. Despite the continuing habitat destruction, however, this general region provides bird watchers with an excellent and exciting introduction to Colombia's birdlife. For example, one party of birders spent twelve days in the general area between Cali and Popayan in the Cauca Valley and returned home with a list of over 400 species of birds! It will be worthwhile to describe some of the better birding areas briefly.

The Buga Marshes and forest, some 80 kilometers north of Cali, offer some fine bird watching opportunities with Spectacled Parrotlets, Pale-breasted Spinetails, Little Cuckoos, Spot-breasted Woodpeckers, Greater Anis, and Apical Flycatchers, all seen in shrubby areas near the marsh, and Horned Screamers, Black-bellied Whistling Ducks, Fulvous Whistling Ducks, Pied Water-Tyrants, and Yellow-hooded Blackbirds reported in the marsh itself. Other marsh birds to be looked for here include White-necked Herons, Pinnated Bitterns, Gray-breasted Crakes, and Least Bitterns.

Another good bird watching location near Cali is at the summit of the Western Andes above Cali where some patches of forest still remain intact near a restaurant. Here Glossy-black Thrushes, Andean Solitaires, Azara's Spinetails, Russet-crowned Warblers, and Green-and-Black Fruiteaters have been seen. A variety of tanagers also apparently occur in the area including Saffron-crowned Tanagers, Metallic-green Tanagers, Golden Tanagers, Scrub Tanagers, Black-capped Tanagers, Beryl-spangled Tanagers, and Golden-naped Tanagers. Other species also seen in these forest patches include Blue-winged Mountain-Tanagers and Dusky-bellied Bush-Tanagers.

Not too far from Cali is another spot called Pichinde, at the 6,000-foot elevation, where some spectacular birds may be found in limited numbers. Perhaps the most exciting is the beautiful Andean

Cock-of-the-Rock, but other species which might come into view here include an occasional Crimson-rumped Toucanet, Collared Trogons, and Masked Trogons. Other species which also occur here and may be seen more or less frequently include Booted Racket-tails, Spot-crowned Woodpeckers, Black-billed Thrushes, Flame-rumped Tanagers, Red-headed Barbets, and Multicolored Tanagers. A great many other species also can be seen at this location.

Still another very important bird watching area in the general Cali region is the Buenaventura Road which leads through some spectacular and bird-rich habitats into the Pacific Colombia region. One can spend days exploring this road and the various side roads which branch off the main highway. For example, in various forested areas in the vicinity of Queremal, Tawny-crested Tanagers and Dusky-faced Tanagers have been seen as well as Purple-crowned Fairies, Spot-crowned Barbets, Golden-collared Manakins, Orange-bellied Euphonias, and a host of other colorful and interesting birds. Some of the rarer species also reported from the area include Barred Hawks, Blue-tailed Trogons, White-headed Wrens, Lemon-browed Tanagers, and Blue-whiskered Tanagers. A great variety of other species, some quite rare, also are likely to be seen in lower areas near Buenaventura.

Many excellent bird watching sites also are available in the vicinity of Popayán, south of Cali. For example, the mountain pass at Cerro Munchique, near the town of El Tambo, is an important and bird-rich area and here one can reach elevations of around 8,200 feet. Blue-and-White Swallows, Capped Conebills, Golden-fronted Redstarts, and Great Thrushes occur here and sometimes large flocks of tanagers of many species are noted. Among the hummingbirds to be looked for are Empress Brilliants and Sword-billed Hummingbirds. The latter are quite impressive.

Certainly another of the important bird watching areas to be visited, this one above the town of Purace, is Purace National Park which saddles the crest of the Central Andes. Here one can reach elevations of 11,000 feet or more, but one should move very slowly at those elevations because of the thin atmosphere.

Wonderful bird watching is possible in this park. For example, at kilometer post 157 near the park entrance a few Andean Condors sometimes perch on rock ledges. Within various sections of the park, Shining Sunbeams, Golden-breasted Pufflegs, Scarlet-bellied Mountain-Tanagers, Black-thighed Pufflegs, Masked Flower-Piercers, and Plumbeous Sierra-Finches are to be seen. In addition, some Oilbirds nest in a cave to which park officials can guide birders.

A short distance off the Popayan-Neiva highway, some 30

kilometers east of the Oilbird cave, one comes to a private farm—
Finca Merenberg—owned by Gunther Buch. Much undisturbed
forest, intact on this farm through the efforts of the Buch family,
provides essential habitat for many birds. Occasional bird watchers
may be allowed to visit the farm provided permission is secured
from the Buch family. Particularly good bird watching
opportunities seem to occur along the forest edge. Sickle-winged
Guans, Maroon-tailed Parakeets, Black-billed Mountain-Toucans,
Capped Conebills, Golden Tanagers, Black-capped Tanagers and
many other species are seen here.

Pacific Slope Region

West of the Western Andes, one finds dense forests and torrential
rainfall on the mountain slopes. Birds in this region tend to exhibit
marked endemism. Tooth-billed Hummingbirds, Empress
Brilliants, White Cotingas, Club-winged Manakins, and others are
notable here. Bird watchers, therefore, will find visits to the Pacific
slope region of great interest.

Ecuador

Ecuador provides excellent bird watching opportunities both on
the mainland and in the famous Galapagos Islands. Indeed, about
1,500 species of birds are known from Ecuador. It is a particularly
scenic and attractive place with a variety of habitats and climatic
zones. On the mainland, for example, between sea level and the ice
and snow fields of the highest volcanic peaks in the high Andes, one
can visit the Amazon zone, the Pacific lowlands, the subtropical
zone, the temperate zone, and the paramo zone. Within each, a
variety of habitats provide the basis for survival of a diversified
wealth of birdlife. In addition, the Galapagos Islands also are a
magnet for bird watchers because of their many endemic birds and
other forms of wildlife and plantlife.

Mainland Areas

Amazon Zone

On the lower eastern slopes of the Andes and eastward from
there, Ecuador claims a portion of the upper Amazon Basin. This is
an area of dense cloud and rain forests. Vastness of the tropical
forests is characteristic of the region with a few important rivers
such as the Rio Pinto Grande and Rio Napo (especially good for
viewing birds) cutting through eventually to join the Amazon River
downstream. Some exceptional bird watching is possible in this
area. Among the species likely to be found are Turkey Vultures,
Black Vultures, Lesser Yellow-headed Vultures, Roadside Hawks,
Ringed Kingfishers, Amazon Kingfishers, Palm Tanagers, Paradise

Tanagers, Yellow-rumped Tanagers, Silver-beaked Tanagers, Barred Antshrikes, Blue-headed Parrots, and Black-capped Mockingthrushes. The Amazon zone also is an area of many primitive Indians who typically live in small huts along the rivers and use canoes for transportation. On the larger rivers, river boats are the main means of transportation for visitors. Some tourist agencies in Guayaquil and Quito have flights into small towns along the Amazon.

Pacific Lowlands Zone

On the western side of the Andes, the Pacific lowlands extend inland from sea level to elevations of about 5,000 feet. This is a tropical region of swamps, marshes, rivers, and streams. Agriculture centers around banana plantations, rice fields, and some dairy and cattle pastures. Bird watching can be very worthwhile here, and it is not unusual to see plenty of birdlife right beside the roads. For example, after the traveler leaves the port city of Guayaquil and heads toward the foothills of the Andes, large numbers of waterbirds appear in many places. These birds include Great Egrets, Snowy Egrets, Cattle Egrets, Little Blue Herons, Striated Herons, Pinnated Bitterns, American Anhingas, and Neotropic Cormorants. Other species frequently seen include Least Grebes, Wattled Jacanas, and Green Ibises. Birds of prey are common: Turkey Vultures, Black Vultures, Roadside Hawks, Savanna Hawks, Snail Kites, and Crested Caracaras. Sometimes Blue-headed Parrots appear and Scrub Blackbirds, Shiny Cowbirds, Groove-billed Anis, Tropical Kingbirds, and other birds also are observed. Frequently it is worthwhile to stop beside marshes and other spots which look interesting to search for birds.

Western Slopes of the Andes

Inland from the Pacific lowlands, there is an area subtropical in character between elevations of about 5,000 and 8,000 feet. It is strikingly beautiful, with many banana plantations and other farms in cleared areas in the foothills and dense tropical forests in higher untouched areas. Birdlife is very rich. In the vicinity of the town of Santo Domingo, for example, birds can be watched without difficulty along the edges of many forests beside secondary roads. Within a few minutes at one Indian village, for instance, I saw a Laughing Falcon, a Blue-gray Tanager, and a Yellow-rumped Tanager, plus several unidentified birds. Around the grounds of the Hotel Zaracay in Santo Domingo, a good variety of birds also can be seen. They include Common Tody Flycatchers, Rufous-tailed Hummingbirds, Blue-gray Tanagers, Yellow-tailed Orioles, and House Wrens. Elsewhere on the western slopes of the Andes at appropriate spots one might expect to see White-bearded

Manakins, Chestnut-mandibled Toucans, Collared Trogons, Masked Tityras, Rufous-tailed Jacamars, Blue-black Grassquits, Variable Seedeaters, and a long list of other species. Sometimes bird watching around the many spectacular waterfalls can be productive.

Temperate Zone

The temperate zone is found higher in the Andes still, between elevations of 8,500 feet and 11,500 feet. Included in the zone, therefore, is the beautiful Central Trough in which Quito, the capital city, is located. Although bird watchers will be impressed with the spectacular scenery on the western slopes of the Andes en route to the Central Trough, and may wish to stop now and again at interesting spots, most bird watching in the temperate zone usually is done within the Central Trough. This is an excellent area in which to observe birds. Indeed, a number of species frequently can be found in the gardens of the larger hotels in Quito. Some species that are likely to be seen include Eared Doves, Green Violetears, Black-tailed Trainbearers, Vermilion Flycatchers, Blue-and-white Swallows, Brown-bellied Swallows, Great Thrushes, and Rufous-collared Sparrows. Other species seen in the vicinity of Quito include White-collared Swifts, Hooded Siskins, Band-tailed Sierra Finches, and Dark-backed Goldfinches. Turkey Vultures and American Kestrels are not uncommon. Good highways and some secondary roads exist in the Central Trough, making it possible for

A typical scene on the bird-rich western slope of the Andes in Ecuador

The Central Trough of the Andes in Ecuador. Bird watching opportunities in this area are excellent.

bird watchers to drive into the countryside around Quito and explore new areas.

Paramo and Puna Zones

Above 11,500 feet in elevation, in the very high parts of the Andes known as the paramo zone, one finds high grasslands and shrubs. Living conditions there are rugged, yet some remarkable birds survive, including hummingbirds such as Andean Hillstars, Glowing Pufflegs, Black-thighed Pufflegs, Violet-throated Metaltails, and Blue-mantled Thornbills. Other species likely to be seen around marshy lakes include Cinereous Harriers, Andean Lapwings, Andean Gulls, and Slate-colored Coots. Sometimes flocks of Andean Lapwings and Plumbeous Sierra Finches may be seen at the higher elevations in the paramo zone.

Just below snowline on the highest peaks, prevailing fog and strong winds demonstrate the very harsh conditions of the puna zone. Bird watchers rarely visit there because the air is very thin and breathing is very difficult. Indeed, activity at any level of the paramo or puna zones involves the danger of altitude sickness. Never exert too much energy at these high elevations. Although the natives are fully capable of great activity, they are born into the conditions of the high Andes. Visitors are not so adapted.

Galapagos Islands

No bird watcher visiting Ecuador should fail to visit the famous Galapagos Islands located on the equator about 600 miles west of

Guayaquil. These islands have been world famous for their endemic birdlife and other wildlife since the time of Charles Darwin's visit on the H.M.S. *Beagle* in 1835. There are thirteen major islands and many smaller ones and rocks. Most are included in Galapagos National Park, which has established strict rules for visitors in order to protect and preserve the many unique species of animals and plants.

Most visitors to the Galapagos join tourist groups which employ the services of trained guides and cruise ships with long experience sailing amid the islands. I recommend that bird watchers join such tours because they will then have the opportunity to visit the most important locations on various islands where wildlife is very abundant. Guides and lecturers usually accompany such tours and are available to help people find and identify the wildlife and plant life they see. Bird watchers will want to make special efforts to try to see as many of the endemic birds of the Galapagos Islands as possible. One cannot see them all on a single tour because a few birds occur in areas or on islands which are not visited, or where visits are prohibited. Nevertheless most of the Galapagos endemic birds listed below can be seen.

Galapagos Penguin	Chatham Mockingbird
Waved Albatross	Small Ground Finch
Flightless Cormorant	Medium Ground Finch
Lava Heron	Large Ground Finch
Galapagos Hawk	Sharp-beaked Ground Finch
Galapagos Rail	Cactus Finch
Swallow-tailed Gull	Large Cactus Finch
Lava Gull	Vegetarian Finch
Galapagos Dove	Small Tree Finch
Large-billed Flycatcher	Medium Tree Finch
Galapagos Martin	Large Tree Finch
Galapagos Mockingbird	Woodpecker Finch
Charles Mockingbird	Mangrove Finch
Hood Mockingbird	Warbler Finch

When attempting to identify the so-called Darwin's finches, particular attention should be given to the *bills* of the birds rather than to patterns of plumage. Most finch identifications are made by critical examination of the bills. At first, it is frustrating to try to identify these important birds, but after a few attempts and careful reference to a good field guide, many (but not all) of the birds can be identified correctly. The illustrations in Michael Harris' *A Field Guide to the Birds of Galapagos* are particularly helpful.

One of the fascinating characteristics of Galapagos wildlife which astonishes people visiting the islands for the first time is the tameness of the animals. It is possible to touch many of the creatures although park regulations forbid doing this. In addition, one never should attempt to feed any of the animals. Nor should visitors venture far from the marked trails provided by the park service in areas selected especially for use by the public. To do so on certain islands could cause serious damage to nesting birds or other wildlife. Most tours to Galapagos visit selected islands. These are the islands discussed here, with details on the birds likely to be seen.

Santa Cruz

One of the highlights of a tour of the Galapagos Islands is a visit to Academy Bay on the south coast of Santa Cruz. Not only are opportunities available to photograph Galapagos Tortoises in natural settings at the nearby Charles Darwin Research Station, but Great Blue Herons, Galapagos Mockingbirds, and Yellow Warblers are frequently seen. In addition, Small Ground Finches, Medium Ground Finches, and Cactus Finches also are seen frequently in the arid zones visited by most tours. Sometimes Audubon's Shearwaters are seen flying low over the water of the Bay, and Brown Pelicans and Magnificent Frigatebirds are not uncommon. Some additional species occur in the interior of Santa Cruz, but time rarely permits visits to such areas, which are somewhat difficult to reach.

South Plaza

This tiny island located just off the east coast of Santa Cruz is one of the ecological jewels of the Galapagos Islands. It is unusually rich

South Plaza Island, Galapagos, is a major seabird nesting island and a delight to visit.

A Brown Pelican soaring over the seabird cliffs on South Plaza Island, Galapagos

in birdlife and usually becomes a favorite of most visitors. Since the island is so small, most tours spend only a few hours here, but such species as Audubon's Shearwaters, Red-billed Tropicbirds, Brown Pelicans, Blue-footed Boobies, Masked Boobies, Magnificent Frigatebirds, Swallow-tailed Gulls, Lava Gulls, Small Ground Finches, Medium Ground Finches, and Cactus Finches are likely to be seen without much difficulty. Large numbers of Swallow-tailed Gulls nest on cliffs on one side of the island and can be observed from a safe distance without much effort.

Baltra

Visitors who fly to or from the Galapagos will land or take off from tiny Baltra Island north of Santa Cruz. Although some finches can be seen near the runway, they will also be seen on other islands, and bird watchers should not be concerned if they do not have time here to devote to serious birding.

North Seymour

This is a small island located north of Baltra. Sometimes visits are made here for a few hours to look at nesting Magnificent Frigatebirds, but Galapagos Mockingbirds and some finches also may be seen.

James (Santiago)

James (or Santiago) is one of the larger islands and it offers bird watchers excellent bird finding opportunities. Generally, several locations on the island are visited. In the morning, for example, many tours go ashore at the southern end of James Bay, walk inland, then to a rocky coastline. Among the birds likely to be seen on such a visit are Brown Pelicans, Blue-footed Boobies,

The shoreline of North Seymour Island, Galapagos

Magnificent Frigatebirds, Lava Herons, Yellow-crowned Night Herons, Galapagos Hawks, Semipalmated Plovers, Wandering Tattlers, Whimbrels, Swallow-tailed Gulls, Lava Gulls, Brown Noddies, Galapagos Doves, Galapagos Mockingbirds, Yellow Warblers, Small Ground Finches, Medium Ground Finches, and Cactus Finches. The North American migrants, of course, would generally be seen only during winter or the migration periods.

A typical view of habitat just inland from the shoreline on James Island, Galapagos

A Yellow-crowned Night Heron standing on lava on the shoreline of James Island, Galapagos

An endemic Lava Gull. The birds occur only in the Galapagos Islands.

Sometimes, visitors also go ashore at the northern end of James Bay near a lagoon in which Greater Flamingoes and ducks are sometimes seen. Bird watching generally is good here and around the vegetation beside the lagoon. Species likely to be seen include Audubon's Shearwaters, White-vented Storm Petrels, Red-billed Tropicbirds, Brown Pelicans, Blue-footed Boobies, Magnificent Frigatebirds, Galapagos Hawks, American Oystercatchers, Whimbrels, Galapagos Doves, Vermilion Flycatchers, Large-billed Flycatchers, Galapagos Mockingbirds, Yellow Warblers, Small Ground Finches, Medium Ground Finches, Cactus Finches, and Vegetarian Finches. The shearwaters and storm petrels, of course, are seen in the bay whereas the best locations to see the various finches are amid the vegetation around the lagoon.

Charles (Floreana)

Charles (or Floreana) Island, located south of Santa Cruz, is one of the larger islands in the Galapagos. Sometimes, visits are made to Post Office Bay, which is mainly of historical interest, but bird watchers will find a visit to the flamingo lagoon at Point Cormorant worthwhile since Greater Flamingoes sometimes are seen here in fairly large numbers. Other birds sometimes seen here include Whimbrels, Black-necked Stilts, Semipalmated Plovers, and Ruddy Turnstones. A variety of other species, including some 211 finches, also may be seen here. Unfortunately, the Medium Tree Finch, which occurs only on this island, is restricted to the highlands and will not be seen.

San Cristobal

This island generally is not visited by most tours, and in my many visits to the Galapagos I have set foot on San Cristobal only once. However, if one wants to see the endemic Chatham Mockingbird a visit to the island is necessary. Fortunately, the birds are common and can be seen without too much difficulty. A good place to look for birds is to walk inland from Wreck Bay along a very rough road for 5 miles to the interior village of Progreso in the humid zone. As one approaches the village, a distinct change in vegetation can be seen. The area is much more green than the coastal arid zone. Caution should be taken, however, because there are some poisonous manzanillo trees along the road. They should not be touched.

Hood

Hood is one of the islands which visitors to the Galapagos always look forward to visiting. It is located in the southeastern part of the

The shoreline of Hood Island, Galapagos. Hood has several endemic species.

An adult Masked Booby on Hood Island, Galapagos

archipelago. Most people go ashore at Punta Suárez where landings are not too difficult. From here one can walk inland for a short distance to large colonies of nesting seabirds of several species. Bird watching is excellent on Hood, and particular efforts should be made to see Waved Albatrosses because this is the only place in the world where these splendid birds nest. However, great care must be taken not to disturb the big birds if they are incubating eggs or engaged in courtship displays.

Blue-footed Boobies on Hood Island, Galapagos

A Waved Albatross on its nest on Hood Island, Galapagos. These birds are endemic to this island.

A pair of Great Frigatebirds at their nest on Tower Island, Galapagos

The Hood Mockingbird also should not be overlooked because it is endemic to this island. Generally the mockingbirds are the first birds seen when coming ashore and not infrequently they hop around the feet of visitors the moment they step onto the island. Birds to be looked for on Hood include Blue-footed Boobies, Masked Boobies, Magnificent Frigatebirds, Swallow-tailed Gulls, Galapagos Doves, Yellow Warblers, Small Ground Finches, Large Cactus Finches, and Warbler Finches. Most of the finches can be seen in low vegetation a short distance behind the landing spot.

Tower

Tower Island is located in the northeastern section of the archipelago. It is not always visited by all tours although it provides excellent bird watching opportunities. Most ships arrive at Darwin Bay and go ashore at two different spots there. At one place, nesting Wedge-rumped Storm Petrels can be seen. Red-footed Boobies are common nesting birds in trees. Great Frigatebirds nest on the ground or in low vegetation or trees. Other birds also seen frequently on Tower include Audubon's Shearwaters, Red-billed Tropicbirds, Blue-footed Boobies, Masked Boobies, Yellow-crowned Night Herons, Lava Gulls, Swallow-tailed Gulls, Brown Noddies, Galapagos Doves, Short-eared Owls, Galapagos Mockingbirds, Large Ground Finches, and Sharp-beaked Ground Finches.

Isabela

Isabela, the largest island in the Galapagos, is about 70 miles long. Its rugged volcanic interior has six impressive shield volcanoes. Most visits to Isabela are to Tagus Cove where Galapagos Penguins, Audubon's Shearwaters, Red-billed

Tagus Cove, Isabela Island, Galapagos, is a popular landing area and a good place to see finches.

Tropicbirds, Brown Pelicans, Blue-footed Boobies, Flightless Cormorants, Magnificent Frigatebirds, Lava Herons, Yellow-crowned Night Herons, Swallow-tailed Gulls, Lava Gulls, Brown Noddies, Galapagos Martins, and various finches are seen frequently. Many of these birds can be seen as one takes a short boat trip around the cove, but a relatively short walk inland along a well-marked trail will produce some finches and perhaps some other birds.

Narborough (Fernandina)

Narborough (or Fernandina) Island contains one of the most active volcanoes in the world as well as impressive wildlife attractions. Most visitors go ashore at Punta Espinosa on the northeastern edge of the island. Here bird watchers will find a small colony of nesting Flightless Cormorants and such other birds (not necessarily nesting) as Audubon's Shearwaters, Brown Pelicans, Magnificent Frigatebirds, Great Blue Herons, Blue-footed Boobies, Brown Noddies, Galapagos Mockingbirds, and Small Ground Finches. Punta Espinosa is a particularly scenic spot offering superb views of nearby Isabela Island and its high volcanoes. In addition, old lava flows also reach down to the sea here from past eruptions of Narborough's volcano and it is possible to walk inland on the sharp, rough lava. Sometimes birds can be seen around a small mangrove lagoon located a short distance behind the beach.

A mangrove lagoon on Narborough Island, Galapagos. Finches and other birds sometimes are seen in the area.

Tropical forest along an Amazon waterway. Birds of many species are plentiful in such areas but sometimes difficult to see.

Peru

Peru is one of South America's outstanding countries for productive bird watching. It is similar to Ecuador in the general types of climatic and vegetation zones both east and west of the Andes. The birdlife of Peru, therefore, is extremely rich, and no fewer than 21 new species of birds have been discovered in recent years by scientists exploring remote sections of this beautiful and fascinating country. For bird watching purposes Peru can be divided into several different zones in addition to the offshore seabird island discussed in chapter 10. Maria Koepcke's *The Birds of the Department of Lima, Peru* is a very helpful field guide covering the high Andes, the western slopes of the Andes, and the Pacific lowlands and coastal areas.

Amazon Zone

Peru's section of the upper Amazon Basin includes extremely lush tropical forests rich in birds and other wildlife. Manu National Park preserves major examples of this primitive wilderness area. In general terms, the Amazon zone extends from the lower eastern slopes of the Andes eastward to Bolivia, Brazil, and Colombia. Much of the area is difficult to visit, even under ideal conditions, although bird watchers will not have difficulty getting to Iquitos near the junction of the Amazon and Rio Napo. Despite oil drilling 217

A Yagua Indian outside his hut in an Amazon forest in Peru

in the area, much superb forest still remains intact. Among birds likely to be seen in the vicinity of Iquitos are Turkey Vultures, Black Vultures, Plumbeous Kites, Black Caracaras, Large-billed Terns, Ringed Kingfishers, White-throated Toucans, Yellow-throated Woodpeckers, Chestnut-crowned Foliage-Gleaners, Tropical Kingbirds, Crested Oropendolas, Green Oropendolas, Yellow-rumped Caciques, and Red-capped Cardinals. Additional birds to be looked for include Roadside Hawks, Yellow-headed Caracaras, Bat Falcons, Yellow-billed Terns, Plumbeous Pigeons, Green Kingfishers, Spangled Cotingas, Black-capped Mockingthrushes, and Yellow-hooded Blackbirds. Others sometimes seen are Black Hawk-Eagles, Chestnut-fronted Macaws, Crimson-crested Woodpeckers, Yellow-tufted Woodpeckers, Thrush-like Wrens, Black-tailed Tityras, Silver-beaked Tanagers, and Blue-gray Tanagers.

Coastal Lowlands

West of the Peruvian Andes, bird watchers encounter a variety of habitats, including the long, narrow coastal desert which extends more than 2,000 miles from northern Peru south to Copiapo, Chile. On the western side of the desert, one finds the Pacific Ocean and coastline, while not too far east of the desert the foothills of the Andes begin their spectacular rise. Not surprisingly many areas within the coastal lowlands are of interest to bird watchers.

Lima, Peru's capital city, is the most logical starting point for bird watchers. In parks and gardens in the city, White-winged Doves, Amazilia Hummingbirds, Vermilion Flycatchers, Blue-and-white Swallows, Chestnut-throated Seedeaters, Rufous-collared Sparrows, and Hooded Siskins are likely to be seen. As soon as possible, however, bird watchers should leave Lima to explore more productive bird watching areas.

One such location, the Paracas Peninsula and nearby areas, is located about 225 kilometers south of Lima. To get there, drive south on the Pan American Highway through a section of the impressive coastal desert. Upon arrival at the Paracas Peninsula, which contains major pre-Columbian archaeological sites and a small museum worth visiting, several habitats will interest bird watchers. Along the bay, for example, gulls and terns easily observed include Southern Black-backed, Band-tailed, and Gray Gulls and Peruvian, Inca, and South American Terns. Chilean Flamingoes also are likely to be seen in some small lagoons beside the road near the archaeological museum.

From the bay, drive out to the tip of the peninsula over a poorly marked track through the desert sands. On the outer coast, most of the seabirds described in chapter 10 for the offshore seabird islands may be visible from atop the cliffs. Particular attention should be given to any Humboldt Penguins seen. Luck might bring a few Andean Condors feeding or flying overhead in the early morning. Many North American shorebirds also migrate and winter along the coast and bay.

On the dry, sandy peninsula itself, birdlife is relatively sparse, but more birds can be seen in the gardens around hotels. In such places, Amazilia Hummingbirds, Blue-and-white Swallows, Long-tailed Mockingbirds, and Rufous-collared Sparrows occur. In the various nearby agricultural fields, Peruvian Thick-knees, Short-tailed Field-Tyrants, Red-breasted Meadowlarks, Slender-billed Finches, Chestnut-throated Seedeaters, and Drab Seedeaters are sometimes seen.

Slopes of the Andes

The Andes form the backbone of Peru and obviously are of major interest and importance to bird watchers. Therefore it is desirable to begin bird watching in these mountains as soon as possible. One of the best routes into all elevations of the Peruvian Andes is the Central Highway, which runs for 400 kilometers from Lima to Huanuco. Bird watchers with experience along this route recommend going slowly and separating the trip into three parts over a period of about three days, so as to explore interesting areas without rushing.

The first part of the trip, from Lima to San Mateo, will provide a satisfactory introduction to the birdlife of the western slopes of the Peruvian Andes. At about the 44-kilometer marker, for example, some flower gardens attract Amazilia Hummingbirds, Oasis Hummingbirds, and Peruvian Sheartails. Along the Rimac River at kilometer 70, a park-like area sometimes produces White-tipped Doves, Eared Doves, Bare-faced Ground Doves, Chiguanco Thrushes, Long-tailed Mockingbirds, Scrub Blackbirds, and other species. At a gas station and restaurant facility near kilometer 99 below San Mateo, there may be sights of Andean Condors, Andean Swifts, and Giant Hummingbirds. A trail behind the restaurant goes to the river where White-capped Dippers occur. Nearby in vegetation, Black Metaltails, Sparkling Violetears, Carbonated Flower-Piercers, Cinereous Conebills, Blue-and-yellow Tanagers, and Rusty-bellied Brush-Finches might be encountered. At San Mateo a narrow road crosses a bridge and railroad tracks and leads upward to a mine in the upper temperate zone at about 10,500-feet elevation. Likely to be seen here are Bar-winged Cinclodes, White-browed Chat-Tyrants, Gray-hooded Sierra Finches, and other species.

After crossing the puna zone (described next), bird watchers will want to continue on the Central Highway past the Cerro de Pasco turnoff and begin the descent toward Huanuco in the valley below. Near La Quinua at about the 335-kilometer mark a park-like zone of trees provides good bird watching opportunities. The species reported here include Giant Hummingbirds, Shining Sunbeams, Black Metaltails, Sparkling Violetears, Red-crested Cotingas, Giant Conebills, Golden-billed Saltators, and Black Siskins.

Puna Zone

The second part of the trip reaches the high elevations of the Peruvian Andes, the puna zone above 11,500 feet, along the so-called Casapalca-Chinchan-Marcapomacocha loop. To reach this area, drive east on the Central Highway past Casapalca to the Marcapomacocha turnoff near kilometer 125. Follow the side road to the puna zone, where as little activity as possible should be undertaken because of the very thin atmosphere. In this area, lakes, ponds, bogs, grasslands, and rocky slopes will be seen and Ornate and Puna Tinamous, Silvery Grebes, Speckled Teal, Andean Geese, Mountain Caracaras, Andean Lapwings, Olivaceous Thornbills, and many others are likely to be observed. Very productive bird watching can be enjoyed in this high puna zone.

Upon finishing birding in the puna zone, return to the Central

A typical scene in the puna zone of the Andes of Peru

Highway for the third part of the trip and continue to the high pass at an elevation of almost 15,000 feet. This is an area of glacial lakes and snowy peaks but few birds. However, Torrent Ducks sometimes are seen near small waterfalls on a stream beside the highway between kilometer 199 and the turnoff to Tarma. In a particularly good raptor area between the Tarma turnoff and the city of Junin, Puna Hawks, Cinereous Harriers, Mountain Caracaras, Aplomado Falcons, and American Kestrels have been reported.

Some 15 kilometers north of Junin, the highway passes Lake Junin, where birdlife is very abundant. Bird watchers should look for Puna Ibises, Andean Geese, Crested Ducks, Speckled Teal, Puna Teal, Mountain Caracaras, Slate-colored Coots, Andean Lapwings, Andean Gulls, and Rufous-backed Negritos in this area.

Temperate Cloud Forest

One of Peru's most extraordinary bird watching areas is the splendid, fog-bound temperate cloud forest near the Carpish Pass at kilometer 467 on the Central Highway between Huanuco and Tingo Maria. Dense stands of bamboo and trees laden with bromeliads and moss are characteristic of the area. A trail near a shed at kilometer 475 leads to a tea plantation lower in the valley. This trail 221 can be used by bird watchers if a small tip of perhaps ten *soles* is given to the man at the shed. Dozens of species of birds typical of Eastern Andean cloud forests occur in this area. Some species sometimes seen along the first part of the trail include Collared Incas, Gray-breasted Mountain-Toucans, Barred Fruiteaters, Mountain Caciques, Yellow-scarfed Tanagers, Hooded Mountain-Tanagers, and Plush-capped Finches. Some of the birds more typical of the higher reaches of the trail include Bronzy Incas, Golden-headed Quetzals, Green-and-black Fruiteaters, Green Jays, Golden-collared Honeycreepers, Blue-winged Mountain Tanagers, and Black-and-white Seedeaters.

Elfin Forest and Pajonal Zones

The Elfin forest (treeline) and pajonal zones extend from about 9,500 feet in elevation upward to about 12,000 feet. This humid area has isolated groves of trees and scattered bushes between which are open meadows and bogs. The area is of particular interest and importance to ornithologists because it is one of the most remote and least explored areas in Peru. A number of new species of birds have been discovered here within recent years.

Unfortunately for bird watchers, visits to these zones are not ordinary bird watching efforts. One requires guides, pack animals, tents, food, water, and a week or more of time in order to properly explore some of the closest examples of these zones where the extremely rare birds occur. Most bird watchers will not be capable of this type of effort, but those few individuals who would like to attempt the adventure can secure full details in Theodore Parker and John O'Neill's article "Introduction to Bird-Finding in Peru: Part II" appearing in *Birding* (1976, 8:205-16).

Argentina

Much bird watching can be done in various sections of Argentina, but one of the most interesting areas is Tierra del Fuego (and even Cape Horn) at the extreme southern tip of South America. To reach Tierra del Fuego, one generally flies from Buenos Aires to Rio Grande, then takes a taxi or bus south to Ushuaia on the Beagle Channel. It is possible to drive from Buenos Aires to Ushuaia, but the trip is very long and difficult.

Bird watchers visiting this isolated section of South America will not have available a good, pocket-size field guide, but some references are available. The most important is *Birds of Isle Grande (Tierra del Fuego)* by Philip S. Humphrey et al. Also helpful because they include some of the birds seen in Tierra del Fuego are George E. Watson's *Birds of the Antarctic and Sub-Antarctic* and Robin W. Woods' *The Birds of the Falkland Islands*. In addition, a tremendous amount of general natural history and tourist information about Tierra del Fuego is contained in Rae Natalie Prosser de Goodall's *Tierra del Fuego*, available in some book stores and camera shops in Ushuaia and perhaps elsewhere in Argentina. The text is in both Spanish and English.

Cape Horn

Most bird watchers will not be able to visit Cape Horn unless they are returning from Antarctica on ships such as the M.S. *Lindblad Explorer*, which approaches the desolate islands of Cape Horn on her return from each Antarctic voyage. This provides bird watchers on the ship with excellent opportunities to watch seabirds. Among the species likely to be seen without difficulty are Magellanic Penguins, Wandering Albatrosses, Black-browed Albatrosses, Southern Giant Fulmars, White-chinned Petrels, Sooty Shearwaters, King Shags, Brown Skuas, and South American Terns.

Beagle Channel

As a ship sails north past the Horn and arrives at the eastern (Atlantic) end of the Beagle Channel, the scenery becomes spectacular. High snow-capped mountains line both sides of the Channel. The Channel is an international border between Chile and

Seabirds are abundant around Cape Horn, South America, and are easily seen from the decks of ships rounding the Horn.

Argentina to a point west of Ushuaia. Argentina claims the northern side, Chile the southern side. As the ship sails westward in the Channel toward Ushuaia, two zones of vegetation are passed. At the eastern entrance, the steep slopes of the mountains and valleys form an Evergreen Forest zone consisting mostly of Winter's Bark, Evergreen Beech, Dwarf Maiten, and hard bogs. Soon, however, the vegetation along both sides of the Channel becomes deciduous forest consisting mostly of high deciduous beech, low deciduous beech, and sphagnum bogs.

Here and there along the Channel's north side one sees houses and farms—the famous *estancias* or sheep farms. There are no roads leading to these places, and all are open to visitors *only by prior invitation.* However, bird watching in the channel is productive from a ship. Species likely to be seen include Magellanic Penguins, Wandering Albatrosses, Black-browed Albatrosses, Southern Giant Fulmars, White-chinned Petrels, Sooty Shearwaters, Greater Shearwaters, King Shags, Southern Black-backed Gulls, and South American Terns.

Tierra del Fuego National Park

Bird watchers visiting the Ushuaia area can enjoy excellent birding in Tierra del Fuego National Park whose entrance is located on Route 3 about six miles west of town. The park is a spectacular mountainous area covering 154,000 acres with splendid snow-capped peaks, forests, bogs, fields, lakes, and rivers, all of which are productive habitats for birds and wildflowers. The park is mostly within the deciduous forest zone and has extensive stands of high deciduous beech and low deciduous beech. *Usnea* lichens are

Tierra del Fuego National Park, Argentina. The park offers excellent bird watching opportunities in an extremely attractive setting.

abundant and hang from most of the trees, adding a great deal of charm to the scene. Abundant displays of wildflowers also appear in the park during the austral summer (December to February).

There are several roads in the park as well as a hotel and restaurant. One road runs to Ensenada—an inlet or cove overlooking part of the Beagle Channel. It is easy to drive along this road but I recommend walking instead and looking for birds en route to the Beagle Channel several miles away. The road passes through a variety of habitats and affords opportunities to see a good cross-section of the area's common birdlife. During one series of short visits to the park, I observed the following species: Great Grebes, Neotropic Cormorants, Black-crowned Night Herons, Ashy-headed Geese, Upland Geese, Flightless Steamer Ducks, Southern Wigeons, Bicolored Hawks, Chimango Caracaras, American Kestrels, Magellanic Oystercatchers, Southern Black-backed Gulls, Dark-bellied Cinclodes, Thorn-tailed Rayaditos, Fire-eyed Diucons, Rufous-backed Negritos, White-crested Elaenias, Chilean Swallows, House Wrens, Austral Thrushes, Gray-hooded Sierra-Finches, Rufous-collared Sparrows, and Black-chinned Siskins.

Camping is allowed in this park and additional information can be secured at the ranger station just inside the park's entrance.

Brazil

Brazil is the largest country in South America and contains an emormous variety of habitats. Perhaps the most interesting portion of the country is the Amazon Basin with its exceptionally rich birdlife, wildlife, and plant life. Since much of Amazonia still remains untouched tropical forest, the only effective way to visit much of the area is by river boats or ships such as the M.S. *Lindblad Explorer* which make voyages of 2,500 miles or more from the mouth of the Amazon upriver. To describe some of the bird watching possibilities along the Amazon it is necessary to divide the river into sections beginning near the mouth at the Atlantic Ocean.

Belém to Rio Pará Channels

About a hundred miles upriver from the Amazon's mouth lies the large port city of Belém, which is the largest city along the Amazon. Despite Belém's large population, virgin tropical forest still exists only a few miles from the city. Even in more disturbed areas closer to the city, however, birdlife is abundant. Indeed, as many as 500 species of birds are known from Belém. By far the most interesting bird watching area in this section of the lower Amazon consists of the Rio Pará channels through which ships of considerable size pass en route to the Amazon River proper and to various cities upriver.

Tropical forest along the Rio Para channels offer excellent birding opportunities from the decks of a ship sailing upriver or downriver.

These channels are unusually narrow, some only a few hundred feet wide. Lush tropical forests crowd against the banks of the channels. Birdlife is everywhere, and one need only sit on the deck of a ship and look for birds with binoculars as the ship passes close to the banks and curtain-like forest. Often, hawks, macaws, and other species fly overhead or cross from one side of the channel to the other. Among the species likely to be seen along the Rio Pará channels are Capped Herons, Turkey Vultures, Black Vultures, Swallow-tailed Kites, Plumbeous Kites, Roadside Hawks, Great Black Hawks, Laughing Falcons, Yellow-headed Caracaras, Crested Caracaras, Bat Falcons, Large-billed Terns, Blue-and-yellow Macaws, Chestnut-fronted Macaws, Mealy Parrots, Smooth-billed Anis, White-throated Toucans, Channel-billed Toucans, Lineated Woodpeckers, Crimson-crested Woodpeckers, Purple-throated Cotingas, Great Kiskadees, White-winged Swallows, Green Oropendolas, Yellow-rumped Caciques, Solitary Black Caciques, and Blue-gray Tanagers.

Rio Pará to Santarém

After leaving the Rio Pará channels, ships sail upriver to the city of Santarém at the mouth of the Rio Tapajós. En route they pass the mouth of the Rio Xingu. The Amazon is very wide in this section but ships often sail close to one forested bank of the river or to the other bank as the river pilots follow the best and deepest navigation channels. The M.S. *Lindblad Explorer* makes one or two stops each day to allow exploration of smaller rivers flowing into the Amazon. Some of the birds likely to be seen in such places include Neotropic Cormorants, American Anhingas, White-necked Herons, Capped Herons, Striated Herons, Great Egrets, Snowy Egrets, Horned Screamers, Black-bellied Whistling Ducks, Muscovy Ducks, Turkey Vultures, Black Vultures, Snail Kites, Slender-billed Kites, Roadside Hawks, Black-collared Hawks, Laughing Falcons, Black Caracaras, Yellow-headed Caracaras, Crested Caracaras, Wattled Jacanas, Southern Lapwings, Large-billed Terns, Yellow-billed Terns, Black Skimmers, Plumbeous Pigeons, Festive Parrots, Mealy Parrots, Greater Anis, Smooth-billed Anis, Ringed Kingfishers, Amazon Kingfishers, Bronzy Jacamars, White-throated Jacamars, Black Nunbirds, Swallow-wings, Toco Toucans, Lineated Woodpeckers, Pied Water-Tyrants, White-headed Marsh-Tyrants, Fork-tailed Flycatchers, Great Kiskadees, White-winged Swallows, Yellow-rumped Caciques, Red-breasted Blackbirds, Blue-gray Tanagers, Red-capped Cardinals, and Saffron Finches.

Rio Tapajós to Rio Negro

The section of the Amazon between the Rio Tapajós and the Rio Negro contains excellent bird watching areas, especially if some of the many smaller rivers are explored by boat. For example, behind the Boca Da Valeria are many placid "lakes" which contain

Birders from the M.S. **Lindblad Explorer** landing along the Rio Tapajós, Amazonia. Such shore trips allow bird watching in remote sections of Amazonia.

Disturbed tropical forest along an Amazon tributary below the Rio Negro. Many land and water birds are seen in such places.

abundant numbers of birds including Neotropic Cormorants, American Anhingas, White-necked Herons, Striated Herons, Great Egrets, Turkey Vultures, Black Vultures, Plumbeous Kites, Snail Kites, Roadside Hawks, Laughing Falcons, Yellow-headed Caracaras, Limpkins, Wattled Jacanas, Large-billed Terns, Plumbeous Pigeons, Chestnut-fronted Macaws, Canary-winged Parakeets, Tui Parakeets, Greater Anis, Ringed Kingfishers, Amazon Kingfishers, Green Kingfishers, Black Nunbirds, Black-necked Aracaris, Spot-breasted Woodpeckers, Green-and-Rufous Woodpeckers, Rufous-tailed Foliage-Gleaners, White-headed Marsh-Tyrants, Great Kiskadees, Lesser Kiskadees, White-winged Swallows, Black-capped Mockingthrushes, Crested Oropendolas, Yellow-rumped Caciques, Blue-gray Tanagers, Silver-beaked Tanagers, Red-capped Cardinals, Lined Seedeaters, and Saffron Finches.

At the junction of the Rio Negro and the Amazon, people always are impressed with the so-called "wedding of the waters" where the cola-colored water of the Rio Negro flows side by side for miles with the muddy Amazon water before finally mixing into the Amazon downriver. Not far upriver on the Rio Negro is the old rubber-boom city of Manaus, to which bird watchers can fly if they wish to make short visits to the middle Amazon region. Untouched tropical forests still exist near the edges of the city. Here bird watchers have opportunities to see an adequate variety of birds without having to hire boats to get into some of the more remote rivers flowing into the Amazon. In addition, a section of the Trans-Amazon Highway passes near Manaus and it can be used to explore some sections of the nearby forest.

Rio Negro to Leticia, Colombia

The long section of the Amazon between the mouth of the Rio Negro and Leticia, Colombia, hundreds of miles upriver, contains many remote tributary rivers and streams which are a delight to explore. These beautiful forest-lined waterways almost always produce good numbers of birds of interest to birders. Unfortunately, most of these rivers are almost impossible to reach unless one operates from a ship such as the M. S. *Lindblad Explorer* which makes special stops at them for the specific purpose of exploring them and finding birds and other wildlife. In some instances, however, river boats sailing from one city or town along the Amazon to another might be able to transport bird watchers to some of the spots and help to secure small boats for use on the smaller waterways. Many birds are likely to be observed on these smaller channels. Some examples include Neotropic Cormorants, American Anhingas, White-necked Herons, Capped Herons, Striated Herons, Green Ibises, Horned Screamers, Black-bellied Whistling Ducks, Turkey Vultures, Black Vultures, Greater Yellow-headed Vultures, Swallow-tailed Kites, Plumbeous Kites, Slender-billed Kites, Roadside Hawks, Great Black Hawks, Black-collared Hawks, Black Hawk-Eagles, Ospreys, Black Caracaras, Yellow-headed Caracaras, Crested Caracaras, Orange-breasted Falcons, Bat Falcons, Hoatzins, Wattled Jacanas, Large-billed Terns, Yellow-billed Terns, Black Skimmers, Blue-and-yellow Macaws, Scarlet Macaws, Chestnut-fronted Macaws, Mealy Parrots, Canary-winged Parakeets, Tui Parakeets, White-eyed Parakeets, Greater Anis, Smooth-billed Anis, Ferruginous Pygmy-Owls, Black-tailed Trogons, Collared Trogons, Ringed Kingfishers, Amazon Kingfishers, Green Kingfishers, Chestnut Jacamars, Black Nunbirds, Swallow-wings, White-throated Toucans, Black-necked Aracaris, Yellow-throated Woodpeckers, Lineated Woodpeckers, Crimson-crested Woodpeckers, Yellow-tufted Woodpeckers, Spot-breasted Woodpeckers, Spangled Cotingas, Masked Tityras, Amazonian Umbrellabirds, Pied Water-Tyrants, Fork-tailed Flycatchers, Tropical Kingbirds, Lesser Kiskadees, Dusky-chested Flycatchers, White-rumped Swallows, Blacked-capped Mockingthrushes, Crested Oropendolas, Yellow-rumped Caciques, Red-breasted Blackbirds, Silver-beaked Tanagers, Masked Crimson Tanagers, Red-capped Cardinals, and Lesser Seed-Finches.

Surinam

Surinam is a relatively small country in northeastern South America. In recent years, it has started to attract the attention of bird watchers and probably will become increasingly popular as a bird watching area in the future. For convenience, the country can be divided into three topographic zones, each of which contains some distinctive birdlife. Some of the best bird watching areas are in Surinam's fine nature preserves scattered throughout the country. The point of departure for visits to any of them is the capital, Paramaribo. Regardless of where one watches birds in Surinam, F. Haverschmidt's *Birds of Surinam* is the basic reference book available.

Coastal Plain

The coastal plain, low swampy country, extends inland for a distance of up to 40 kilometers. Extensive mangrove areas fringe the coast, and many brackish and freshwater lagoons lie behind the coastal mangroves. Sandy ridges also are found within the marshes behind the mangroves. Two outstanding preserves on the coastal plain, Wia-Wia Nature Reserve and Galibi Nature Reserve, provide excellent bird watching opportunities. Some of the birds which occur on the coastal plain in suitable habitats are Brown Pelicans, Neotropic Cormorants, White-necked Herons, Striated Herons, Great Egrets, Black-crowned Night Herons, Yellow-crowned Night Herons, Wood Storks, Jabirus, Scarlet Ibises, Roseate Spoonbills, Black-bellied Whistling Ducks, White-cheeked Pintails, Black Vultures, Hook-billed Kites, Snail Kites, Slender-billed Kites, Savanna Hawks, Roadside Hawks, Rufous Crab Hawks, Ospreys, Peregrine Falcons, Orange-breasted Falcons, Limpkins, Rufous-necked Wood-Rails, Gray-necked Wood-Rails, Wattled Jacanas, Yellow-billed Terns, Black Skimmers, Blue-and-yellow Macaws, Painted Parakeets, Orange-winged Parrots, Mangrove Cuckoos, Greater Anis, Barn Owls, Spectacled Owls, Great Potoos, Common Potoos, Green-throated Mangos, Black-throated Mangos, Tufted Coquettes, White-chinned Sapphires, Glittering-throated Emeralds, White-tailed Trogons, Green-tailed Jacamars, Pied Puffbirds, Arrowhead Piculets, Spot-breasted Woodpeckers, Lineated Woodpeckers, Straight-billed Woodcreepers, Yellow-throated Spinetails, Great Antshrikes, Common Attilas, Cinereous Becards, Yellow-breasted Flycatchers, Shiny Cowbirds, and Yellow Orioles.

Savanna

Inland from the coastal plain is a narrow savanna, consisting of open grassland and bushes growing on sandy soil. There also are forested areas in the savanna.

Some examples of savanna birds are Little Tinamous, King Vultures, Turkey Vultures, Gray-headed Kites, White-tailed Hawks, Roadside Hawks, Black Hawk-Eagles, Little Chachalacas, Crested Bobwhites, Common Ground Doves, Blue Ground Doves, Red-shouldered Macaws, Squirrel Cuckoos, Striped Cuckoos, Common Potoos, Lesser Nighthawks, White-tailed Nightjars, Band-rumped Swifts, Fork-tailed Palm Swifts, Ruby-topaz Hummingbirds, Green-tailed Goldenthroats, Barred Woodcreepers, Barred Antshrikes, Spangled Cotingas, Purple-throated Fruitcrows, Golden-headed Manakins, Black Manakins, Bran-colored Flycatchers, Black-billed Thrushes, Green Oropendolas, Red-shouldered Tanagers, and Grassland Sparrows.

Interior Forests

In the interior of Surinam, bird watchers will find vast tropical forests, largely untouched and containing a splendid assortment of birds. Many of these areas are unexplored, but two of the more accessible locations where bird watchers can sample some of the birdlife of the interior forests are the Brownsberg Nature Park and the Raleighvallen/Voltzberg Nature Preserve. The former can be reached by road in about two hours from Paramaribo. It is an extremely interesting and scenic area with trails and a few roads leading into excellent virgin forest which provides exciting bird watching opportunities.

Some examples of the birdlife of these interior forests include Variegated Tinamous, Lesser Yellow-headed Vultures, Crested Eagles, Harpy Eagles, Red-throated Caracaras, Black Curassows, White-headed Piping Guans, Scarlet Macaws, Caica Parrots, Black-bellied Cuckoos, Long-tailed Hermits, Blue-chinned Sapphires, Black-tailed Trogons, Black-throated Trogons, Blue-crowned Motmots, Barred Woodcreepers, Red-billed Woodcreepers, Rufous-rumped Foliage-Gleaners, Fasciated Antshrikes, White-plumed Antbirds, Ringed Antpipits, Guianan Red Cotingas, White Bellbirds, Guianan Cock-of-the-Rocks, Musician Wrens, Guianan Gnatcatchers, Tawny-crowned Greenlets, Swallow-Tanagers, and Paradise Tanagers.

Venezuela

Since Venezuela has 352,141 square miles of rich wildlife habitat, this country is obviously of major importance to bird watchers. Indeed, its recorded avifauna numbers no fewer than 1,296 species—roughly 44% of the entire South American avifauna! Moreover, 46 species of birds are endemic to Venezuela. Thus bird watchers have splendid opportunities to see an exciting sample of South America's rich birdlife. *A Guide to the Birds of Venezuela*, written by Rodolphe Meyer de Schauensee and William H. Phelps, Jr., is the standard field guide to the country's birds; it is well illustrated with many color plates.

Part of the reason why the birdlife of Venezuela is so rich is that its varied habitats extend through four major life zones: tropical zone (sea level to 4,500-5,500 feet), subtropical zone (4,500-5,500 to 7,500-8,500 feet), temperate zone (7,500-8,500 to 9,500-11,500 feet), and parámo zone (9,500-11,500 feet to snow line). In addition, the country has several major river systems of which the Orinoco (more than 1,500 miles long) is the most important. Some others include the Rio Guaviare, Rio Atabapo, Rio Meta, Rio Ventuari, and Rio Catatumbo. Lake Maracaibo also is an important aquatic area.

The mountain ranges of Venezuela also are major wildlife habitats. Among them are the Sierra de Perijá, Cordillera de Mérida, Cordillera de la Costa Central, Cadena del Interior, Sierra de San Luis, Sierra de Aroa, and the Cordillera de la Costa Oriental. Llanos, grassy savannas, forested lowlands, rain forests, and other areas provide still more habitats for birds.

Travel within Venezuela is relatively easy by South American standards. Caracas is the usual port of entry into the country. From there one can use modern highways to visit all major cities, birding along the way, and follow other paved roads to reach many important towns. To reach smaller, more remote villages, a network of good unpaved roads is available. Commercial airplane flights also make visits to remote locations possible. Finally, river boats offer adventurous bird watchers colorful opportunities to explore many river systems. However, a good knowledge of Spanish would be necessary to take full advantage of this type of birding.

Additional Reading

Bates, H. W.
  1975   The Naturalist on the River Amazons. Dover Publications, Inc., New York.

Besch, D.
  1976   Travel Notes. *Animal Kingdom*, 79 (6): 33-34. (Contains helpful information on travel in Surinam.)

Davis T. H.

1974   Supplement to a Birding Expedition to Western Colombia. *Birding*, 6 (3): 114-15.

1975   The Tinalandia Hotel, Pichincha Prov., Ecuador. *Birding*, 7 (6): 322-27.

Dunning, J. S.

1970   Portraits of Tropical Birds. Livingston Publishing Co., Wynnewood, Pa.

Gochfeld, M., and G. Tudor

1974   A Birding Expedition to Western Colombia. *Birding*, 6 (3): 101-14.

Hanebrink, E. L.

1974   Birding in Ecuador. *Birding*, 6 (6): 273-80.

Mittermeier, R. A., and K. Milton

1976   Jungle Jackpot. *Animal Kingdom*, 79 (6): 26-32. (Information on nature study in Surinam's nature parks.)

Morrison, T.

1972   Land Above the Clouds: Wildlife of the Andes. Universe Books, New York.

Murphy, R. C.

1925   Bird Islands of Peru. G. P. Putnam's Sons, New York.

Parker, T. A., and J. P. O'Neill

1976a   An Introduction to Bird Finding in Peru: Part I. The Paracas Peninsula and Central Highway (Lima to Huanuco City). *Birding*, 8 (2): 140-44.

1976b   Introduction to Bird-Finding in Peru: Part II. The Carpish Pass Region of the Eastern Andes along the Central Highway. *Birding*, 8 (3): 205-16.

Thornton, I.

1971   Darwin's Islands: A Natural History of the Galapagos. Natural History Press, Garden City, N.Y.

White, A., B. Epler, and C. Gilbert

1972   Galapagos Guide. Charles Darwin Research Station, Santa Cruz, Galapagos.

21
ANTARCTIC BIRDING

Until recently, people wanting to bird watch on the biologically rich Antarctic islands and surrounding waters, let alone the equally rich edges of the Antarctic continent, were unable to do so because of enormous transportation and related problems. Such remote and exciting polar regions were accessible only to explorers and scientists engaged in full-scale exploration and field studies, some of which required "wintering over" in Antarctica.

During the past decade or so, however, visits to these high latitudes have become possible on the M.S. *Lindblad Explorer*, which makes several Antarctic voyages each austral summer. Hence, bird watchers can now visit areas where, until just a few years ago, only world-famous explorers had set foot. Although Antarctic voyages are expensive, they are extraordinary experiences and produce a number of life birds which do not occur elsewhere.

Most of the *Lindblad Explorer*'s voyages to Antarctica are restricted to the South Atlantic-Scotia Arc-Antarctic Peninsula-Drake Passage sector where there are outstanding islands rich in birds and mammals, splendid scenery, and necessary support facilities. Areas of particular interest to bird watchers include the Falkland Islands (discussed in chapter 10), the Antarctic Convergence, Shag Rocks, South Georgia, islands in the South Orkney and South Shetland groups, the Antarctic Peninsula, and islands off the west coast of the Antarctic Peninsula. During the austral summer, air temperatures are relatively moderate, generally around the freezing mark or a little higher. Sometimes parkas are unnecessary, and only rarely do temperatures drop far below freezing. Therefore, people who do not like intensely cold weather should not be discouraged from visiting this part of the Antarctic. Indeed, the Antarctic Peninsula sometimes is referred to as the "banana belt," and by polar standards it usually lives up to that description during the austral summer (December through February).

Bird watchers visiting the Antarctic will want to carry with them a copy of George E. Watson's *Birds of the Antarctic and Sub-Antarctic* which illustrates all of the birds known to occur on the continent, surrounding islands, and seas.

Antarctic Convergence

Ships such as the *Lindblad Explorer* generally sail south en route to the Antarctic islands and Antarctica after first visiting the Falkland Islands. While at sea en route to these southern islands, bird watchers have many opportunities to enjoy spectacular pelagic birding—particularly when the ship crosses an invisible line known as the Antarctic Convergence where colder Antarctic waters meet with warmer Sub-Antarctic waters. The birdlife along the Antarctic Convergence often is extremely abundant; thousands of prions and other species frequently are seen over the expanses of the ocean around the ship. In December 1975, for example, I crossed the Convergence at about 53° 16'S, 45° 00'W and had splendid views of Wandering Albatrosses, Black-browed Albatrosses, Gray-headed Albatrosses, Southern Giant Fulmars, White-chinned Petrels, Cape Pigeons, Antarctic and/or Slender-billed Prions, Wilson's Storm Petrels, and Black-bellied Storm Petrels.

Shag Rocks

Occasionally ships such as the *Lindblad Explorer* sail past a remote group of islets known as Shag Rocks. Landing on the rocks generally is impossible, but birds such as Wandering Albatrosses, Black-browed Albatrosses, Light-mantled Sooty Albatrosses, Southern Giant Fulmars, Cape Pigeons, prions of various species, Wilson's Storm Petrels, and Blue-eyed Shags can be seen flying around the islets. Apparently the shags nest on them.

South Georgia

South of Shag Rocks, one of the islands sometimes visited by the M.S. *Lindblad Explorer* is South Georgia. Bird watchers landing on this large island will soon discover that it is a very exciting place to observe a variety of nesting seabirds. In addition, it is a place exceptionally rich in history because of its many decades of use as a major whaling station. Fortunately, it is no longer used for that deplorable activity, but one can still walk among the old, well-preserved buildings at Grytviken on Cumberland Bay.

Upon seeing the coastline of South Georgia for the first time, most people have the impression of being thrust back into the Ice Age and are awed by great glacier-filled valleys, rugged snow-covered mountains, and impressive ice- and snow-covered coastal cliffs. Viewed against these spectacular backgrounds are countless

The snow and ice covered coastline of bird-rich South Georgia in the Antarctic

seabirds which live along the outer edges of the island. Bird watchers will have a glorious time watching the comings and goings of these birds as a ship sails along South Georgia's coastline.

Exciting as bird watching is from on board a ship along the coast, South Georgia has much more to offer on land during the austral summer when the climate is relatively gentle. Here and there are valleys, coastal bays, and little satellite islands which become relatively free of ice and snow for a few months. In these areas are impressive concentrations of wildlife, such as the great breeding colonies of albatrosses, penguins, and other seabirds. Here, too, are fine colonies of Elephant Seals and other sea mammals.

One of the most exciting of these areas is beautiful Bay of Isles where, in 1912, the greatest of all students of seabirds, Robert Cushman Murphy, made some of his first studies of pelagic birds. Here, too, he made the first accurate map of this part of the South Georgia coastline, including the naming of many islands, points, glaciers, and other geographic features. Today, just as in Dr. Murphy's time, everyone who lands here is captivated by three special attractions.

The first is a very large and easily reached colony of King Penguins located half a mile inland between Grace and Lucas glaciers. King Penguins are the second largest species of penguins and are superb birds to watch and photograph coming ashore, walking inland, or at their nesting colonies. Nowhere in the

Antarctic is there a setting more spectacular than this one on South Georgia.

The second outstanding bird watching attraction, also in Bay of Isles, is Albatross Island (so named by Dr. Murphy) on which one finds a large nesting colony of Wandering Albatrosses. These great birds are a never-to-be-forgotten sight. Here, too, one can also see South Georgia's smallest and rarest native bird—the endemic South Georgia Pipit. On the main island this species has been seriously reduced in numbers by introduced rats and other animals, but the birds are still relatively common and easily observed on Albatross Island. Sometimes the recently arrived Speckled Teal and the native Yellow-billed Pintail also are seen on the island.

Elsehul is another of South Georgia's ornithological attractions. It is located north of Bay of Isles along the coastline. Its steep, tussock-grass-covered cliffs provide ideal nest sites for large numbers of Light-mantled Sooty Albatrosses, Gray-headed Albatrosses, and Black-browed Albatrosses. Above the tussock grass, on talus slopes, a large Macaroni Penguin colony also is of interest to bird watchers because this is the only spot where these birds can be seen in such large numbers on most voyages to the Antarctic.

Bird watchers should not expect to see large numbers of bird species on South Georgia, but those which do occur there are

King Penguins, and a Gentoo Penguin, walking along a beach in Bay of Isles, South Georgia. A large King Penguin rookery is located a short distance inland.

A colony of nesting King Penguins, Bay of Isles, South Georgia

unusually fascinating. Listed here, for example, are the birds I observed on South Georgia during a four-day visit in December 1975: King Penguins, Gentoo Penguins, Macaroni Penguins, Wandering Albatrosses, Black-browed Albatrosses, Gray-headed Albatrosses, Light-mantled Sooty Albatrosses, Southern Giant Fulmars, Cape Pigeons, Snow Petrels, Antarctic Prions, White-chinned Petrels, Wilson's Storm Petrels, South Georgia Diving Petrels, Blue-eyed Shags, Speckled Teal, American Sheathbills, Brown Skuas, Southern Black-backed Gulls, Antarctic Terns, and South Georgia Pipits.

South Orkney Islands

The South Orkney Islands, about 1,440 kilometers southeast of Tierra del Fuego, sometimes are included on the voyages of the *Lindblad Explorer* when she visits Antarctica. Signy Island, one of four main islands, and the one of greatest biological importance, sometimes is landed upon if weather and ice conditions are favorable. In December 1975, for example, I spent an afternoon ashore on Jepson Rocks and at Jepson Point. A variety of seabirds were seen there, including a few Adelie Penguins. In addition, Cape Pigeons were found nesting along with Snow Petrels and Antarctic

A nesting Snow Petrel, Signy Island, South Orkneys

Terns. These species are typical of true Antarctic birds and characteristically were exceptionally tame. It was possible to take close-up photographs without difficulty. Some Southern Giant Fulmars, including some birds in the beautiful white color phase, also nest on Signy Island.

A white phase Southern Giant Fulmar on its nest on Signy Island, South Orkneys

A Cape Pigeon on its nest on Signy Island, South Orkneys

South Shetland Islands

The South Shetland Islands are located about 480 kilometers west of the South Orkneys and 770 kilometers south of Cape Horn. They are exciting islands for birds watchers to visit because they form a roughly parallel line west of the west coast of the Antarctic Peninsula. Among the islands in this group which are visited on most Antarctic voyages are remote Elephant Island, King George Island, and Deception Island.

Landing on isolated Elephant Island is particularly memorable because few places in Antarctica are as famous, yet as remote and rarely visited, as this. In addition, few places occupy as important a role in the history of Antarctica and the expeditions to that continent. It was here on these rugged, inhospitable coasts that Sir Ernest Shackleton and his crew from the ice-crushed exploration ship *Endurance* made a desperate landing months after they took to the ice of the Weddell Sea. Since then, all who have landed on Elephant Island think first of Shackleton and his life-and-death struggle here in 1916.

Despite the difficulty of landing on the island, which has only a few ice-free rocky beaches, bird watchers will find much of interest, including impressive colonies of nesting Chinstrap Penguins along with lesser numbers of Macaroni Penguins scattered among the Chinstraps. Cape Pigeons, Snow Petrels, Wilson's Storm Petrels, Blue-eyed Shags, and Brown Skuas also nest here. Weather and ice

Chinstrap Penguins on the shoreline of Elephant Island, South Shetland Islands

Gentoo Penguins walking inland to their rookery on Ardley Island, a small island off King George Island, South Shetlands

conditions in this area are very unpredictable, and most visits to the island usually last only a few hours. They are, however, well worth the effort.

In comparison to Elephant Island, visits to King George Island are relatively simple to carry out. In addition to Chilean and Russian field stations, visits also are made to the Fildes Peninsula where colonies of Elephant Seals are seen and some nesting Southern Giant Fulmars can be observed on top of a headland. In addition, little Ardley Island is located within sight of the Chilean and Russian stations and landings often are made there. The island contains fine colonies of Adelie, Chinstrap, and Gentoo Penguins. There also are exceptional examples of lush Antarctic lichens and moss flora. These plants are especially colorful during the austral summer and offer visitors sights contrasting to the ice and snow normally expected in Antarctica.

Deception Island is the last of the islands in the South Shetland group to be visited by the M.S. *Lindblad Explorer*. Unlike the others, it is still volcanically active while also being one of the few calderas in the world flooded by the sea. Ships enter the flooded caldera by way of the narrow and spectacular Neptunes Bellows. Once inside the caldera, Port Foster and the island's central harbor are reached. At one time the island was used as a whaling station.

Bird watchers will find Deception Island unusually interesting because it has a rich avifauna by Antarctic standards. In the vicinity of the abandoned whale factory named Hector, for example, I have observed Emperor Penguins (unexpected here), Gentoo Penguins, Adelie Penguins, Chinstrap Penguins, Southern Giant Fulmars, Cape Pigeons, Wilson's Storm Petrels, Blue-eyed Shags, Brown Skuas, South Polar Skuas, Southern Black-backed Gulls, Antarctic Terns, and American Sheathbills. Some of these birds nest here. In addition, as already described in chapter 6, important penguin colonies are located on the island's outer coastline. One Chinstrap Penguin colony contained about 25,000 birds in December 1975.

Antarctic Peninsula and Other Islands

In addition to the islands already discussed, bird watchers visiting the Antarctic generally are able to visit the tip of the Antarctic Peninsula, Anvers Island in the adjacent Palmer Archipelago, and the Argentine Islands group near the Antarctic Circle. Many birds are seen on these sites. Also, visitors have here views of some of the most spectacular scenery in the Antarctic.

Hope Bay, for example, faces the Weddell Sea at the northern end of the Antarctic Peninsula and provides ideal landing opportunities on the continent. Not far from the Argentine base, Esperanza, are

Nesting Adelie Penguins at Hope Bay, Antarctic Peninsula, Antarctica

large colonies of nesting Adelie Penguins. Skuas, gulls, terns, sheathbills, and storm petrels also occur around Hope Bay, as do fossil plants on the nearby slopes of Mount Flora.

Good bird watching also is possible on several of the islands located just west of the Antarctic Peninsula. At Port Lockroy, for example, visitors to Anvers Island can visit a small nesting colony of Gentoo Penguins and see many Blue-eyed Shags nesting. Nearby Palmer Station (a United States Antarctic Research station established for biologists) provides bird watchers with the opportunity to see both Brown Skuas and South Polar Skuas nesting and interbreeding. A few examples of hybrid skuas sometimes are kept in outdoor pens at the station. A small colony of Adelie Penguins occupies a small island, Torgesen Island, a few hundred yards from Palmer Station.

Directly east of Anvers Island, on the Antarctic Peninsula, visits can be made to the Argentine station, Almirante Brown, which overlooks spectacular Paradise Bay. A small nesting colony of Blue-eyed Shags is located on the side of a cliff here, while at the northern end of the Bay, near another abandoned station, bird watchers will enjoy seeing colonies of nesting Gentoo and Chinstrap Penguins. Paradise Bay also has some of the finest scenery in the Antarctic. It is particularly well known for its attractive icebergs.

South of this area, one comes to the Argentine Islands, which are almost within sight of the Antarctic Circle. Sometimes, if ice conditions permit, ships stop at a British Antarctic Survey base on

Galindes Island. Bird watchers will want to take full advantage of this opportunity because a small colony of nesting Wilson's Storm Petrels occupies a moss-covered cliff half a mile behind the station buildings and usually can be walked to without much difficulty. It is delightful to stand there late in the austral evening and watch the birds flutter in front of their nest burrows while behind them the pack ice extends south to the horizon. Brown Skuas and South Polar Skuas nest near the storm petrels.

When visits are made to this part of the Antarctic, a high point of enjoyment is the beautiful Lemaire Channel through which ships pass en route to the Argentine Islands. This strikingly beautiful place is perhaps the most splendid spot in all Antarctica. Snow-and ice-covered mountains tower high above the deck of a ship moving through the channel. Sometimes pack ice covers the sea ahead of the ship and she is forced to push her way through. If this happens, everybody on board hangs over the rails watching the action below.

Bird watchers, however, always manage to keep one eye alert for unusual birds. One of the species occasionally seen in the area is the Antarctic Petrel. Not many are seen, sometimes none, but it is an excellent bird to add to one's life list if possible. Antarctic Petrels sometimes occur among flocks of Cape Pigeons with which they can be confused if the birds are not studied carefully.

The M.S. Lindblad Explorer enters the beautiful Lemaire Channel, Antarctica, as bird watchers and photographers stand on deck enjoying the view.

The final days of most Antarctic voyages are spent crossing the Drake Passage en route back to Cape Horn and the Beagle Channel in Tierra del Fuego. Tradition claims that the seas in this area are the worst in the world. Sometimes they are—but not all of the time. When relatively calm conditions prevail, and bird watchers are not seasick, they can enjoy much excellent birding in these waters.

Additional Reading

Heintzelman, D. S.
    1976   An Antarctic Christmas Bird Count. *Birding*, 8 (5): 330-31.

Matthews, L. H.
    1978   Penguins, Whalers, and Sealers: A Voyage of Discovery. Universe Books, New York.

Murphy, R. C.
    1947   Logbook for Grace. Macmillan Co., New York.

Peterson, R. T.
    1972   A Guide to Antarctic Birds and Seals. Lindblad Travel, Inc., New York.
    1977   Penguins and Their Neighbors. *National Geographic*, 152 (2): 236-55.

Simpson, G. G.
    1976   Penguins: Past and Present, Here and There. Yale University Press, New Haven, Conn.

Stonehouse, B. (ed.)
    1972   Animals of the Antarctic: The Ecology of the Far South. Holt, Rinehart & Winston, New York.
    1975   The Biology of Penguins. University Park Press, Baltimore, Md.

Wilson, E.
    1968   Birds of the Antarctic. Humanities Press, New York.

APPENDIX: FAMILIES OF BIRDS OF THE AMERICAS

CHECKLIST OF BIRDS

- ☐ SPHENISCIDAE: Penguins
- ☐ RHEIDAE: Rheas
- ☐ TINAMIDAE: Tinamous
- ☐ GAVIIDAE: Loons
- ☐ PODICIPEDIDAE: Grebes
- ☐ DIOMEDEIDAE: Albatrosses
- ☐ PROCELLARIIDAE: Shearwaters
- ☐ HYDROBATIDAE: Storm Petrels
- ☐ PELECANOIDIDAE: Diving Petrels
- ☐ PHAETHONTIDAE: Tropicbirds
- ☐ PELECANIDAE: Pelicans
- ☐ SULIDAE: Boobies
- ☐ PHALACROCORACIDAE: Cormorants
- ☐ ANHINGIDAE: Anhingas
- ☐ FREGATIDAE: Frigatebirds
- ☐ ARDEIDAE: Herons
- ☐ COCHLEARIIDAE: Boat-billed Heron
- ☐ CICONIIDAE: Storks
- ☐ THRESKIORNITHIDAE: Ibises
- ☐ PHOENICOPTERIDAE: Flamingoes
- ☐ ANHIMIDAE: Screamers
- ☐ ANATIDAE: Ducks
- ☐ CATHARTIDAE: New World Vultures
- ☐ ACCIPITRIDAE: Hawks
- ☐ PANDIONIDAE: Osprey
- ☐ FALCONIDAE: Falcons
- ☐ CRACIDAE: Curassows
- ☐ TETRAONIDAE: Grouse
- ☐ PHASIANIDAE: Pheasants
- ☐ MELEAGRIDIDAE: Turkeys
- ☐ OPISTHOCOMIDAE: Hoatzin

☐ GRUIDAE: Cranes

- ☐ ARAMIDAE: Limpkin
- ☐ PSOPHIIDAE: Trumpeters
- ☐ RALLIDAE: Rails
- ☐ HELIORNITHIDAE: Finfoots
- ☐ EURYPYGIDAE: Sunbittern
- ☐ CARIAMIDAE: Cariamas (Seriemas)
- ☐ JACANIDAE: Jacanas
- ☐ ROSTRATULIDAE: Painted Snipe
- ☐ HAEMATOPODIDAE: Oystercatchers
- ☐ CHARADRIIDAE: Plovers
- ☐ SCOLOPACIDAE: Sandpipers
- ☐ RECURVIROSTRIDAE: Avocets
- ☐ PHALAROPODIDAE: Phalaropes
- ☐ BURHINIDAE: Thick-knees
- ☐ THINOCORIDAE: Seedsnipe
- ☐ CHIONIDIDAE: Sheathbills
- ☐ STERCORARIIDAE: Skuas
- ☐ LARIDAE: Gulls
- ☐ RYNCHOPIDAE: Skimmers
- ☐ ALCIDAE: Auks
- ☐ COLUMBIDAE: Pigeons
- ☐ PSITTACIDAE: Parrots
- ☐ CUCULIDAE: Cuckoos
- ☐ TYTONIDAE: Barn Owls
- ☐ STRIGIDAE: Typical Owls
- ☐ STEATORNITHIDAE: Oilbird
- ☐ NYCTIBIIDAE: Potoos
- ☐ CAPRIMULGIDAE: Nightjars
- ☐ APODIDAE: Swifts
- ☐ TROCHILIDAE: Hummingbirds
- ☐ TROGONIDAE: Trogons
- ☐ ALCEDINIDAE: Kingfishers
- ☐ TODIDAE: Todies
- ☐ MOMOTIDAE: Motmots
- ☐ GALBULIDAE: Jacamars
- ☐ BUCCONIDAE: Puffbirds
- ☐ CAPITONIDAE: Barbets
- ☐ RAMPHASTIDAE: Toucans
- ☐ PICIDAE: Woodpeckers
- ☐ DENDROCOLAPTIDAE: Woodcreepers
- ☐ FURNARIIDAE: Ovenbirds
- ☐ FORMICARIIDAE: Antbirds
- ☐ CONOPOPHAGIDAE: Antpipits
- ☐ RHINOCRYPTIDAE: Tapaculos
- ☐ COTINGIDAE: Cotingas

☐ PIPRIDAE: Manakins
☐ TYRANNIDAE: Tyrant Flycatchers
☐ OXYRUNCIDAE: Sharpbills
☐ PHYTOTOMIDAE: Plantcutters
☐ ALAUDIDAE: Larks
☐ HIRUNDINIDAE: Swallows
☐ CORVIDAE: Crows
☐ PARIDAE: Titmice
☐ SITTIDAE: Nuthatches
☐ CERTHIIDAE: Creepers
☐ TIMALIIDAE: Babblers
☐ CINCLIDAE: Dippers
☐ TROGLODYTIDAE: Wrens
☐ MIMIDAE: Mockingbirds
☐ TURDIDAE: Thrushes
☐ ZELEDONIIDAE: Wren-thrushes
☐ SYLVIIDAE: Old World Warblers
☐ MOTACILLIDAE: Pipits
☐ BOMBYCILLIDAE: Waxwings
☐ PTILOGONATIDAE: Silky-flycatchers
☐ DULIDAE: Palmchat
☐ LANIIDAE: Shrikes
☐ STURNIDAE: Starlings
☐ CYCLARHIDAE: Pepper-shrikes
☐ VIREOLANIIDAE: Shrike-vireos
☐ VIREONIDAE: Vireos
☐ PARULIDAE: Wood Warblers
☐ ICTERIDAE: Troupials
☐ TERSINIDAE: Swallow-tanager
☐ THRAUPIDAE: Tanagers
☐ CATAMBLYRHYNCHIDAE: Plush-capped Finch
☐ PLOCEIDAE: Weaverbirds
☐ FRINGILLIDAE: Finches

INDEX

249